Singers Die Twice

THE
SEAGULL
LIBRARY OF
GERMAN
LITERATURE

Singers Die Twice

A JOURNEY TO THE LAND OF DHRUPAD

PETER PANNKE

Translated by Samuel P. Willcocks

LONDON NEW YORK CALCUTTA

This publication was supported by a grant from the Goethe-Institut India

Seagull Books, 2021

Originally published as *Sänger Müssen Zweimal Sterben* by Peter Pannke
© Piper Verlag GmbH, Munich, 2006

First published in English translation by Seagull Books, 2013
English translation © Maria Pakucs, 2013

ISBN 978 0 8574 2 829 5

British Library Cataloguing-in-Publication Data
A catalogue record for this book is available from the British Library

Typeset by Seagull Books, Calcutta, India
Printed and bound by WordsWorth India, New Delhi, India

CONTENTS

Singers Die Twice

I	Monday, 29 July to Tuesday, 30 July 2002	3
	A Garland of Sound	16
II	Wednesday, 31 July 2002	93
	The Rainmakers	104
III	Thursday, 1 August 2002	112
	Hither I Carry My Heart Once More	118
IV	Thursday, 1 August 2002	149
	The Emperor of Dhrupad	164
V	Friday, 2 August 2002	221
	Flight through Darkness	232
VI	Saturday, 3 August 2002	252
	Do These Clowns Have Anything to Do with You?	263
VII	Sunday, 4 August 2002	272

The Mallik Family Tree	284
Glossary	286
Select Discography	294

Before anything else, India is a smell. Lightning fast, it finds its way deep into the brain. Next, you hear sounds, then images start to flicker. Sight comes later, thought last of all. The brain takes in the outside world through the nostrils, the retina, the eardrums, the skin, until everything is turned into memory.

Every time I arrive I experience India piercing its way into me, unfolding in a trice. The first breath is the biggest shock; later, when I've picked up the scent of this great animal, I can't smell it any longer. Hardly have I left the country than it fades away, nothing but a vague shadow, beyond the grasp of nose or brain.

I try to remember.

I

Indira Gandhi International Airport, New Delhi, Monday, 29 July 2002

It was just before midnight but the road downtown from the airport was still busy. When I had arrived the previous winter, the city lay like a lazy lizard, the blood in its veins cold, almost at a standstill, only now and then shifting sluggishly and stretching its legs. This time, there were no fires burning at the roadside where those out at night could warm their hands. Everyone was awake, out and about, up and at it. The people outside the taxi window were seizing the chance to breathe freely in the shadows, in the night, before the next day dropped on them like a stone from heaven, heavy, hot.

July was almost over but not a drop of rain had fallen yet. Delhi was smothered by a pall of dust and groaned like a woman spurned by her lover. Her desire had mounted ever higher as she waited for the monsoon, burning with her need, and now she blazed yet more fiercely in disappointment that it had not come. The air shimmered, yellow as sulphur, with a dirty gunmetal taint. During the day it sucked up tonnes of lead from the car exhausts, which rained down at night as sour soot all across the city. Drifting mist melted before the light from the headlamps as we approached the city.

New Delhi, 1978

Years ago in India, I dreamt of my death.

I'm standing in a long queue of people, all of them waiting for Death, who has taken the shape of a black-clad woman. She embraces everyone waiting in line and slips a slim blade into their back. Behind me, I see a group in turbans and long white robes, who are in a fearful hurry. Every so often, some of them run as fast as they can past the rest of the queue, to the left and the right, shoving others aside, and hurl themselves eagerly into the black-clad lady's arms. I can't see her face; she wears a black mask with a pattern of silver lines incised.

When it's my turn, she embraces me. I note how the blade strikes me between the shoulder blades. It's only a tiny sting but I feel it sharply. Then she turns me upside down, sets me on my head and embraces me a second time. This time, the sting strikes me in the lower spine, at the sacrum.

I look at her questioningly. 'Singers have to be stabbed from both ends,' she says. 'Singers must die twice.'

New Delhi, Monday, 29 July 2002

When my friend Premkumar called from Allahabad, I was in Berlin. His father, singer Vidur Mallik, whom I had known for almost thirty years, had died and had been burnt the same evening as tradition demanded. He had been cremated at Triveni, the confluence of the Ganga, the Yamuna and the mythical Saraswati. The family was beginning to gather for the last rites in his home village in Bihar.

Amta, the village of the Malliks, is near the former royal capital at Darbhanga. The maharaja had granted it to the forefathers, who founded the family line, as a reward for bringing the rains with their song. That was in 1785; East India Company annals record the worst famine of the eighteenth century in those years. It hadn't rained for three years and the land was parched. The two founding fathers, Radhakrishna and Kartaram, had sung up a storm with their magical rain raga, a storm so intense that the land was flooded. Premkumar Mallik had told me the story over and over again, lifting his hand to his chest to show how high the water had risen.

The puja that must be performed after the death of a patriarch from the Gaur brahmin caste, as Vidur Mallik had been, is long and laborious. It dates back to the beginning of creation. The ancestors are invoked, gods and demons are invited to the ritual feast. A hundred and twenty-five thousand yonis must be fed, the cosmic vaginas that gave birth to all life, to insects, animals, birds and every other creature, including the pretas and the bhutas, the hungry demons. The manushya, the human race, were born last. Villagers from all round are invited to the feast that would conclude the puja.

Although I had booked the next flight to Delhi, it would still take me several days to reach the remote spot. The puja had to be performed within thirteen days and I hoped to be there for the final rites at least.

5

Old Delhi Railway Station, Tuesday, 30 July 2002

On the way to the railway station, the images at the side of the road flickered in the hot air rising from the asphalt. Heat lay over the houses in a venomous yellow haze. Vultures wheeled above downtown. Rickshaws, taxis and buses crawled agonizingly through the furnace air. The drive took us across the broad square that spreads out between the Jama Masjid and the Lal Qila. Pedestrians trotted across the open space, drenched in sweat, trying to reach the shade of the next tree as quickly as they could.

The Old Delhi Railway Station is the less busy of the city's two large stations. The New Delhi station is for passengers to the metropolises of Bombay or Calcutta, while the Old Delhi station offers connections to the wide plains that stretch away northward as far as the Himalayas. Darbhanga is in the northeast. Only a few years ago, the journey would have taken several days, changing several times from train to bus to rickshaw, but now there was a direct connection, a train called the *Shaheed Express*, the Martyr Express.

It's a train from one no-man's-land to another. It sets out in the west from Amritsar, the last Indian city before the border with Pakistan. It was in Amritsar that Indira Gandhi had ordered the storming of the Golden Temple in 1984 when her protégé, the rebel leader Sant Bhindranwale, broke loose and declared an independent Sikh state. The Amritsar temple precinct became the last refuge for his armed followers. There was never any official death count but the rusty red bloodstains left behind on the marble tiles are still shown off like stigmata. When the prime minister was shot by her bodyguards—also Sikhs—shortly after Operation Blue Star, thousands of Sikhs were massacred on the streets of Delhi, car tyres hung round their necks, set alight with kerosene. It was two days before the army intervened. The bodyguards were hanged in their turn. Martyrs wherever you turn. *Shaheed Express*—the name sounded rather ominous for my journey.

Indian trains are generally overcrowded but there was no such trouble with the *Shaheed Express*. Clearly Darbhanga didn't draw in visitors, but there was another reason the compartments were so empty—the east of India was largely under water and no one knew whether the train would reach its destination. In the west, by contrast, not a drop of rain had fallen and not even the meteorologists could say whether this year the monsoon might not miss Delhi entirely. It was notoriously unreliable and had grown even worse since the late eighties; there had been several catastrophic droughts and floods since then. It was already apparent that this year would be worse than the year before.

A four-line report in the *Times of India*, third page, noted that thirteen million people in Bihar had been affected by the floods. Seven thousand villages round Samastipur were apparently under water. Samastipur is the stop before Darbhanga. That was where I was going.

Hamburg, 1967

Voices always fascinate me if I can feel the human being behind the voice. I can't get interested in European classical singers—the strained pathos, the weary way they hide their own feelings behind the composer's dusty emotions always struck me as artificial and contrived. I was crazy about Snooks Eaglin, the blind New Orleans street singer with his indescribable loneliness, about Muddy Waters' razor-sharp elegance, about Lightnin' Hopkins' Texan nonchalance, about John Lee Hooker's demonic conjurations. Above all, about Big Bill Broonzy, whose songs just floated away like clouds, so easy, so simple—this was music that came straight from the singer's heart, not from a sheet of paper.

Big Bill Broonzy became my first guru. Night after night, I sat up listening to his songs, trying to figure out how to play them on an old lute that my father had left me. He had played me the first chords I ever heard on this instrument, when I was perhaps two or three years old. We had an old songbook in our house from the glory days of the German ramblers' clubs, the *Zupfgeigenhansl*. On one page was a curiously attractive picture, the silhouette of a girl in a diaphanous gown, asleep under a branch where a bird of paradise perched, and on the opposite page, the music for a fine old love song from the fifteenth century. This book too gave me a glimpse of a world where feelings make themselves truly heard, in chiming crystals of song.

India drew nearer. I put the Incredible String Band onto my record player, *The Hangman's Beautiful*

Daughter, an album where they used a Bengali dilruba brought back from the hippy trail to the East. The sleeve of *John Wesley Harding* showed two bauls, smiling mysteriously, the mystic clowns who are called 'God's fools'. One was dressed in a jacket and bearskin hat with a mala of Indian beads round his neck, while the other seemed to be wearing a dressing gown and peering from beneath a three-cornered hat. 'Are you experienced?' asked Jimi Hendrix; the album cover showed him as an aspect of the god Vishnu. 'Rites that the Vedas ordain, and the rituals taught by the scriptures: I am the clarified butter, and this world's mother and grandsire. I make all things clean. I am Om, Om, Om!' chanted John Coltrane, in an incantation to the Creator Spirit, while Pharao Sanders on second-tenor sax scaled icy heights. In Donaueschingen I saw Don Cherry live on stage with his wife Moqui, their three-year-old son Lanou Eagle Eye and their dog Stup. It was said that he had meditated for four days before the concert; he began his suite 'Humus—the Life Exploring Force' with Bhairav. It was the first raga that he had learnt from his teacher, the enigmatic singer Pandit Pran Nath. Don Cherry and his other disciples, Terry Riley and La Monte Young, used to say that the pandit had spent years living in a cave in the Himalayas as a naked sadhu.

It was the year of Flower Power when I first heard an LP of Indian songs. I felt hypnotized. The singers' voices seemed to shrink time and space in some magical way. They floated weightlessly in a space created for them by the droning strings of the tanpura that accompanied the recording from the beginning to the end. It seemed that every note had its own clear and unmistakable meaning, which I could never put into words, which could only be expressed by these soaring voices. They climbed and wheeled, intertwining, to a tremendous crescendo where every tiny impulse was clearly heard, nothing was hidden, nothing held back, every feeling flowed directly into the voices. No constraints or contrivance and no words but the strange syllables that fit the voices seamlessly at every turn—an endless calm, a nameless stillness, a solitude where none could follow. I could feel the desolation when they sank downwards to abysmal depths. I heard tenderness and ancient weariness; they were terrified by the prospect of being overwhelmed by some unspeakable force and at the same time yearned for this fate. At last, the singers were seized by an uncontrollable trembling and I felt that I was being torn apart, that I was soaring and flying, that I had found that magic tone that carries the soul away to unknown realms.

Then a grumbling drum joined in. The singers began to articulate words which were unknown to me, yet unmistakable in their meaning. I found a translation of the song on the LP sleeve, a tale of a secret ravishment in the forest at night by Krishna the black god, who uses trickery and magic to take the woman he has drawn to him with his music. With his friends he surrounds her and breaks her pearl necklace. I recognized myself in that image. They had taken me prisoner and there was no escape. I knew that I had to find these singers and learn their secret.

The music on the LP was called dhrupad. It had an inner relationship to old lullabies, or to the blues, or to the heartfelt hollering of Andalusian *cante jondo*. The singers' breath opened the door to an inner world which could not be reached except through song. Only the fearless could enter here. 'She cut her heart quite open,' someone once said of Billie Holliday—that was it. She stripped herself bare, showing her naked soul.

At that time, the LP in the light grey sleeve, published by Alain Daniélou in the UNESCO series in 1964, was the only recording of Indian songs available in the West. In his sleeve notes he said that dhrupad was almost a vanished art, that only a single family of singers still practised it. It would take years before I would find out what dhrupad meant but this first time that I heard it, it struck a chord within me that has never died away.

Shaheed Express, *Tuesday, 30 July 2002*

Two young men came and sat in the compartment. They were on their way back to Samastipur. When they heard that I wanted to get to Dar-bhanga, they grinned and told me they reckoned it had probably rained there just as much as in Samastipur. The air conditioning was turned right up and the compartment was ice cold. The two of them switched on a fan as well, that rattled and coughed above their cots. Then they lay down to sleep, smiling blissfully in the cool.

The wagons swayed from side to side on the rails and I surrendered myself to the gradual accelerando of the wheels. I love this sound which can put me into a trance within moments with its intricate, labyrinthine rhythms, the clicking and squealing of the metal confounding all my attempts to count, to find the beat or pattern. It followed a line that led nowhere, though new paths opened on every side. Very briefly, it would point towards a regular rhythm, then fall away. Every sleeper added a new beat and when two rails met end to end, they unleashed a cascade of staccati and hard syncopation. We crossed a bridge. The empty space between the water and us scattered the sound, adding new tones and colours. The wheels ground over the rails, carrying tonnes of weight across a tracery of iron—heavy metal.

When the train crossed a set of points, I was almost thrown clear of the narrow bunk, jolted with every motion. My internal organs quivered in time with the furnishings in the wagon. The aluminium panels, the simple fretwork fittings screwed to the walls by hand, trembled in rhythm with the journey, while the chrome reading lamp and the grasp bars thrummed along. On my way down the corridor to the toilet, I saw a hand-painted wooden frame glowing in the twilight, lit up by red and green control lights winking through the pane. Ages ago, someone had pasted a tourist poster across the glass but it was so shabby and peeling that I could barely recognize the temple towers in the picture.

At the next stop, I tried to peer out of the blacked-out compartment windows. A few dim lamps glimmered faintly on the station platform.

Munich, Summer 1973

A new picture flares into my sight. Straight in front of me I see a musician sweep his right arm away from his instrument flamboyantly, as though waving onward the note that he struck so elegantly, ushering it through the room. The sound mounts up into the dome as though in slow motion and fades away in the heights. A moment later the applause begins. The musician sets down his instrument, puts his right hand on his breast and bows his head slightly.

I come to myself at exactly the moment when the echoes die away in the vault. The concert is over. I remember that when I entered the church, the Indian musician was sitting on a carpet spread out in front of the altar, his instrument in his lap. His left foot supported the sound box, a huge dark brown pumpkin. Fixed to the pumpkin was a broad neck, its gleaming metal rungs running up to curving scrollwork, an ornamental spire whose steps led upward like a Jacob's ladder.

The benches were all full but in front of the steps leading to the altar carpets were spread on the stone floor. I sat down and leant against a pillar. It was pleasantly cool. I had been driving across country all day, then had got out of the car and smelt the perfume of the trees and the earth; the sun was still glowing warm on my face when I arrived at the church. Weariness overcame me. Happy to surrender myself to the music, I tipped my head forward onto my knee. When the first note sounded, I shut my eyes, relaxed.

Then memory stops. I only remember a vague shadow, a gleaming orange light that shone into my closed eyes as the music began. I looked into the flame and then nothing. When I come to myself again, the last note has just died away. I'm astonished.

It unnerves me not to know where I have been. The concert must have lasted at least an hour, but I remember nothing. In the meantime, something has happened, I know that I've been on a long journey. I have the feeling that it must have been important, but I can't remember what or why. I hear the applause round me as though through a fog.

With the others, I leave the church. I don't want to talk to anyone. It would be too difficult to have to say what's going on within me. The question throbbing behind my eyelids would vanish if I spoke even one word. I sit up all night, unable to sleep.

The next morning I summon up the nerve to go and see Imrat Khan, the musician who played the surbahar the night before, the only one who can answer my question. 'What happened?' I ask him. 'When the first note sounded, I was away, gone, and I only knew where I was when the last note died away. Where had I been?'

Imrat Khan laughed. 'I don't know,' he said. 'For me it's just the same! It happens again and again. When I play, I disappear, I don't know where. It has been like this since I was a child. Sometimes I played all night and only came to myself in the morning, sitting behind my instrument, in my room at home in Calcutta. I begin to play and time stands still. I only notice when it's over. It's not always like this, but often enough.'

'You're lucky that it happened to you,' he added. 'Come to India. Perhaps you'll find the answer there.'

A GARLAND OF SOUND

Benares, Autumn 1973

I came to my senses with a jolt standing in the middle of the crossroads. I had already been in Benares for more than two weeks but as they say in the Orient, the soul does not fly as fast as a jet, it travels at the speed of a camel. It had hurried to rejoin my body and now it was here.

I think it was a rickshaw driver who woke me. All at once I heard a whole symphony of bicycle bells. Nowadays, the Benares soundscape is dominated by the coughing and clattering of petrol engines but when I came to myself at the Godowlia crossroads in October 1973, it was still the bells on the rickshaws that led the chorus on the city streets. Not the little metal bells on European bicycles which are struck just once and then fall silent; the rickshaw drivers had mounted great contraptions onto their vehicles. They lashed a short rod against the spokes of the front wheel with a cord, so they could set a clapper rattling and hammering against the bells—not merely one but often a whole battery of bells, installed on both sides of the front wheel.

The result was a high-pitched trill that never stopped because the rickshaw drivers tugged on the cord continuously. The bells were not exactly the same size, so their pitch varied minutely from one to the next. To my ears, the resulting panorama of chirruping, warbling and harmonic interference sounded like music, not set down in any score but composed and directed by the sheer joy of sound and the need to be heard.

The performance reached its high point in the evening rush hour. The Godowlia quarter is at the heart of Benares and its main road runs parallel to the Ganga, above the ghats, the broad interlocking steps and terraces that lead down to the river. It begins in the south of the city at the gate of the BHU, the Benares Hindu University, and then leads over a crossroads to the quarters up on the hill where the great bazaars are. It ends at the bridge by which you leave the city to reach the river's other, undeveloped bank.

The main road crosses another that runs from the Cantonment (Cant for short), the former garrison quarter which the English set out with military precision and which now holds the great tourist hotels and the railway station. This second road runs down to the Ganga to Dashashwamedh Ghat, where all the pilgrims and tourists stream in, and the cremation platforms at Manikarnika Ghat. The Godowlia crossroads is the largest traffic node of the city. Traffic floods in from all four directions and in the evenings the rickshaws regularly get snarled up in hopeless tangles. Policemen in khaki uniforms then rush in from the traffic island in the middle of the crossroads to break up the knots, swinging their lathis across the rickshaw drivers' backs.

Benares is a percussionists' city. The rhythm is set by the damarus, the hourglass-shaped Shaivite drums rattling from the temples, and the citizens join in with their hammering, clattering and knocking. Metal clangs on metal and tin, or thumps on rubber and wood, punctuated by human voices, by bells, conch horns, braying donkeys, barking and howling dogs, cawing crows, twittering sparrows, chattering monkeys, snorting buffaloes and at night the tremolo of the croaking of frogs by the river, not forgetting the bone-shaking blare of horns from the lorries and the booming feedback whine of loudspeakers, playing everything from Vedic recitation to the latest film song. The whole performance has a percussive character, the rhythms shift and surge and repeat in many different ways—day sounds different from night and summer different from winter.

And everyone joins in. The policeman's lathi beats the rhythm of the city onto the rickshaw driver's back while craftsmen in the bazaars beat silver leaf with rubber mallets, thin enough to spread across the sweets as decoration. Dhobis beat their laundry on the stones down by the river, oil-smeared workmen in the metal shops hammer replacement parts and fold sheet metal into storage trunks. Rhythmic microcycles are written into every hour, minute, second; silversmiths with their hammers chisel fine ornamentation into the city soundscape, while the Benares tabla masters, famed for their fast tempo, brash stage presence and thundering strokes, chop time down into the tiniest moments, perfect masters of their art. Benares is a living music, a percussive symphony which the city writes for itself each day anew.

I found this symphony's conductor only a few hundred yards from the Godowlia crossroads, hidden in the tangle of alleys between the main roads and the old city. Under the golden roof of a temple to Vishwanath, Lord of the Universe, Shiva the Divine Drummer resides. He is the city's patron deity and the beat of his drum creates not merely Benares but the whole universe.

In the little alley that leads to the temple I passed the shrine of the city's guardian, called Dandapani from the dandi that he carries in his hand, just as today's policemen carry their lathis. He is the sheriff of Benares. The two deputy sheriffs who guard the gate are called Udbhrama and Sambhrama, doubt and awe. They decide who may enter Shiva's sacred grove; anyone who does not pass through doubt and awe cannot reach the sanctum.

Cologne, Summer 1973

'How can someone who studies comparative musicology want to make music himself? There's really no time left for that!'

The professor sat across from me in his study, his glass eye gleaming. I had gone to see him because I wanted to apply for a grant to study music in Benares. He was the recognized authority on Indian music and occupied the only university chair for the subject in Germany. Every grant application had to go through him.

It was hopeless though. He believed that a student should only be allowed out into the field after he had spent at least two years transcribing field recordings, listening to tapes and writing them down in Western musical notation. I didn't know enough about Indian music to explain why such transcriptions were pointless but I knew that I didn't want to waste my time in a dusty seminar room smelling of chalk, listening to a man who thought that playing music was dangerous. He was an acoustic accountant; elegance, beauty, magic—none of these could raise a smile from him. A mycologist who collected mushrooms in order to classify them. I wanted to taste, to enjoy.

I didn't care for the way he said 'informants' when he meant musicians. He talked of India as though it were hostile territory, to be entered only for a short time and with a particular end in mind, to obtain information, and then to beat a retreat as quickly as possible. He warned me in no uncertain terms of the risk of being overwhelmed by India. Perhaps his warnings were not unfounded but how could I believe him? He didn't even speak the language of musicians. That would detract from the music as such, he had decided.

I wanted to stay in India for as long as possible though. From all I had learnt, it would take years to uncover the secrets of these strange and magical sounds. I gave up the idea of a grant. There would be no point simply studying, I would have to go to the musicians themselves if I wanted to learn about the music. I looked for a job, worked as a packer in a wallpaper factory for a couple of weeks and sold newspapers at the Oktoberfest, until I had enough money to buy a ticket to India.

Benares, Autumn 1973

At first I wondered whether I was in the right place. I took my first lodgings with an Indian singer I had met at a concert in Munich before I set out.

Pandit Patekar lived with his wife and two daughters on the first floor of a house on the main road, near the great gate to the university campus. He taught music at the Girls' College, and also directed student theatre productions. His problem was that he came from Bombay. He couldn't get along with Benares. Granted, he had found a job here that put food on the table for him and his family but he thought it his bad luck to have ended up in this crude and uncivilized city, where the locals saw strangers and pilgrims as welcome bounty sent to them by the gods. He told me that he yearned to be back in glittering Bombay, where they knew how to treat artistes of his calibre. It was an endless source of worry to him that here, up against the old, established Benares musician families, he would never make it.

He told me about his doubts. 'In India, you must be either very rich or very poor, only then can you do what you want,' he liked to complain, his sad eyes fixed on some unreachable goal far off in the distance. 'If you are from the middle class, you are lost.'

In Germany, he had lectured on the spiritual aspects of Indian music but at home he had to contend with his wife who wanted to sell the motor scooter he'd just bought, because the price of petrol had gone up. When I reminded him that I wanted to know more about music's spiritual depths, he took me to a temple to meet his guru.

A stage had been built in the garden in front of the marble temple. A pastel curtain fluttered in the wind; bolts of yellow and sky-blue cloth gleamed in the sun, and pale green, pink, all worked with gold and silver braid. The curtain was pulled aside, children dressed up as gods danced and sang, then the guru came and sat upon a throne. He was a bearded and long-haired holy man who looked like Allen Ginsberg. He talked at length about the life of Rama, then began to sing in a deep bass voice. The audience joined in unhesitatingly, full of enthusiasm. Afterwards, Pandit Patekar took the stage, a tabla player sat down next to him while he too sang of Rama and Sita, and his eyes shone again with the light that I had seen in Munich.

We visited the guru in his little house in the tangled alleys of the old town. The walls shone green in the flickering light of a neon tube and underneath it, the holy man sat surrounded by figures of gods painted on wooden pallets. 'He threw his old murtis, his figurines of the gods, into the Ganga when his son was shot,' Pandit Patekar whispered to me. His only son, a promising student, had been hit by a stray police bullet during campus riots. At first, his father had raged against the gods and thrown their images into the river but since then he had gathered a new pantheon round himself and continued to preach.

I camped down in the front room where the pandit taught his students. Every morning, a young Japanese man came, who tried to sing the notes the teacher demonstrated for him. I joined in these lessons but was irritated that he seemed to have no ear for music and always sang too low. It was an effort to have to ignore this but I had heard that a shishya, a disciple, was not supposed to complain to his guru. The teacher set the tasks and could not be questioned.

When I plucked up the courage to ask whether he could give me individual lessons after all, the pandit simply looked at me in sadness and shook his head. He had no time, I had to be patient, I would get used to his method and to my fellow student. I doubted that this would ever happen. It seemed to me that he couldn't see Benares on his doorstep, the Benares that I wanted to discover, that I wouldn't find as long as I stayed with him.

This was the dilemma for many Western music students I met in Benares. They had no yardstick by which to judge their teachers' quality and since not a few of the musicians were engaged in bitter feuds, their students were at loggerheads as well. Students of one tabla master would freeze in disdain when they heard the name of a rival master. I felt as though I'd entered the world of the mediaeval trade guilds, who jealously guarded their art and mystery. There were great rivalries; rumours flew that the disciples of one singer had poisoned another who threatened to outshine him. Everyone knew stories about the sacrifices that students had made simply to be allowed to draw near to the masters.

Ravi Shankar—born in Benares in 1920—in his autobiography tells the story of how his teacher Allauddin Khan resolved to commit suicide when he was turned back from the door of Wazir Khan, the greatest veena player of the day, from whom Allauddin wished to learn. He bought himself a fatal dose of opium. A mullah in whom he confided his plan advised Allauddin to throw himself in front of the car of the nawab of Rampur, whom Wazir Khan served as a court musician. Then he could beg the prince to ask for him the favour of being allowed to become a student. The plan worked. Allauddin Khan, one of the greatest twentieth-century Indian musicians, found his way to the very heart of the tradition although he was an outsider, not from one of the old gharanas, the musical dynasties. Other stories told of rejected students who would bribe a guru's servants to be allowed to hide behind curtains and eavesdrop on their secrets, to steal their knowledge that way.

As long as there were no such things as phonograph records and cassette tapes, music could exist in its own hermetically sealed world to which only a few initiates had access; the musicians still remembered this time vividly. In the age of radio and public concerts, absolute secrecy and seclusion was no longer possible but a veil of secrecy still shrouded those exercises through which the student prepared himself mentally and spiritually for musical mastery. Indian students knew how much the times had changed and could judge whether the masters really meant it when they demanded homage and obeisance but Western students all too often took this at face value.

For the Indian teachers, it was a matter of prestige, as well as income, to teach foreign students, but the first thing that a new arrival learnt from his guru was to sneer at the rival teachers. This was, after all, easier to learn than the complicated musical technique, which could only be grasped—if at all—after long practice. He would first learn to imitate his guru's bad habits, to stand at the street-corner paan booths shoving betel leaf into his mouth, as he had seen his teacher do, and repeating the snide remarks he'd heard from the master's lips about the competitors and their competence or lack thereof. Others, though, were troubled by the thought that this long, possibly vain, discipleship might last for years and they might never quite know where they stood.

In the early seventies, there were several dozen music students in Benares from the West. And just like at the beginning of a new school year, new arrivals asking silly questions were looked down upon as nuisances. Older students told awe-inspiring stories reminiscent of the self-mortifying practices of Indian ascetics. In the tea shop at the street corner they talked of an American who would tie his long hair to a hook on the ceiling while he practised; when he drooped and drowsed after hours of playing, his hair would bring him up short with a jerk and he would awake. He was said to have practised a single raga fourteen hours a day for a whole year, just as the old masters had done. Others made do with eight or ten hours' practice; these many hours each day were the threshold you must pass to reach the promised land of complete artistic freedom.

But the Indian musicians I got to know had begun their training as children. There was no chance at all of catching up on their enormous head start. Music was a family trade. Outsiders who tried to join a gharana were expected to make heroic efforts. How could I keep up? And what should I be practising? I didn't know.

Riding three in a Rickshaw
—it is unlawful—
ABANDON IT!

stood in large letters on the student pass issued to me by a stern young man in the secretariat of the BHU but the rickshaw drivers who pedalled their way through the great gate of the campus seemed never to have heard of this prohibition. Two people could sit comfortably on the narrow bench of a rickshaw in its cheerful red or blue plastic upholstery but the vehicle had room for plenty more. You could squeeze a third person onto the bench and then one, or maybe two, crouched on the footboard and a slim passenger could worm in between the bench and the frame at the back where the canvas cover offered the passengers some shade on hot summer days. A simple bicycle had space for three—one sitting at the front on the handlebars, the rider pedalling away, a third balanced on the carrier at the back. A motor scooter was ideal for a family with three children.

The university campus in south Benares is big enough to be called a city quarter in its own right. On a sunny morning, it was fun to cycle along the university's shady avenues, flanked by tall trees, from the departments and colleges to the sports grounds and the new Vishwanath Temple, an imposing marble building that complemented the older, smaller temple in the old town—even if it could not compare for holiness and number of visitors. To the right and left of the street the faculty bungalows, the dean's office and the student dormitories stood on carefully tended grounds. Gardeners watered the rose beds, donkeys trotted along the avenues with bundles of grass on their backs. Their herdsmen had mowed grass from the sports grounds and were taking it to a goshala to feed the cows. Chipmunks skittered across the lawns, hoopoes called in the trees, here and there a peacock shrieked reproachfully.

I turned in from the long avenue to the Music College precinct, a rounded building curved about an inner courtyard. The classrooms all opened out onto the courtyard and from their doors I could hear the metallic twangings of a sitar class and voices chanting tabla syllables. I found myself looking at a picture of Saraswati, the four-handed goddess of music and scholarship, that hung over the entrance. She had one hand on the neck of a veena and strummed at the strings with another; the other two hands held a book and a mala.

'Do you see those two gourds?' asked a student who saw me looking at the picture.

He pointed at the two sounding chambers of the instrument. 'She uses these to stay afloat in the ocean of sounds, for otherwise she'd be sunk!'

I nodded. 'Like us!' he added and shrugged, apologetic, smiling.

I eagerly joined the small group of students studying musicological texts with the dean of the school, Premlata Sharma, dressed in a modest sari and with her hair bound up in a tight braid. She was one of the greatest scholars of the Sangeet Shastras, the labyrinthine texts on music that have been written in India for more than two thousand years. The Indian term for the music that we in the West call Indian classical music is shastriya sangeet, music based on the canonical books. The shastras are composed in verse and intended to be learnt by heart, in order to be available to the memory at all times. Written in an archaic and highly specialized language, they are so terse and succinct that it would be impossible even to begin to understand them without a teacher.

Sangeet Ratnakara, the ocean of music, which Premlata Sharma was translating with her students, was written by the Kashmiri brahmin Sarangadeva in the thirteenth century. He begins at the very beginning of creation and then goes on to all the complex ramifications of the musical system. The first chapter begins with a paean to Shiva, embodied as sound, Nada.

Nada is an ambiguous term. Sarangadeva devotes hundreds of verses to a very thorough description of its two aspects—the eternal, unheard anahata Nada and the audible ahata Nada caused by two objects striking together. He explains that the human body is created to make the inaudible anahata Nada heard and thus he begins his work with an intricate description of how human life comes about.

He explains how the self-aware intelligence, jiva, descends from the highest element, the akash, the substance of thought and of music which Classical Europe called the aether. Thence it descends to the subordinate element of air, which condenses into clouds; the sun's fiery gaze makes the clouds draw up water and they rain down the aetheric intelligence into plants, trees and bushes. The vegetation becomes earth whence men take their food and turn it into semen.

His description of pregnancy fills several pages. 'In the seventh month the embryo hides the hollows of its ears between its thighs, while the jiva within remembers the terrors of earlier births and, self-sustaining, contemplates the possibility of liberation,' writes Sarangadeva, always keeping music's ultimate aim before his eye. Then he analyses the infant body, how characteristics are shaped and formed, the development of the sensory organs. He describes the nerve centres, counts the bones, numbers the veins and the arteries, the blood vessels, the lymphatic nodes. Three and a half million hairs grow on a human body, says Sarangadeva; of those, three million in the beard and on the head; he gives the total number of blood vessels, nerves, veins, arteries and hairs as 564,750,000.

'Such is the body,' writes Sarangadeva at the end of the first chapter of his *Sangeet Ratnakara*, 'A heap of filth, surrounded by all kinds of squalor—but yet a wise man may use it as a way to achieve pleasure or as an instrument of liberation. Turning towards the manifest side of creation, saguna, will lead to worldly pleasure, and turning to the unmanifested side, to nirguna, will lead to redemption.'

In the next chapter, he describes this path—the worship of Brahman as sound, Nada Brahman. But Brahman, the absolute and transcendent cosmic principle, the fount of all being, can no more be translated than can Nada. A chasm opens up between name and form, between the holy formula and the reality towards which it points. It is a mystery, a riddle which can never be solved because its meaning is ever-changing. 'That which cannot be expressed in speech but is the source of speech—know that this is Brahman,' says the Kathopanishad.

Historical commentators agree that Nada Brahman is untranslatable because Brahman and Nada are identical. If we were to imagine Nada as a sound, it would imply a division into a hearing subject and an object that is heard—but that would not be the all-encompassing Brahman. No more can it be said that Nada Brahman means 'the world is sound.' Brahman is not the world, it is absolute reality beyond any description.

And yet, there is a way to approach the unheard and inaudible. The Upanishads teach that if we cover our ears with our thumbs, we can hear the sound of Nada in our heart. It has a sevenfold resemblance—it is like the rushing of water, the ringing of bells, the sound of a vessel beaten, the spinning of a wheel, the croaking of frogs, the sough of rain and the murmur of voices in an enclosed vault.

'Lila, lila!' someone called to me. 'Come along, there will be a lila!' I let the crowd carry me along, flooding downward towards the river. It was as though the whole city quarter had turned out to be at the shore. Every inch of the ghat was taken, people had climbed onto rooftops of houses to get the best view. They sat on the balustrades and the outside staircases, they were crammed onto balconies, little boys had clambered up trees and faces even peered from the temple towers. The boatmen had drawn up their vessels at the shore and invited so many passengers aboard that the gunwales were only an inch or two above the water. I climbed into one of these dangerously swaying boats; the boatman rowed us out into the river and took his place in the line of boats ranged in a ring round the scene.

At first, I couldn't make out the reason for the throng but when I followed my neighbours' gaze, I saw that they were all staring at a tree trunk that jutted out over the water from the bank. Musicians grouped round the trunk struck up songs and the audience joined in and clapped their hands. Then there was some movement. A boy climbed the tree trunk, decked out in all the insignia of the god Krishna—the peacock-feather crown, the pearl necklaces, the yellow dhoti, the flute. He climbed up to the highest point of the trunk, where he executed a few neat dance steps, then struck the pose in which Krishna can be seen on countless posters—one leg bent across the other, the flute at his lips.

'Look, look over there!' Excitedly, my neighbour was pointing at a papier mâché figure floating on the water. It was a serpent with several heads, manouevred by a group of swimmers who brought the figure to a standstill beneath the tree trunk. For a moment all was perfectly still and then the boy jumped down from the trunk and landed on the papier mâché figure, quivering a little. A cheer rose from the crowd.

Across from the serpent and between the boats came the craft of the maharaja of Benares. It was unmistakable, shaped like a winged swan. One of the spectators declared that it was a vahan, the steed of the gods; another contradicted him, explaining that it had been a present from the Queen of England to the maharaja as a sign of her favour. Maharaja Vibhuti Narayan Singh had crossed over from his glowering fortress on the other bank of the river to beg Krishna's blessing.

Very slowly, the boatmen rowed the great white bird towards the serpent until at last it stopped in front of little Krishna balancing on the monster's many heads. The maharaja bent down and placed a garland round the boy's neck and again a collective shout arose. 'Krishna Yogiraj ki jai! Kashi Maharaj ki jai!' the spectators called out as one—'Hail Krishna, king of the yogis! Hail the maharaja of Kashi!' In Benares, the age of princes was not yet past, tens of thousands of people cheered for their maharaja as, on behalf of them all, he presented the garland to the child god.

An old man with snow-white hair and gleaming eyes was sitting next to me in the boat. He had been watching me the whole time.

'You have witnessed Kaliyadaman Lila!' he explained. 'Krishna danced on Kaliya's head!'

I asked him what the spectacle meant. He told me that a lila is a mystery play, a piece of ritual theatre showing Krishna's deeds and sport. There were dozens of them. Kaliyadaman Lila showed how Krishna defeated the water serpent Kaliya, a demonic nag from the underworld sent by Krishna's wicked uncle Kans, usurper of his father's throne, to swallow the little prince.

The boatman rowed back to the shore and the crowd dispersed, but the white-haired man hung back. He introduced himself as a jyotishi, the honorific title accorded to an astrologer. His father had held this position at the maharaja's court but the son had never learnt the craft and the maharaja no longer needed an astrologer. He had inherited the title along with his father's house on the riverbank but he had had to sell the garden across the street, with its flame-flowered gulmohur tree, to a temple.

I told the white-haired man with the friendly face that I was looking for a room and he offered to take me in to live in his house. In fact, there was no room free in the ancient house at Assi Ghat, only a windowless chamber that the women had used for giving birth to their children and that otherwise served as a lumber room.

I asked his name.

'The people in the neighbourhood call me Guruji but that doesn't really mean anything,' he said, smiling bashfully. 'I call myself Vishwamitr, friend of all the universe, after a sage of Vedic times.'

I too became his friend. He brought workmen in to make a hole in the wall, making a little window, and I moved in.

Everyone called him Guruji, including his wife, Mataji. He radiated a cheerful serenity that made him seem almost a saint, and shared his house with family and others. Guruji was a gentle soul; over the course of weeks and months other guests would arrive—distant relatives, friends—and no one would be turned away. A young pakhwaj drummer from Bihar occupied the room next to mine, living rent-free in the house thanks to Guru Vishwamitr's passion for music. The only person in the household who held down a regular job and brought in a salary was his son-in-law, who worked for the railways.

They scrimped and saved however they could, throwing a cable with a little hook from their first-floor window to the overhead power line on the telegraph pole, tapping off unmetered electricity. It was mostly used for the electric pump that brought up water to the tank on the roof. The only other electrical devices in the house were a black-and-white television in the son-in-law's room and a few dim light bulbs.

Life was largely lived in the courtyard—open to the sky but deep and narrow enough to offer shade at any time of the day. In the middle of the yard was a deep well whence we would fetch water with a bucket when there was a power cut, which happened for a few hours every day. A balustrade round the first floor connected all the rooms and a steep narrow stair led up through a lightless passage to the roof. A mesh cage across the parapets stopped roaming monkeys from getting into the house. Sometimes, one of them would manage to sneak in down the stairs and steal a potato or leap gleefully into the heap of dal that was meant for lunch.

Because of the way the house was built, everyone could always hear everyone else. Since the doors were almost always open, I always knew who was in the house, and the sounds of the city and the street came in through the ceiling and the windows. It didn't bother me—on the contrary, it made me feel that I was living among people, that I was tuned in to the same wavelength as the family in this house, the mood of the neighbourhood and more.

Almost every other house in Assi was a temple or had a temple somewhere within it. The bigger ones had loudspeakers permanently installed, so that the whole neighbourhood could share the blessing of hearing the sacred texts recited. Lesser households made do with hiring loudspeakers from Ahuja's radio shop on the high street when they were celebrating a particularly important ceremony.

The loudspeakers laid a carpet of sound across the whole city, seeming soft from far off but scratchy and rough up-close. One morning, Sanskrit verses boomed and screeched into my room from the beaten-up old speaker that hung on the wall of the temple opposite, barely two yards away. The children in the house knew just what to do about this—a trick they had thought up when the recitation distracted them from their homework. A boy from the neighbourhood was given five rupees and a pair of pliers to cut through the cable.

Guruji would go down to the street-corner market every morning to buy fresh vegetables and whatever else might be needed for lunch. Often I went with him on this little errand. We would walk down past the goshala at the corner, where cattle and water buffaloes were tied up, past the women drying cowpats mixed with straw on the alley wall for kitchen fuel. I liked the rural face of Benares. The smell of the cows filled my nose, warm and pleasant, and I stroked their hide as I went past; it was soft, and their liquid eyes gleamed darkly.

Urban Benares began with the asphalt on the next street, where costermongers spread out their wares on a bit of sackcloth each morning. The quarter's intellectuals, students and music lovers would meet at Pappu's tea shop, which didn't open until four in the afternoon. The owner sat cross-legged in front of his shop and sold hundreds of cups of tea and, under the counter, little green golis, globules of bhang made from freshly ground cannabis which the menfolk used to take at the end of the day just as naturally as we in Germany drink beer. Not quite though; there is a difference—the correct dose of bhang sharpens the senses and frees the spirit but doesn't make you tired. Students use bhang to help them learn texts by heart, since without Shiva's help it would be impossible to commit these long passages to memory. And above all, bhang is seen as a gift from Shiva, the lord of ecstasy—how better to draw near to the god than by enjoying his favourite intoxicant?

While Mataji and her daughters prepared the meal, the old man and I would sit on the floor in the upper room where the children unrolled their mattresses to sleep; a wooden cot was also kept there for the grown-ups. Rice, dal and hot chapattis came in from the kitchen, and then the season's vegetables, saag, potatoes or peas. Onions and garlic were off the menu since, Guruji explained, they were too stimulating for a brahmin to eat. He would scrutinize every food for how well it could be digested and whether it suited the season. Bananas or yoghurt in winter? Unthinkable; they would cool the body too much. When the summer heat drew in he would split the hard rind of the bel fruit, sacred to Shiva, as round and smooth as the breasts of his consort Parvati, and strain the dark yellow fibres in water to make a refreshing drink. On Ekadashi, the eleventh day of the lunar month, only uncooked food was served, and on other days, if we were remembering Rama's exile with his beloved Sita and his brother Lakshmana, sweet potatoes appeared on the thali, the food which the gods had eaten in the forest. Once a week, Mataji would serve us a roasted papadam and laddu, a sweet ball of sugar and gram flour.

I could watch the street from the tiny balcony in front of the window. Like the windows, the balcony too was caged in to protect us from the monkeys. A birdcage hung from the mesh and the green parrot perched there watched his kin freely flying round outside. Scratch his head and he would call, 'Sitaram, Sitaram!' and Mataji, who had taught him the words, would beam with pleasure. She drew aside the curtain from a little niche, showing me the gallery of gods she had set up here in her home shrine. She introduced them all to me, explaining how they were related and what their special characteristics were.

Guruji told stories while we ate. Mythological tales mixed seamlessly with news from the mohalla, the neighbourhood. He juggled the kalpas effortlessly, so that the creation of the universe led naturally to the latest events of the day. When the gods called the demons to help them churn the primaeval ocean of milk and bring up the nectar of immortality, this was at least as newsworthy as the latest campus riots or the aeroplane theft at the weekend. A love-struck young man had stolen a sports plane and flown over his beloved's house downtown, waving his handkerchief at her with bravado.

Guruji showed me how to tie my dhoti, the elegant and comfortable garment that all the well-dressed men of Benares wore; Guruji persuaded me that I simply had to stroll along the Ganga at sunset to refresh myself with a cool bath and a little chillum; Guruji taught me the local ways of communing with the gods. Washing your clothes on a Thursday—the day sacred to Brihaspati, guru of the planets—was immensely disrespectful to Lakshmi, goddess of wealth, and you would surely wash the money out of your pockets. It was just as unwise to shave on a Saturday, for that would cut short your life as well as your hair. Guruji also taught me some of the nuances of Hindi. It was as though he were putting money in my palm with every word he taught; I noticed that when I used the right words in the shop at the corner, the price went down straight away. Gradually, I was able to follow conversations, to understand why people got worked up and why they laughed, to understand the puns they cackled over and the jokes they made about one another and about the tourists.

'It's wonderful that you speak Hindi! I'm sure that you were an Indian mahatma in your last life, you were simply reborn in the West to be punished for your sins. Now you've found the way back here. Welcome to Varanasi!' Our neighbour wagged his head enthusiastically. 'I always thought that tourists are all mute like the water buffaloes—they never answer if you ask a question, they just plod on through the puddles of urine with a fixed gaze!' Guruji quoted a proverb that everyone knew hereabouts, 'Rand, sand, siri, sannyasi—inse bache to jive Kashi.' The harlots, the bulls, the stairs and the saints—if you can keep clear of these, you can survive Benares!

It didn't much matter whether you said Varanasi or Benares. On the All India Radio news, read out in a highly Sanskritized Hindi that hardly anyone understood, the city was called Varanasi, while the English, who couldn't pronounce the Indian name properly, had named it Benares. For the old married couple, the city was still called Kashi—the old name, meaning 'light'. It is the light that Shiva carries on his trident—which is why the city is the only place that will not be destroyed when everything else sinks into the ocean of annihilation at pralaya, the moment when the universe ceases to be.

But no one worried much about the future in Kashi. Guruji laughed when I asked him how he thought the world would end. For him, it was all old hat, a perfectly normal process which had happened countless times already and would happen again and again. 'Don't you know that we are in the Kali-yuga, the last and worst of the four ages of the world?' he asked. 'We are experiencing catastrophes, plagues and wars but these are nothing but the signs of the approaching pralaya. It won't be long now before Shankar Bhagwan dances on the ruins of the universe.'

No cause for alarm. No future? He just laughed at the idea. Brahma would lie down to sleep for some millions of years and then when he woke up, would create a new world for himself.

Out of my window I could see a door on the other side of the street, which led to a little temple. Long before sunrise, bells, drums and human voices would sound from the doorway and the spectacle would be repeated every evening. I asked the priest whether I could look inside. He laughed and invited me to take part in the ceremony. Lights were waved, bells struck, a brass plate struck with a wooden hammer by one of the congregation to set the rhythm. Prasad was shared, the sacred food of the gods—little crumbs of laddu, a slice of apple, a disc of banana, a piece of sugar candy, a cashew.

'This is our arti,' the priest explained. 'Lights are swung before the statues of the gods in temples all across India at this time of day.'

He showed me how he would draw a figure in the air with his oil lamp which represented the Sanskrit syllable Om, the cosmic sound that contains all other sounds within itself. 'We offer the gods the best of everything we feel, smell, touch, hear and see—the purifying flame, the best smells, the loveliest flowers, the most beautiful songs, the tastiest food.'

Only a few old people came along to the dawn ceremony but after sunset the congregation was much larger, when the neighbourhood rowdies flooded in, grabbing all the drums and bells and cymbals they could find to play themselves into a trance. Old people and children joined in with the rhythm. The temple was open to all, for anything they liked, not only for spiritual needs but for pleasure too. This was no Sunday school—ecstasy was an everyday affair. It was a welcome interruption, a necessity, a way to shake off all the dross of the day. Arti was a daily observance, a chance to get rid of all the day's troubles.

One morning, I heard the beating of drums and chiming of bells at an unaccustomed hour. I looked out. A parade of children was just about to start in the narrow alleyway under my window. They told me that a young monkey had touched the high-tension cable above the roofs and had fallen down dead to the street. Monkeys would climb up the power masts and cling on to the top, shaking the mast until the tangle of cable and lines leading in all directions snapped. But this monkey had gone too far and had touched one of the power lines. Perhaps he had even just been careless and lost his grip on his mother's back as she jumped across a street canyon carrying him.

The neighbourhood children had gathered to see him off into the next world. They wrapped the small body in a yellow cloth and put it on a little bier, as grown-ups do with human corpses. But there were no grown-ups involved; the children had taken it upon themselves to fetch cloth from the bazaar and bamboo sticks for the bier and had borrowed the drums and bells from the little temple across the street to make the noisy procession that wound its way along the alley to the ghat. A genial boatman volunteered to row some of the children out to the middle of the river to sink the little monkey's body. According to the rites, only adult corpses were burnt, children and saints were given to the river.

I tried to imagine the reaction in a German church if a group of children wanted to borrow the cross and some holy water to bury a hamster or a rabbit. I now learnt that religion was something quite different from what I had been used to. It was like a game. Religion provided the pretext for playing out scenes, for celebration, ornament and music. The children were playing with death. Life was a game, death was a game and religion was a game of life and death.

The monkeys played a leading role in the city performance. They ruled the air; whole armies of them, led by a fat general, would roam across the rooftops, swing through the trees and climb up the balustrades and oriels on the houses, always on the lookout for plunder.

Sometimes, a whole horde would appear on the roof of our house and steal laundry hung out to dry. One of the monkeys would sit on a high spot where we could not reach him, a stolen shirt or dhoti in his paws, and take the cloth between his teeth and chew it provokingly. He seemed to be waiting for something. I soon found out what—the only chance to get the clothing back was to hold something up for him to eat. When I fed him a chapati or a banana, he would disdainfully drop the shirt down the canyon of the street, where it would get tangled up on a power line and I would have to fish it down with a long stick.

The monkeys were a menace in the bazaar where they would squat on the telegraph poles, the roofs and brickwork, watching closely to see what they could snatch. The grocers and costermongers always had a stick handy to protect their wares but as soon they let their attention drift, a monkey would leap down from a porch and pounce. It was quite common to see them snatch fruit or vegetables that a customer had just bought, straight out of their hands. The locals, well used to the monkeys' presence, took good care not to carry about anything tempting too openly. They defended themselves from theft but, otherwise, they tolerated the hairy acrobats who lounged about on roofs and in the trees. The monkeys' only enemies were the dogs. They ruled the ground while the monkeys ruled everything above what a dog could fasten its jaws onto.

New arrivals had a lot to learn. Once, when I was sitting in front of a tea stall, daydreaming, with a bunch of bananas on the bench next to me, a monkey leapt down lightning fast from a wall, seized the bunch and jumped to the tea stall's roof with a mighty leap. He didn't leave it at merely eating the bananas—but, to make me look even more foolish to everyone watching, he also bent down and dangled the bunch before me, taunting.

He knew exactly how far he could go. Helplessly, I grabbed for the fruit but he snatched them away before I could get close. The passers-by laughed and applauded, then as his *coup de théâtre* he ate the bananas calmly and threw the skins down at my feet, scornful of my earthbound incapacity.

Tourists who come to Benares carry in their heads the pictures they expect to see—the temple silhouettes, the cow chewing the cud in the middle of the crossroads, the morning sun over the bathing ghats, the pilgrims raising their hands in prayer, the matted hair of the sadhus, the glowing colours of saris hung out to dry, the boat trip on the river when the tourists gaze into the water and watch for the corpses that the travel brochures have promised them, the obligatory stop at the burning ghat. One cliché after another is spooled out until the ventrilo-quial words of the tourist guides have fixed themselves in the memory.

Mark Twain was the first in a long line of Western authors to visit the Domra, the guardian of the pyres on Manikarnika Ghat. He was to become a central figure in all future travel reports from Benares, featuring in the German newspaper *Frankfurter Rundschau* as 'the most untouchable of all India's untouchables'. Gabriele

Wenzky writes in indignant tones, 'But at the same time he is one of the city's most respected citizens, because he's one of the richest, which is all that counts in this money-centred country. The man smells of booze even in the morning. His father died of drink as well. It's the only way to bear all this.'

The sun rises glowing red and the pilgrims rush down to the bank and drink the dirty water straight from the river. The skulls crack in the fire and corpses are sunk into the stinking channel sandwiched between stone plates. Josef Winkler promotes the Domra, already the hero of innumerable documentaries and travel shows, to a character in his novel. His story from the shore of the Ganga ends with the sight of a bitch chewing on a charred human bone, still bloody in places. The next television team is already on its way to gather the requisite pictures.

Even writers capable of nuance and discernment in other parts of the world reduce this lively, noisy city to a 'city of the dead', despite the multitude of people who live here in so many different ways. To Pier Paolo Pasolini, who portrays himself as a hound on India's pestilential trail, the 'breath of India' is a dreadful whirl-wind, a hellish tornado that streams out a horrid and indefinable stench. His travel book is a document of paranoia. In the Clarks Hotel in Benares, a Sikh holds out his hand and Pasolini sees that the doorman is wearing gloves—probably, he decides, because his hand is eaten away by leprosy. With Alberto Moravia he goes down to the burning ghat. While the two poets warm their hands at the pyre, India grants them one of the few happy moments of their journey. 'At no other time or place in our whole visit to India, nowhere else did we feel such a deep sense of community, of peace, almost of joy.'

'No, you shouldn't go to India for just two weeks,' Cees Nooteboom decides but then he can't resist a day trip to the burning ghats. A hand grasps his wrist and leads him to a terrace where he will have the best view of the smouldering pyres. The undertaker wants a donation, which Nooteboom duly presses into his hand. For a moment he feels connected to what happens here, then he goes back to his hotel and tells the reader about the seven corpses he counts on a photograph he had taken from a safe distance.

You can't see death but you breathe it in. The smoke rises from the pyres and merges into the air and the dust, blowing through the city's alleys and settling on its roofs. You can feel the fine grains in the hide of the cows you stroke and you wipe it from the bench or rock that you're about to sit on. You can see it lying in a fine grey film on your skin, you feel it when you run your hand through your hair, you breathe it in, you see the dark traces on your handkerchief when you wipe your nose. Death is in the air, everywhere.

Mark Twain reckoned that Vishnu should have called the place Idolville or Lingamburg, confusing Vishnu with Shiva. For him, the city is 'a vast museum of idols—and all of them crude, misshapen, and ugly. They flock through one's dreams at night, a wild mob of nightmares.' But he knows the truth about the wonders the traveller wants to see. 'I find that, as a rule, when a thing is a wonder to us it is not because of what we see in it, but because of what others have seen in it. We get almost all our wonders at second hand,' he notes. 'By and by you sober down, and then you perceive that you have been drunk on the smell of somebody else's cork.'

And in fact, there are far stranger things swimming in the Ganga than human bones—dolphins, for instance. Freshwater dolphins only live in three places on the globe—in the Orinoco, where Alexander von Humboldt listened to them puffing and blowing, in the Mekong and in the Ganga. They swim blindly through the murky water. The boatmen have seen them and say that they change the expressions on their faces, that they laugh and cry. One told me that they had driven the fish into his net.

Another foreigner has moved into the house, an American anthropologist. He wants to collect these dolphin stories and announces prizes for the best—one for the best tall tale and one for the best true story. The competition is held on a houseboat, where dozens of boatmen assemble, but it's impossible to tell the true stories and the fishermen's yarns apart. The men egg one another on, they are masters of the art, as though telling tales were a daily sport.

'Why didn't you catch this giant dolphin that you're telling us all about?' one asks another.

'You know quite well why not!' comes the reply. 'They're too clever. You can only catch a dolphin if it lets you. A fool like you would never be able to!'

What makes this city so exciting is the unpredictable, the almost impossible. When I set foot in the street in the morning, I have no idea what will happen to me. Benares is more diverse than any other city I know; here, different ages of the world, different ways of thinking, different religions meet and mingle. To reach Godowlia from Assi takes me a quarter of an hour but in this short time I cross the territory of two different religions. In the Muslim quarter there are no temples to be seen, the men on the street are bearded and wear little white caps, the women sit in the shops sewing saris. Buddhist monks live in the Nepali temple at one of the ghats, carved in wood like the temples in Kathmandu. Every region of India is represented in Benares and you hear countless languages on its streets—Hindi, the broad Benares dialect, Vedic Sanskrit, Urdu, Telugu, Tamil, English. The tourist guides at the ghats throw snatches of Japanese, Italian, French, German and Spanish into the mix.

Sometimes, I seem to cross years merely by crossing the street. The cinema in Assi only opened a year ago but after a single rainy season, the building, richly ornamented like an Oriental gingerbread house, looks a hundred years old. In Vishwanath Gali, the narrow alley that leads to the temple, Indian Barbie dolls are sold next to Shivalingams. There's a power cut and the young man in the bookshop holds his customers spellbound with mythological stories from the Puranas.

One night I wander the streets aimlessly. Hearing songs in the distance, I follow the sound and enter a room

crammed full of people. Men are sitting round a microphone on the stage; there is a poetry recital taking
place. Whoever is up next is handed a candle and he
begins to recite a verse in a melodic voice but the audience are already cheering and clapping before he has
finished speaking. He waits until the hubbub dies down
and repeats the verse. A shudder runs through the room
and some listeners beat their breasts. The poet sings and
a tumult breaks out, some leap up and stand on the
wooden folding seats of the theatre.

I watch, enthralled. The recital simply doesn't stop.
A new group takes the stage. Several poets recite their
verses in a dramatic, melodic manner; most of them
don't hold back from really singing their verse. I understand hardly a word. They use a poetic form of the language, expressions that you never hear in everyday
Hindi, but from the listeners' responses I can read
which verses move them most. It's noisy, the audience
chatter away and call out enthusiastically.

I wander onward through the night. I catch another
sound, someone playing the drums. I enter a hall where
they are performing kathak, the storytellers' dance. An
adolescent in a gleaming green costume stands on the
stage, looking at the audience with eyes made huge by
make-up. He shimmers with a golden light, his cheeks
are red and he looks flushed. The show is in full swing.
The spectators clap, a tabla starts up and the boy dances,
graceful steps that come faster and faster. Then he lies
on the floor and covers his legs with a shawl so that
only his feet can be seen. The audience are almost hypnotized as they follow the minute, almost imperceptible

49

movements of his feet, until one of the many bells tied about his ankles begins to chime, then another, then a third, then all of them. The dancer breaks off as they reach their crescendo and begins a new movement. The spectators stare at his feet in fascination.

The night is giving way to morning. I leave the building. It's quite silent outside though I rouse a couple of dogs who follow me down the street, barking. The contrast between the lively scene in the brightly lit hall and the dark and silent street makes what I have seen and heard seem like a dream. I rub my eyes, find my way back to the river and stroll along the bathing ghats back to Assi Ghat. The first pilgrims arrive before dawn. A new day begins.

Benares is a city of early risers. Long before the sun rises, I hear pilgrims murmuring below my window, on the way down to the river. Even without looking out, I knew how they appear—old men, often with their white hair cut short, in a faded dhoti from which all the colour has been washed out. In one hand they carry the staff that shows they have been ordained as sadhus, wandering monks, and in the other the brass pot with which they will take the holy water of Mother Ganga back to their hermitage, to pour over Shiva's holy stone. They draw the shawls closer about their shoulders to ward off the early-morning chill but their footsteps are full of purpose.

One morning, I heard a strange sound mingling with the chiming of bells, the tap of the staves against the pavement and the sadhus' voices. I followed the sound to a shack beneath a temple balustrade on the waterfront, only a few steps from our front door. A young Irishman had set up house in a doorless niche in the temple wall, like one of the many sadhus who live on the ghats. He was sitting on the straw mat where he slept at night and was playing a small bowed instrument that he held in his lap, calling forth the strange, yearning tones that had woken me. I sat down next to him.

At first, I could not see how he was making the notes. Though their pitch and tone certainly varied, he didn't seem to touch the strings with his fingers at all; he simply glided his nails up and down the strings.

'It's a sarangi,' he told me, setting down the instrument.

'How is it played?' I asked him.

He held out his hands and showed me the grooves that the strings had worn into his fingernails.

'That's how you can tell how long someone has been practising,' he explained, not without pride in his voice. The way he glided his fingers over the strings seemed playful but, in fact, he had to press his nails very hard against them, until over time the gut strings cut deep into his nails.

He put the instrument in my hand. I looked at it, an ornate and neatly constructed object, made of wood, bone, leather and parchment. It reminded me of the human body. I ran my fingers over the curve of its hips. The belly of the instrument was a single carved block of wood, covered with a sheet of parchment. Dozens of sympathetic strings of steel and copper ran beneath the three thick gut strings along which he had been sliding his nails. Some of these resonating strings were tightened by pegs on the side of the instrument and ran through ivory eyelets set into the wood. Others were grouped in bunches that fed through little windows and across a complex system of tiny channels and secondary bridges, and joined the three main strings at a bridge of carved camel bone that vibrated on the parchment skin. The Irishman ran his finger over the tightly tuned metal strings, producing a shimmering arpeggio. The bow never touched these secondary strings but they resonated when the instrument was played, lending it a yearning tone that seemed to come from far away. The wooden body of the instrument served as a sound chamber that picked up the notes, drawing the sound together.

The Irishman told me that the sarangi is the instrument that most closely resembles the human voice, ideal for playing the gliding notes essential to Indian music, but it was a hard taskmaster—it had taken him many weeks even to learn to tune the strings.

It was the first time I had seen a sarangi up-close.

'Where did you get it?' I asked.

'I found it in Dalmandi Bazaar,' he answered. 'Sarangis are really rare these days. There aren't any craftsmen left in Benares to build them. If you want to have one, you need to find an old instrument you can still play. Watch out that they don't sell you something worthless though—with most of them, the wood is so warped that you can't use them at all.'

He explained how I could find the little alley where the drum- and kite-makers had their shops. The craftsmen sat left and right, filing, sawing or hammering at the wooden and metal drums in various stages of completion. Most of the shops were simply a single small room opening directly onto the street. At night the shutters were pulled down; the shop-owners sat on the stoop before their doorway. Behind them, in the darkness inside the shops, were piles of animal skin, dusty wooden planks, metal rings and broken parts of old musical instruments. Above their heads hung finished drums, ready for sale.

Next to these hung colourful paper kites, twisting and fluttering. In January, young and old took to the rooftops to duel—the aim was to bring down your neighbour's kite, by crossing the strings and cutting through theirs. To this end, the strings were coated with a mix of glue and finely ground glass. The festival took place in winter, the only time that kites were up for sale, the only time the drum-makers took on this extra business.

All the craftsmen in this alleyway were Muslims, since they worked with skin and leather—work which is unacceptable for Hindus. I had sometimes seen signs in front of temples asking visitors to remove all leather items from their person before entering the temple—bags, belts and shoes. Pious Hindus not only recoil from killing animals but even from touching animal pelt. Musical instruments were excepted from this prohibition but leather and parchment were regarded with mixed feelings.

The tabla players of the long-established Benares musical dynasties were mostly Hindus and usually turned a blind eye to the fact that the drums they played were covered with goatskin. But they belonged to a lower caste in the musicians' hierarchy anyway. Since the human voice is the most noble instrument of all, singers held first place, followed by sitar players, who had gradually been winning over public favour from the singers over the last few decades. The instrument makers also observed this hierarchy; the sitars were made only from wood and metal and were sold in a different part of the bazaar. The drum-makers who handled animal skins kept themselves apart.

In the musicians' hierarchy, the sarangi players were even lower than the drummers. There was a stigma attached to the instrument and sarangi players were held in contempt. Although some of them were highly gifted musicians, they were seen as thieves and pimps. In earlier times they had accompanied the singing of courtesans in the kothis—the refined brothels where the women entertained a male audience with poems, songs and dancing. These courtesans had brought the arts of thumri, chaiti and kajari to a high degree of perfection in Benares, Lucknow and Patna. The soulful sound of a well-played sarangi could follow every turn of the voice like a shadow, lending these romantic songs a particular charm. This tradition had flowered under the Mughals but the British regarded it as immoral and by the time the colonial rule ended, so had the tradition of the brothels.

In the street of the drum-makers I found a sarangi that had fallen into three pieces. The shop-owner,

Roshan Ali, pulled it from a heap of broken instruments. He showed me how he could put it back together and cover it with the skin. I sat for days watching him work; three times he had to put me off with excuses, four times I came back. The work took him more than a week but he succeeded.

When I asked him about a teacher, he took me through the winding streets of the bazaar to a house where a sarangi player lived with his wife and an immense horde of children. Pandit Mathu Mishra was a Hindu, belonging to one of the old Benares musical dynasties. He took me on as a disciple in the traditional manner. I had to bring sweets, flowers and incense, a new dhoti and a gift of money, after which he tied a red thread round my wrist in the name of Saraswati, goddess of music, and showed me the first exercises.

He came pedalling along on his bicycle to teach me almost every day. The bazaar in his neighbourhood was loud and his twelve children made the house even more raucous. For him, the lessons he gave me were a welcome opportunity to escape the uproar at home. As soon as he entered my room, he would lie down on the bed and tell me to play whatever I had been practising since the last lesson. Usually he fell asleep at the very first notes. When he woke up again, he would praise my playing, get on his bicycle and go back home, thankful for the respite that my playing had allowed him.

Bangalore, 1978

When I recall the plangent sounds of the sarangi on the banks of the Ganga at Benares, I see myself fishing the strings with a hook through the holes where the tuning pegs sit; gleaming bright steel, soft yellow brass worn dull in places, red copper wire wound round the pegs. It's a complicated process—dozens of strings must be threaded through and tuned, each one in its place. They run through little windows at the top of the instrument and over the tiny balconies like those of a miniature haveli, or a shrine. I can't wait for the sounds I heard on the riverbank in Benares. My hands are calloused from tuning and tuning the instrument. I turn the key of one of the pegs, the string tightens, the note approaches its pitch and another string begins to hum in resonant sympathy.

A new image. Early October 1974. I'm standing in West Berlin's Tempelhof Airport waiting for Ram Narayan, who is to play at the Meta Music festival in the Neue Nationalgalerie. The festival is a great symposium of sound. Its founder, Walter Bachauer, calls it a 'cross section of world music'. This is at a time when no one even speaks of world music; it will take twenty years to trim his vision down to a narrow-gauge version that fits neatly on the shelves in record shops and online music stores. The Meta Music festival was a spark that lit up everyone who attended during these three weeks, sitting on foam cushions on the floor of the Neue Nationalgalerie.

Ram Narayan will play the sarangi. He comes through the gate, his face drawn and tired from the long flight. It's as though we've known each other for a long time. When he opens his suitcase and shows me his sarangi, he smiles. I listen to him, he has shut his eyes, his hair floats in the winds of sound, his face is like that of an old Native American.

Then we're sitting in a Mercedes, driving over snowy roads to a concert in Nuremberg, or looking out together over Marine Drive in Bombay, we're sitting in his living room in Bandra, clinking glasses, next I'm watching him on the stage, his hair has turned white now and is thinning but the look on his face, the excitement as he goes in search of sound, is still the same.

Another picture now. I'm standing in front of a hotel in Bangalore. At the end of the seventies, the city is still a long way from being India's Silicon Valley; Bangalore is still a garden city. The hotel is a colonial villa. The garden is walled, a raked path crosses it and leads outside, edged with neat white-painted stones. The first violin of the Bombay Philharmonic Orchestra stands next to me. Ram Narayan isn't about yet, perhaps he's still having breakfast, but he's the reason for our journey since he's the soloist for the orchestral piece written by Peter Michael Hammel and sponsored for this tour by Germany's cultural institute, the Goethe-Institut, known in India as the Max Müller Bhavan.

A little white-haired Indian man with a sack on his shoulder and a cloth wound about his head turns up at the gate. He squats in front of us and fishes out a tiny musical instrument from his sack. The sounding chamber is nothing but a little earthenware bowl, the kind of clay cup that you drink your tea from and throw away after use, but he has pasted a sheet of paper across it, affixed a strip of bamboo and stretched a string across the whole thing.

The violinist acknowledges the street musician as his colleague—low-ranking perhaps but a colleague all the same. He points loftily at the instrument and invites the man to play something for us. The white-haired musician picks up a little bow. This too is only a strip of bamboo threaded with a single string. He touches it to his instrument and plays us a popular song from a film that's in all the cinemas right now. He plays perfectly; it's incredible what he can conjure up from the teacup, which looks like a mere child's toy. The violinist is astonished and enthusiastic. He asks to be allowed to look at the instrument and tries his hand but can only summon a couple of squeaky, scratching notes.

We fall into conversation. The little white-haired man tells us that he's from Hyderabad. He tells us his name; he's a Muslim. Do we want to see something else? He lays his sack carefully on the ground, kneels down and heaps up a little mound of earth with his hands. Then he looks about and plucks a leaf from a nearby shrub, along with its stalk. He looks at it carefully, turning it this way and that in his fingers, before he sticks it stem-first into the little mound so that the leaf points straight upward. He shuffles back a pace or two on his knees and shows us that he's not touching the leaf on its mound in any way. Then he takes up his instrument and begins to play. We begin to clap again but he points to the leaf with his chin. We look at the little mound. The leaf is turning about on its stalk, as though under its own power. We simply can't explain this phenomenon.

The man gets up and points at his mouth. We can see something there, glowing white. He spits it out and a hot stone falls to the ground, slowly turns red and then grey. We clap again and give him some money. To finish, he sells the teacup fiddle to the violinist for five rupees. He offers to bring a few more tomorrow but the violinist declines. We don't have the time, tomorrow we fly.

Benares, Winter 1973

The glass over the photograph was sooty from the fire crackling under a little tea kettle. Behind the glass, the contours of the face were blurred in the twilit interior of the hut beneath the banyan tree at the Assi cross-roads but I knew that I had seen that face somewhere. The hut was a tea shop where Chai Baba, a slight, curly-haired young man in a thin T-shirt and lungi, served tea. When I asked him who the man in the photograph was, he pointed over his shoulder towards the ghat. 'Shiva Sharan!' he rasped, his voice dried up from smoking innumerable chillums. 'That's what we called him. In Europe his name was Alain Daniélou but here he took the name Shiva Sharan, "protected by Shiva". He used to live in Rewa Kothi down on the shore, with Raymond Burnier, the photographer. Good man! He bought a house for his servant when he went back to Europe.'

Rewa Kothi was one of the most impressive houses in the quarter, an imposing building of several storeys which reared up from the ghat like a fortress, flanked by two round towers. It had originally belonged to the maharaja of Rewa, although it had passed into new ownership long since, its earlier inhabitants now part of the folklore of Assi Ghat.

I had first seen Daniélou's name on the LP record that had brought me to India. Everyone who was interested in Indian music knew of Daniélou. He was the first European to take not merely a theoretical interest in Indian music but to put it into practice, to learn how to play. He was a highly controversial figure among ethnomusicologists. There were a few who hated him quite openly. He had published several books on Indian music but his interests went far beyond music; he was one of the last of the species *uomo universale*, now extinct. During the fifteen years he lived in Rewa Kothi, it had become a meeting place for artists and intellectuals, scholars and politicians, where Eleanor Roosevelt was just as much a guest as photographer Cecil Beaton or director Jean Renoir.

Perhaps there was a certain amount of envy at work too. His companion Raymond Burnier was an heir to the Swiss Nestlé concern, and Daniélou could afford to live in India for decades with no monetary worries, devoting himself to study without having to answer to a university. He had always refused to take a professorship and submit himself to the Western academic system. He had reached the conclusion that Indian classical music was the equal of Western music in every way and should be judged on its own merits. He thought it undignified and misleading to consider shastriya sangeet from the ethnological perspective. Only by following the local tradition could anyone understand Indian musicology, and this he duly did.

He was also astonishingly industrious. He learnt to play the veena, translated texts, collected an extraordinary number of manuscripts and published several books not only about music but on a number of topics, from the symbolism of the phallus to a comparison of the cults of Dionysus and Shiva.

He hated Nehru, considering him a product of Western thought who only knew Indian spirituality from reading English books on the subject, and blamed him and Gandhi for India's bloody Partition. In 1954, when post-Independence India was on a path that he could not bear to see, he left the country for good.

He saw signs that the ancient Indian culture he had come to know and love was doomed to disappear, just like traditional musical cultures round the world. With the help of UNESCO, the Ford Foundation and the Berlin Senate, he founded an institute tasked with bringing musicians from other cultures to Europe and publishing their music. For Daniélou, India was the very pinnacle of these other cultures. The first LP he issued was of Vedic recitations recorded in Benares and the second was the album of dhrupad singers that had led me to India.

But now he was long gone from Berlin as well. Musicologists had banded together against the grand seigneur, who lived in the institute in the exclusive

Grunewald district. When they started a whispering campaign against the homosexual Daniélou, the Ford Foundation withdrew its funding. UNESCO would not be fooled so easily however and the institute moved to Venice. Daniélou's successors in Winklerstrasse in Berlin were unable to persuade the city bureaucrats of the necessity of continuing his work there. In 1996, the institute was 'dissolved', as the paper-shufflers say, despite international howls of protest.

Zagarolo, Autumn 1992

It took two decades before I came face to face with the man I had seen on the sooty photograph in the Assi tea shop. I visited Alain Daniélou in his enchanting villa on the Colle Labirinto, a hillside south of Rome that had once been a stop on the pilgrimage to the temple of Fortuna in today's town of Palestrina. I was there to invite him to a Berlin festival charting the course of Indian music into the West. He had withdrawn from public life long ago but agreed to come.

We sat on the terrace in front of the house and looked out onto the autumnal colours of the park. It was an extensive property, with a little copse and broad meadows surrounding a swimming pool with travertine balustrade and rose bushes growing round. Over his shoulder I could see the hillside where he grew the vines for his wine. The liveried chef who poured us the wine at lunchtime had a rip in his white glove and his thumb poked out but he served the meal adroitly. The wine had a golden gleam, the house was yellow, the garden too glowed with colour in the sun.

'Do you hear the birds?' he asked. 'They feel at home here. We don't use any artificial fertilizers, so lots and lots of birds come. Snakes as well. This is a blessed place. All those who come here feel at home.'

He sat across from me, an old man, well past seventy, his wise blue eyes glittering in a narrow face beneath thin grey hair, carefully combed. In India it is said that the ears are a clue to musical talent; his were enormous, with impressive long lobes. A sly humour shone from the depths of his eyes and a small, winged golden phallus hung at his chest. He had a long nose; I felt that I was sitting across from a member of a rare species of bird.

'Do you know what the Sanskrit texts say about sacred geography?' he asked me. 'They describe where you should live and where not. Benares of course stands on a quite excellent spot. People say that it is connected to the underworld and the stars—that an underground river flows beneath the city, and the Akashaganga, the Milky Way, flows above. In Benares, these two meet the Ganga, making it the perfect place to live'—he chuckled happily—'and to die.'

I asked why he had gone to Benares.

'I never really thought I would go there,' he replied. 'I wasn't one of those people who dream of mystic India. I wasn't at all interested in that. It was a happy coincidence, I simply discovered it on the spot.'

He had grown up in Brittany, the son of an anti-clerical father who had been a minister in successive French governments and a devout Catholic mother who had founded a religious order. She was shocked to discover that Alain had taught himself to play the piano. His elder brother became a cardinal of the Roman Catholic Church, whereas he was the family's *enfant terrible*, a sickly child who did not go to school but was tutored privately. He went to Paris to study composition; he painted, sang Schubert's lieder and performed as a dancer. He quickly got to know Igor Stravinsky, Jean Cocteau, Jean Marais and Maurice Sachs. The Swiss Raymond Burnier was the love of his life and in 1932, they went travelling the world together. They visited Daniélou's friend Zahir Shah, the king of Afghanistan, ventured into Kafiristan though it was forbidden to foreign visitors and then went on to India. Nobel prize winner Rabindranath Tagore invited Daniélou to take over the music department at the Santiniketan university in the forests of Bengal but he went onward to Benares.

'Almost at once, I started to study with a great veena master,' he told me. 'From the beginning I studied under a living guru—after all that is the only way to learn Indian music!' he added emphatically.

In 1936, he settled down with Burnier in Rewa Kothi. Daniélou took the boat almost every day to visit Shivendranath Basu, a reclusive zamindar from East Bengal who spent his time playing the rudra-veena, Shiva's instrument, which only a very few musicians still played. It may seem archaic but the rudra-veena is a perfect tool for meditation; two hollowed gourds bridged by a bamboo tube where the frets are affixed, while the player sits between the gourds, swathed in sound—an instrument primarily meant for the player himself, to listen to the subtle sounds.

'My teacher never played in public,' Daniélou continued. 'He was a wealthy man who considered it beneath his dignity to steal work from the professional musicians. He performed privately for his friends but would never take money. Moral scruples prevented him from giving concerts!'

He laughed. 'He was right! It's a matter of caste and of what you consider your dharma, your duty. For me, he played every day, one raga after another. I asked him questions, he explained matters, and I wrote everything down. At first he was reluctant to teach me; then at long last he gave me a small veena but refused to listen to my playing. "You would only ruin my ears," he said, "I couldn't stand that." But after a while he began to praise me. "Alain is my best student," he would say, "but only when I am not there."'

'When I went to India I was primarily considered a musicologist,' he continued. 'It was something entirely different to become a musician myself. The professional ethnomusicologists were stuck in their European mind-set and rejected the idea outright. "Daniélou? He's no scholar, he's a musician!" they would say. Playing music was seen as the absolute antithesis of scholarship.'

The old gentleman took a cigarette from a case with his slender fingers and lit up. He seemed a little tired but memories of Benares made him more lively.

'When I came to Benares, I found myself in the midst of an ancient culture,' he said. 'I found it extraordinarily interesting. If you wish to be accepted in a society, the first thing you must do is to follow its rules. It's a question of comportment and good manners. When people know that you won't put them in some awkward situation, that you take your ritual bath in the Ganga, that you do not break taboos, that you don't touch what is polluted, that you don't behave in an unseemly manner—then there's no problem! Most Europeans just aren't ready to shed their habits and their prejudices, so they are constantly offending the locals. If they can be quite sure that you know how to behave like a civilized person, then there's no problem! But first you must set aside all your preconceptions of good and evil, purity and pollution, moral and immoral.'

He laughed, half ironically, half sadly.

'I have never encountered a more consistent worldview than the Indian worldview. The ancient Indian, please note,'—he raised his hands as if to fend something away—'I am quite allergic to modern India!' He raised his brows. 'Today's dreadful religiosity, its moralizing sentimentality—there was no such thing in old India.'

He shook his head.

'According to Hindu belief, life's only purpose is to appreciate what the Creator has made. Something that no one is looking at cannot be said to exist. Creation would not exist if there were no one to look at it, to appreciate, to try to understand it; and that is the only true religion.'

I told him how I had followed his footsteps at Assi Ghat in the early seventies. Westerners coming to study Indian music in Benares had become an international horde since he had left. Most were Americans, since the American universities gave their students generous stipends; then the British, French, Italians, Israelis, a few Germans. None of the German music students had a grant; the German professor I had met made sure that no young ethnomusicologists got the idea that they could pick up a sitar or a tabla, at Assi Ghat or anywhere else.

'These people have the mentality of slaves,' he commented. 'They sell themselves, they sell their work and their bodies to some organization which they are not truly interested in, just so that they can have a pension in their old age.' He sighed. 'What a sad view of life!'

He was silent for a while, then took another cigarette from the leather case and lit up.

'I've never been serious,' he concluded. 'I believe there's an advantage in not being taken seriously by the establishment. By staying out of it—you stay free.'

'I thought perhaps you might like to take a stroll in the park?' he asked, ending our conversation. 'The apples are ripe. Fruit that you pluck from the tree yourself always tastes better than what is handed to you on a plate!'

Benares, May 1974

It's too hot to sleep indoors. I spread my bedding on the roof at night and listen to the city. Frogs croak in chorus down by the river, a donkey brays, tormented. The chime of bells and the muzzy melodies of a harmonium drift across the rooftops. In the temple at Dashashwamedh Ghat, the microphones are switched on round the clock. One of Shiva's names means 'the god who never sleeps'. It's quite true; Benares never sleeps. There's always someone awake in this city.

When the loudspeakers fall quiet, it is the dogs' hour. Packs of mutts roam the neighbourhood. Sometimes I hear them fighting, a low, husky, rumbling growl, shrill yelps when one has been bitten. As soon as one starts howling, the others join in, running barking through the streets towards the sound. I can track their path by hearing alone.

During the day, as I move through the tapestries of smells, faces and conversation, when I jump out of the path of a rickshaw that blares its horn in warning or step aside to let a cow pass, when I go to the bazaar, watchful to be sure that the shopkeeper has not sold me a dhoti that will rip in two when I unpack it, other impressions bury the sounds of the city, but in the darkness the panorama of sound becomes clear. I lie on the roof and look at the stars. A soundscape of the city unfolds in my ears. In the distance, a steam engine hoots and whistles, announcing its arrival at the station, I hear the low grumble of wheels on the bridge as a train crosses the Ganga at the other end of the ghats.

Far off in another quarter, a procession is on the march. In the spring wedding season, numberless bands parade through the city, laying down criss-crossing trails of sound. Their costumes are their trademarks; bands in Roman legionary dress, in togas, in tiger-print or in colourful uniforms that mimic English military bands, all marching through the streets at once. A man with a microphone walks in front to announce the event, followed by a lackey who carries the speaker set balanced on his head. A third man has hoisted onto his head the car battery that powers the speakers. After the brass band follows a sound system on a four-wheeled cart blazoned with the band's logo and festooned with batteries of bullhorns. Up among these sits the DJ, shoving cassettes into his tape deck and feuding with the brass band. Behind him marches a traditional band with shehnais and small drums, sometimes drowned out by the loudspeakers. They are the poorest among the musicians, without any amplification, but they do their best to compete by blowing into the wooden cones of the shehnai with their cheeks puffed out mightily, while the drummers beat their clay drums for all that they are worth, slamming the sticks onto the skins. These groups are called naubat shehnai; the naubat are the drums and the shehnai the woodwind. In Mughal times, they played from the minstrels' galleries leading to the princely courts to mark the hours, to greet dignitaries and give a fanfare for the guests. Times meet and clash—the naubat shehnai is a survival of the princely courts, the brass bands were imported by the British colonial regime, the sound systems stand for modernity. Yet, no one would think to do away with the older parts of the procession. Everything exists together at once, a crossing of times that lends Benares its particular character.

A second procession approaches from the opposite direction. It crosses paths with the first. A spontaneous battle begins; men shout and laugh, firecrackers and squibs make their mark, adding to the tumult, until the processions gradually fade into the distance. The last blinds rattle down in the bazaar; somewhere in the neighbourhood, distorted snatches of a sarod concert blare from a badly tuned radio. A wooden staff clacks on the pavement of the alley in front of the house, water drips from the courtyard tank, mosquitoes whine right by my ear.

I love to sound out the three dimensions of acoustic space, listening to depths and distances. The sounds overlay without dampening one another, instead forming a perspective. The distance makes them almost hallucinatory, lends them tone and colour, as though I am looking upward into a sky full of sounding stars in which I can recognize each and every star by its tone, its position and the way it moves through space, until at last the outlines fade away in the distance. The aether above the city is a palimpsest of sound, an old parchment on which new sounds have been inscribed since time immemorial—drumbeats, strings, wind, speech, song. The older layers can still be seen, shimmering through.

The old texts play with this idea of an ancient page overwritten with sound. The Tandya Maha Brahmana describes how Vac, the primal word of all languages, escaped the gods to settle first in the watercourses and the trees, then in the drums and the veena, in bows and the axles of carts. They are still all around. At Assi Ghat, a brook babbles down to join the river, a stream after which the ghat is named, with the river Varana on the other side, after which the city is named. For thousands of years, people have played the drums and plucked the strings of the veena on this riverbank. There are bows as well, in the thrumming of strings on a device which a particular caste of workers uses here to plump up the wadded cotton of mattresses which their customers have lain flat. I soon make out their sound even from afar. The axles of the auto rickshaws grind metallically, wooden oxcarts squeak along the streets, urged on by the carters' hoarse cries.

Another text, the Satapatha Brahmana, tells how Indra himself, after he had drunk the intoxicating soma, divided the unarticulated primal language into four— humankind was given one of the four parts, while the other three went to the four-footed creatures, to the birds and to the insects. They too are all around; the lowing of buffaloes, the chattering of monkeys, the crowing of cocks, the melodious calls of parrots, the tremolo of frogs and the whining of mosquitoes—all are older than the Sanskrit texts booming from battered old bullhorns on a ghat where a Vedic rite is being performed.

In the Benares soundscape, bragadaccio rules the day. Everyone wants to be heard but at the same time must also listen to everyone else. This sensitive self-regulating system reminds me of the locust populations that I had taped in the Borneo jungle with a friend of mine, a professor specializing in bioacoustics. Innumerable species of locust roam through the treetops, far more than could ever be collected and identified visually before they become extinct, so instead, we recorded their acoustic signals and compared them, using a highly specialized computer programme developed by NASA for analysing acoustic signals from space. A locust population never occupies the same range of the frequency spectrum that another horde has already taken. Humans intruding into the rainforest had a hard time coping. As we crept along the ropeways stretched across the treetops, our eardrums rattled and scratched as though about to burst, but the locusts understood one another.

I follow the sounds. The cassette recorder I have brought with me was actually intended for music, but that is only a part of the many-layered performance, unplanned, spontaneous, running through ever new variations, yet clearly structured and making use of the most refined techniques. The way they deal with loudspeakers is phenomenal; there are public address systems that broadcast some acoustic event over a whole city quarter via relays of loudspeakers and portable speaker systems perfectly attuned to the fragile Indian power grid, brought to perfection by generations of skilled craftsmen.

Sonic art, *Klangkunst,* is a Western concept derived from the Futurists' loud-hailer concerts, from Pierre

Henry's *musique concrete*, from John Cage's theories and innovations. Indian sound artistes have never had anything to do with this Western art that so pompously tries to define itself as a genre in its own right, removed from any older definition of music. They've never needed to; since India celebrates it as a collective and continuous achievement for which no curator must be retained and paid. Benares residents do not need a sound artist to tell them to put their radios on the windowsill to create a sound cloud over the city; this cloud has been there for a long time now, the whole city is nothing but a cloud of sounds, and everyone joins in.

One morning, I am woken by the shriek of a bird diving close in over my head. A vulture; apparently checking to see whether this shape wrapped up in a sheet on the rooftop is edible.

Time to go.

Benares, February 1995, Maha Shivaratri

'The clouds of Heaven are weeping tears of joy!' the two men cried out, pointing excitedly upwards. They were respectable gentlemen, pandits dressed in white kurta and dhoti, but looked as though they were about to break into a jig. They ran hither and yon on the roof of the building in astonishment, watching the raindrops splatting darkly on the flagstones. Their faces beaming, the men pointed at a small cloud that hung directly above them. It was unusual to see rain falling at this time of year and even more extraordinary that the rain seemed to fall only on this rooftop terrace. It was not a real downpour, just single drops pattering onto the roof and down into the courtyard. Everything round this little area stayed dry.

The pandits were dancing on the roof of a massive building of dark red sandstone, towering over the river-bank, several storeys high. The entrance lay halfway up, only reachable via one of the many winding stairs that lead up from the waterfront to the city. A balustrade surrounded the open courtyard where the raindrops fell. From there, the visitor could enter a wide, roomy hall that had once been the palace kitchen. A spiral staircase led downward to the lower storeys, which had served as storerooms for the enormous quantities of flour, rice and lentils for the meals prepared here. A peshwa, a Marathi prince from western India, had built this house to feed a thousand brahmins every day.

Sattra, the feeding of the brahmins, was an act of virtue, but the time of princes was long past now. The empty building belonged to a cultural foundation that had given us permission to hold a festival of sound there. Bill Buchen came from the Lower East Side of New York and was studying tabla with Vidur Mallik's son Anandkumar; at home he made sound sculpture with his wife Mary. I had accompanied Andres Bosshard, a sound artist from Zurich, on his voyage to the Santhals, an Indian tribal people whose acoustic traditions are as old and as complex as the songlines of the Australian aborigines. The three of us had decided to revive the sattra tradition, this time feeding not merely brahmins but everyone in the neighbourhood—not with food but sound. We called our festival the Sound Sattra.

We went to Ahuja's radio shop at the corner of the high street to borrow some amplifiers and speakers for the installation. Ahuja, founded in 1926, was everyone's first port of call for sound systems and still thoroughly dependable.

'How many speakers do you need?' the owner asked us. He was dressed in jacket and trousers, a 'suit-bootwallah' as they say in North India to describe someone who has traded his dhoti and sandals for Western attire. 'One hundred? Two? Three? I have as many as you will need!'

Though we wanted only thirty-six speakers, we also needed technicians to instal the mixing desk and the amplifiers, to hang the speaker boxes across the many storeys of the building where our festival would take place. They brought along their bamboo ladders lashed together with hempen rope and clambered up and down three storeys with the heavy boxes on their backs. They were nimble and in a few hours the installation was ready. The technician who plugged us in to the power mains had a way with current that rather reminded me of yogic technique—he loved to feel electricity flowing through his body. In the West, electric current is a rather abstract commodity; in India, it's physical, tactile. It comes and goes, surging in rhythmic pulses, ebbing and flowing. The more appliances are connected, the weaker the current, with the voltage fluctuating between 110V and 360V. The man who was connecting our cables to the sockets didn't use a volt-meter or warning light to check whether current was flowing—he simply moistened his finger and touched it to the bare wire, nonchalantly, as easy as that. When the current flowed, he'd feel a tingling in his finger, he told us.

The visitors poured in through the gate where a shehnai band played in the minstrels' gallery, and scattered through the rooms on every floor. Tea was served. It was a sunny afternoon on the eve of Maha Shivaratri, the night of Shiva that is celebrated at new moon in the month of Phalgun. I had called the sound installation that opened the festival 'Shri Kashi Vishwanath Shabdanath', a garland of sounds from the city of light. The piece, commissioned by West German Radio's acoustic arts studio, was composed in the tradition of the Kashi mahatmya, hymns that scholars and saints had sung in and for Kashi for thousands of years.

These songs aren't stored in any digital media but in the human brain. People remembered them and at some point wrote them down on palm leaves, then printed them on paper, but these were only aides-memoire. I was the first to ever record a Kashi mahatmya on tape—a sonic palimpsest, a book of sound containing many of the tones I had recorded in Benares over the last twenty years.

I owed the arrangement to Saket Maharaj, the Bihari pakhwaj player who had been my neighbour in Guruji's house at Assi Ghat. He lived in a dark alcove that had just enough room for his mattress. Come evening, he would light a candle and invite friends over.

Evening after evening, a group of aficionados gathered on his mattress to hear him play.

The pakhwaj has a mellow tone. It is made from a hollowed, seasoned section of tree trunk and two drum-skins lashed together with sinew. The left skin, the bass face, is smeared with wet wheat dough before it is played, mixed up fresh each time just as though the drummer were preparing a chapati. The chapati is fed to the drum, the drum duly speaks; the drumskin is its mouth. It is a complicated art, taking one weeks or months to learn how to strike the skin with a hand cupped like a cow's ear and then immediately let go so that the skin can reverberate. Drum and drummer speak the same language, for every beat has its own mnemonic syllable. The mouth repeats what the hand has struck, syllables build up into words, sentences, whole stories. The drummer speaks, the drum answers. It knows the names of the gods and can recite their attributes and their deeds. Every combination of syllables in the Sanskrit language can be translated for the drum to speak.

After playing, the drummer scrapes the dough off the drumskin before it can dry. 'If a child has trouble speaking, we give him this drum-cake to eat. It has drawn in the vibrations as we play and his tongue will surely be loosened,' explained Saket Maharaj.

One evening he recited a jaw-cracking series of syllables that sounded different from the rhythmic patterns or eulogies to the gods that I had heard from him before. I asked him what they meant.

'These are the syllables which Shankar Bhagwan shook from his damaru at the beginning of Creation, establishing human language,' he answered, raising his right hand like the priests in the temple when they shake the damaru.

'These syllables go back to Panini,' the drummer added. He recited the Sanskrit formula once again. In the last line, the grammarian, who lived two and a half thousand years ago, announced his name.

'I have recited the beginning of Panini's grammar, a sequence of fourteen combinations of syllables called the Maheshvarani Sutrani, the Shiva Sutras.'

I later learnt that Panini's grammar is a work of genius, unsurpassed to this day. It is the oldest-known grammar setting out rules for every formal logical language. In 1958, John Backus devised the Backus-Naur Form, BNF, which underlies every computing language. In 1998, Indian linguists T. R. N. Rao and Subhash Kak suggested that the BNF be renamed PBF, or Panini-Backus Form, since Panini had already discovered the governing principles of a universal metalanguage two and a half thousand years ago.

A sutra is an aphorism, meant to be learnt by heart, and must be formulated as concisely as possible. Panini's sutra is the crown and keystone of all other sutras. I read Otto Böthlingk's German translation, published in Leipzig in 1887. 'The composition may perplex us at times but it is rigorous and pithy and marvellously consistent. It aims at the greatest possible concision and to avoid any repetition, and these aims it undoubtedly achieves. The more carefully one studies Panini's grammar, the more one is astonished at his acuity and felicity in mastering such a mass of material. It is a masterpiece of the first order in its field. Later grammars deranged Panini's sutra from its fixed order, trying to bring together material under common themes, but they are utterly incomprehensible without extensive commentary that must always refer to what lies far back or is yet to come, and they are to be regarded as failures.'

I used Saket Maharaj's recitation of the sutra that he had spoken onto my tape recorder, to structure the grammar of the sounds that I developed in the Shri Kashi Vishwanath Shabdanath. For each of the fourteen combinations that Panini had used to represent vowels, consonants and combinations, I assigned one of the characteristic sounds that I had discovered in Benares. I wandered through the city's soundscape in fourteen sonic chapters, from dawn through day and night and on to the next sunrise, through seasons and festivals, Vasant Panchami, Shivaratri and Holi in spring, Durga Puja and Diwali in autumn; I paced the sacred fields, walked through the forest of lingams that Lord Shiva had planted, followed the pilgrim routes to the temples, followed too the horse carts and the wedding bands, the bicycles and rickshaws on their way through the city, followed the men carrying corpses wrapped in red and saffron down to the burning ghats, calling 'Ram nam satya hai!' as they went, the eternal formula proclaiming the god's name as truth; I watched the monkeys shaking the bells in the temples, making them chime as men would.

The longest chapter follows the river. It begins at the great water tower whose groaning pumps suck water up from the river bed, goes past the pipes that belch sewage out into the Ganga, past the rhythmic slap as the dhobis beat laundry against the stones. I drift on a boat past the ghats, listening to the pilgrims singing. One can hear the scrape of the oars on the gunwales, then the voice of Ambika Datta Upadhyaya, the first of the learned pandits of his city to teach the sacred language to a mleccha, a non-Hindu. Daniélou had studied with him and many Western students and professors frequented his house, famous folk from Harvard and Oxford. He agreed to instruct me as well. Whoever wanted to meet him had to visit his house at Assi Ghat, which he only left once a year to take the obligatory ritual bath in the Ganga. I found him on his veranda, whence he could watch the street—a tall man, a little stooped with age, with grey hair and a generous, infectious sense of humour, dressed in the kurta and dhoti of the conservative brahmin.

Lessons took place in the small garden behind his house. His teenage sons waved me onward past the white cow who gave the family milk. You had to take care, since she could kick out or lower her great horns pointedly at anyone who came too close. She only made an exception for the pandit, who radiated such calm that the cow too became placid. I think he liked the fact that I didn't want to solve the riddles of mythology or ask clever questions about the Puranas, leaving it up to him which texts we would read. Reading meant reciting and recitation meant singing. He knew the melody for every strophic metre. The pandit sat on a dais, while I took my place on a low stool in front of him. He would take up a text and sing, I would repeat each line. Sometimes he would gloss single words or phrases but mostly we would just sing. I loved the sound of his voice, the garlands of melodious Sanskrit syllables shining forth from the abysm of time, accompanied by the birds twittering in the garden, sometimes interrupted by the clatter of the milk pail as the cow kicked it over or by the creaking of the rope as the women of the household drew up water from the well.

'You know that one can achieve moksha, liberation, if one drowns in the Ganga?' he asked me.

I nodded.

'Today we will read a text written by a great poet,' he continued. 'A great sinner, whom the river washed clean of all his sins!'

He raised his brows and waited for my reaction.

'Who was he?' I asked.

'Jagannath Panditraj, the king of the pandits, lived in the time of Emperor Akbar and wandered all over India. He was a famous man and like all great men he committed many sins. At last, he came to Benares to purify himself but the priest did not let him take the bath in the Ganga because he had married a Muslim woman—an unforgivable sin for a brahmin. So he sat on the top step of Tulsi Ghat and began to compose the 'Gangalahari', a love song to the Ganga that he so longed for. You will certainly have noticed that the ghat has fifty-two steps!'

I nodded and the pandit winked jovially.

'It is a very beautiful song! He sang the first strophe and the river rose one step to hear his song. When he sang the second strophe, the river rose two steps and when he sang the third, the river rose three steps. When he sang the fifty-second verse, the water of the Ganga rose all the way and took him in.'

He laughed. 'He was drowned!'

We fell silent for a moment, thinking of the poet whose song the Ganga had heard. The birds twittered in the background, the cow kicked against the rattling bucket, inside the house workmen hammered at a sheet of metal.

The paean to the Ganga and the pandit's commentary are on one of the first cassette tapes that I recorded in Benares. The tape brings back memories of the atmosphere in the garden where I spent so many hours listening to the pandit's gentle voice, and I wove the story of the drowned pandit king into the 'Shri Kashi Vishwanath Shabdanath' that played in the palace on the riverbank twenty years later. By then the pandit was long dead. I remember him telling me that as you die, you must hold a cow's tail in your right hand to be sure of reaching the other shore. I was not there but I am sure that he held a cow's tail as he died.

Meanwhile, the pandit's sons, who had led me into the garden once upon a time, were grown men. They had accepted my invitation to the Sound Sattra and stood on the roof of the house on the ghat to listen to the wreath of sound that I had woven for Kashi. At the very moment when they heard their father's voice for the first time since his death, that little cloud appeared and rained a few drops down onto their rooftop terrace.

With beaming faces they called to me, 'The clouds of Heaven are weeping tears of joy!' They looked as though they were about to break into a jig.

Benares, February 1975, Maha Shivaratri

Cross-fade, twenty years back, same place, same night of the year.

I was walking along the main street of Assi once again. That first winter that I spent in Benares, I had not been able to find any singers of dhrupad. The voices of the Dagar brothers had brought me to India but I learnt that Moinuddin, the elder brother, had died; his younger brother Aminuddin lived reclusively in Calcutta. Dhrupad seemed to have vanished from Benares.

The following year I returned. Maha Shivaratri was approaching, the Phalgun dark of the moon, when Kashi's patron god dances down from the Himalayan heights to marry Parvati, daughter of the mountains. The festival follows the Hindu calendar, usually falling in February or March.

In Pappu's tea shop they were discussing that evening's doings as announced by the loudspeakers hung on the telegraph poles, spread across the walls, the houses and the kiosks. Miles of cable strung from box to box delayed the sounds, to reach the farthest speaker last of all. The closer you came, the more the speakers were in sync, so that the listeners might move through layered cascades, delayed and distorted sound, towards its source, until they arrived at the real time of the Dhrupad Mela, the festival celebrated down on the ghat for Maha Shivaratri.

Maha Shivaratri is the high point of the Benares year, so rich in festivals. The ancient scriptures tell how on this night Shiva dances the dance of destruction, the tandava nritya, whereby he lays waste the old world to make way for a new one but for the women of Benares, it is Shiva's wedding night. They honour the lingam, garlanding it with flowers, pouring water upon it; married women pray for their husbands and sons, while the unmarried ones pray for a suitable bridegroom. Mataji had told me the story of how Shiva appeared for his wedding in the form of a dishevelled old yogi, naked, smeared with ash and riding a bull, wearing scorpions as earrings and poisonous cobras as necklace. His eyes were turned to Heaven in ecstasy and a horde of demons accompanied him. When his mother-in-law saw him, she fainted. Only when his bride begged him did he assume the form of a respectable young bridegroom.

For the residents of Benares, Shiva's wedding feast was the ritual occasion to drink bhang. Young and old, child and greybeard, boatman and university professor— all took at least a sip of the drink to share in Shiva's ecstasy. The city hummed and thrummed; a curiously weightless, hallucinatory mood prevailed.

All the temples stood open, and on this night when earth and heaven meet, many pilgrims hurried round the forest of lingams that Shiva planted at Kashi. Thousands of times they invoked the god of ecstasy, uttering wild cries of 'Hara Hara Mahadev!' Their course took them past Tulsi Ghat, scurrying up the steep stairs from the Ganga that flowed as black as night. Torches were swung, electric lamps shone from the tent set up at the top of the ghat. A generator roared, voices and drums could be heard from the tent all through the night till dawn.

Tonight the first Dhrupad Mela was celebrated on Tulsi Ghat. Mahantji, the high priest of the Sankat Mochan Temple, had invited all the living dhrupadiyas to sing their venerable verses that had not been heard in the great cities' concert halls for so long.

Everyone in the quarter knew the white-haired Pandit Amarnath Mishra. He was not only the mahant but also the president of the Akhara Goswami Tulsi Das, one of the traditional wrestling clubs for whom wrestling was a religious observance as well as a sport. At the same time, he played pakhwaj, the heavy bass drum used in dhrupad—a common combination, for wrestlers are frequently drummers as well.

Pandit Amarnath had told me that it was a song from one of the first Indian sound motion pictures that had awoken his passion for the pakhwaj, a song in praise of the sound of the damaru in Shiva's hand. Since then he had followed his passion. But dhrupad was so old-fashioned that there were only a handful of initiates who remembered it at all, in traditionally minded temples and in the hinterlands. Western ethnomusicologists had already declared dhrupad as good as dead. Daniélou had believed the Dagar brothers to be the last of their kind when he recorded them.

But Pandit Amarnath knew better. He had word of the singers and drummers who played in this style in the backwoods and the boondocks and now, towards the end of his life, he wanted to gather them round.

What is dhrupad? The word is an abbreviation of dhru-vapada; Dhruva means fixed and unmoving, like the Pole Star which is called Dhruvatara, and pada means foot—thus also verse, metre. When I asked one of the singers on Tulsi Ghat about the meaning of the word, he answered, 'Dhruvapada—achala pada'—dhrupad is the unalterable verse. He wagged his finger at me, then pointed it straight upwards at the dark night sky where no moon showed. 'Do you see, it does not move, it does not vary—it is eternal!'

Another singer demonstrated the rise and fall of the syllables in which the Samaveda had been recited for thousands of years, the codex of ancient knowledge that only a few today could decipher. It is possible that it goes back to Vedic recitation but dhrupad's histori-cally attested roots are much younger. Dhrupad was the soundtrack for the Bhakti cult of loving submission spread through India by ecstatic poets and wandering saints towards the end of the fifteenth century, singing of the visions they had seen in the sacred groves of Braj.

The new way of singing soon became so famous that the princes inclined their ears to it. Emperor Akbar exempted the temples in Braj from the tax that Hindus in the Mughal Empire had to pay and made the great singer Tansen, whose guru lived in seclusion in the forests of Vrindavan, one of the jewels of his court. While pious sadhus in their temples and hermitages continued to recite the verses of the Bhakti poets, a new generation of singers developed an almost abstract form of the vocal art at the princely courts. This was the origin of the ragas, which would later be called 'North Indian classical music'.

Yet dhrupad is a demanding art, associated with magic and ritual, and its rules must be strictly followed; it is also a style of music performed only by men. New, ornate styles arose that women too could sing. By the nineteenth century at the latest, the flamboyant khayal—literally imagination or fantasy—had won the audience's favour and supplanted dhrupad, along with newly developed instruments such as the sitar that replaced the veena and the tabla which overtook the pakhwaj. To this day, the ornamented and playful khayal dominates North Indian classical music. Dhrupad always strove to free its melodic lines of all decoration, to reveal the lineaments of the raga in clarity and simplicity. It gained a reputation as a difficult art which only a few old people fussed and fretted over, mathematical, devoid of feeling; Baroque music probably had the same reputation in nineteenth-century Europe. Many Indians did not even recognize the word dhrupad. Musicians still knew the style, at least by name, for the dhruvapadas continued to provide the models for every other raga.

A mela is not quite a festival but, rather, a religious gathering that happens in and round a temple, rather like a parish fair in old Europe. The word mela literally means a mixture, a mixing. Someone had painted the names of the musicians who would perform over the three nights of the Dhrupad Mela on the wall outside the tent. I tried to decipher the careful brushstrokes but I did not know any of the names. Then I joined the people thronging into the tent.

Maharaja Vibhuti Narayan Singh had sent his son to represent him at the event. The podium was decked with fresh green leaves, surrounded by clay vessels painted with a calligraphic design that turned the word dhrupad into a conch, and a banner hung at the back of the stage proclaiming the importance of the occasion. A lamp was lit, Mahantji played his pakhwaj to bring Shiva's blessing down on the mela. A group of aged temple singers climbed up onto the podium, which was draped in white sheets, and others followed; some of them seemed to have trouble remembering the old verses. A pakhwaj master rolled up his sleeves, invoked the gods and beat his drum with rugged piety. A cow wandered onto the stage, drawn by the sound of the pakhwaj, and was courteously escorted away.

Then the names of Vidur Mallik and his sons Ramkumar, Prem-kumar and Anandkumar were announced. A middle-aged man took the stage, not even fifty. A curtain of deep black hair fell down to his shoulders and he wore a sharp and stylish moustache. The growling sounds that came from his mouth were repeated by his sons, sitting beside their father like young lions beside the leader of the pride.

A dhrupad concert follows a fixed formula—it begins with the first breath of the alap, the introduction. The voices sink slowly ever deeper through the octaves and the singers explore the shape of the raga note by note. A pulse forms and the voices make patterns, spiralling, until a melodic formula appears, a caesura. The voices leap to a new level, the tempo is doubled again and again, until at the high point they reach the greatest speed that human lips can articulate, a perfect rap, spoken in resounding syllables that follow the rhythm, then a long arc, and the alap is over.

This first part takes at least half an hour. So far, the pakhwaj player has sat motionless next to the singers. Now he tunes his drum. The singer recites the verse, for the performance is a poetry recital as much as it is a concert. Often, several singers will perform together, dhrupad being a demonstration of physical strength as well. A proverb says that you must have the strength of four elephants to sing it.

The drum rolls out to join the voices in a precisely modulated rhythm while the singers build up the majestic structures of the verse. The singers beat the rhythm on their thighs, clap their hands, first in the simple tempo, then double, triple, quadruple, sextuple, octuple, accelerating the recitation in leaps. Again, they break off at the high point.

Then begins an improvised passage, a game in which words, syllables and notes are created to fit the rhythmic structures, then changed and remade. It is the drummer's task to follow these spontaneous patterns. Nothing has been planned beforehand, though the game has been played ten thousand times—what new thing will be created today? The singer and the drummer seem to be engaged in a duel. The singer stops for a fraction of a second amid the cascading syllables, looking at the drummer who must hold his gaze, waiting for the next syllable to fall. Ever and again they meet in the rhythmic cycle, the singers' hands clapping in inexorable time. The audience follows; when you raise and clap your hands, your body is part of the performance, the rhythms run right through you. If you do not join in the game, you have missed this dimension of the recital. For the uninitiated, it can be as baffling as a cricket match. Even so, you can appreciate the song; the majestic contours of the notes tracing a cosmos of shapes in that mysterious part of the brain where we understand music, the sounds drawn up from deep in the belly, syllables shot out at breathtaking speed when the concert reaches its high point and the wild movements of the arms.

Vidur Mallik followed this set path with his teenage sons who joined in his song. 'New clouds, new love, a new bridegroom, a new bride, a new green earth!' began the dhrupad verse that they would sing this evening on Tulsi Ghat. The text went on to enumerate, in the sweet honeyed words of Braj, everything that was now new: 'A new spring, the chataka and the kokila birds call anew, new flowers bloom on a new sari with which Shri Radha bedecks her limbs, the poet Nanda Das has wound a new yellow turban about his head!'

They radiated an indomitable strength, undaunted, proud of the majestic form of the raga handed down by their ancestors, a wild swagger which I had never experienced before. The father poured out honey and hurled lightning bolts, while the sons growled like young tigers.

The February night was cold. Some of the audience made their way home, some made for the tea stall at the entrance. Those who had stayed behind pulled their shawls closer round their shoulders or wrapped up in sleeping bags.

Long after midnight an old man in a long black sherwani took the stage. A pupil supported him as he walked and helped him to sit, for the old singer was partially lame. I heard that he was from the same family but I had never heard of the Mallik family or the dhrupad tradition of Darbhanga, whence the old singer came. I had a little Hindi but I hardly understood a word of what Ram Chatur Mallik said. He spoke a strange, choppy dialect, its words oddly broken up. His tongue too was partly paralysed and he could not fully articulate except when he sang but he had the regal aura of an old prince. Among musicians, he was treated like a king.

That night on Tulsi Ghat, he sang a composition in the midnight raga of Darbari Kanada, with his great-nephew Abhay Narayan. Ragas are sung at particular times of day, the twenty-four hours of the day being divided into eight three-hour praharas; the period after midnight belongs to the majestic Darbari, the raga which was sung in the Mughal princes' darbar, their audience chamber.

The audience warmed themselves after the concert at the tea stall at the entrance. 'Look at those men!' someone next to me said as Ram Chatur Mallik went past us after his concert, supported by Abhay Narayan. 'Don't they look like warriors?'

To me they looked like magicians, whom one may not approach without leave. I could never have imagined exchanging even a word with these people. I found them rather uncanny but they fascinated me as well.

II

Shaheed Express, *Wednesday, 31 July 2002*

I awoke as the train arrived in Gorakhpur. During the morning, the countryside had become greener. We passed ponds, and trees slipped past; slender sal trunks with their light green silvery leaves, a dark mango grove, the fiery red blossoms of the gulmohur, banyans, each a little forest in its own right with its aerial roots spreading out, sometimes a palm tree. Even through the darkened glass of the train window, everything seemed lush and green.

I wondered what feelings might overwhelm me in Amta or what I would hear there. Vidur Mallik's death had been a shock for the whole family; he was only sixty-seven and no one had thought that he might die so suddenly, even though he had been suffering from diabetes for a few years now. For many years, I had arranged concert tours in the West for him and his sons. On the last tour, his teeth had been giving him trouble and in every town we had to take him to a dentist. He kept spitting out the temporary crowns that they had fitted onto teeth worn down to brown stumps by a lifetime of chewing tobacco and betel. He livened up for the concerts, opening his soul, but it was obvious that he had lost his wanderlust. He yearned to be back where they would serve him the food they knew he liked.

He had been living in Vrindavan for the last twenty years. At first, he occupied a room in a gurukul, a traditional music school where the guru lives with his students. After I went back to Germany, he had built a little house at the edge of town and brought his wife, Mataji, from the village. He lived like a sadhu, like one of the ascetics who make up a considerable part of the population. For Hindus, Vrindavan is a sacred place since Krishna spent his childhood here on the banks of the Yamuna. When I visited Vidur Mallik, I witnessed how he was invited almost every evening to the huts at the edge of town, where the sadhus lived, old men in tattered but scrupulously clean dhotis. They celebrated arti every evening, swinging oil lamps before the statues of the gods and sprinkling the congregation with holy water. Afterwards there was something to eat. The evening ended with music; an ancient harmonium was fetched out, and he would glide his fingers up and down the clattering keyboard. Usually one of the sadhus would accompany him on a tabla that seemed as old as the player himself.

He had completely set aside a concert singer's impressive postures: mostly, he shut his eyes or looked downward at the harmonium keys moving under his fingers but he always held his listeners in the palm of his hand.

Foamy bubbles burst on the dark surface of the canals by the railway embankment. Women were working in the fields, stooped over with their saris hitched up. An iron telegraph pole was bent down at an improbable angle, which must have taken enormous force; the wires had snapped and were dangling down left and right. Children played on the embankments. A couple of dirty oil tankers glided past.

It was raining. Farmers sat in puddles, planting rice. Herds of black water buffaloes wallowed in the dark brown ponds. Over and over, I saw telegraph poles with only a few crazy wires swaying at the top. Some were so overgrown with creepers that they were barely recognizable.

This is the forgotten land, they seemed to say, no messages from the outside world reach here any more.

Vidur Mallik was a dhrupad singer, one of the few surviving masters of the art who could send their voices gliding, spiralling seemingly endlessly, swooping majestically through the ancient melodies of the ragas, but in these temples he sang simple bhajans, hymns to Radha or Krishna that tell of the vanity of earthly life and the unquenchable yearning for the divine; feelings that his audience shared with him.

He would teach almost anyone who came to ask for it, which was most unusual for Indian musicians who look at their art as capital that they have to live off for a lifetime. They guard their treasures well, only opening the storehouse of songs for hard cash or if they are providing some musical knowledge as a dowry for their daughters, but Vidur Mallik had always been very generous. He called it his gurudhan, the service that a guru performs for the gods. In return he claimed the right to turn up to give lessons only when he felt like it. Almost every evening, the youth of the town would come to visit, in ones and twos or in greater numbers, and he would listen patiently while they sang back to him the old songs he had taught them. Some of them he helped to get jobs at the All India Radio station in the nearby town of Mathura. He was having trouble with his diabetes, and when his condition worsened, his youngest son Premkumar would bring him to Allahabad. Premkumar had been teaching at the university there for twenty years and had built himself a comfortable middle-classs Indian house.

Vidur Mallik would always camp out on the sofa in the reception room where otherwise Premkumar taught his private pupils, mostly young daughters of well-to-do parents who came to him to complete their classical education. After a little while in Allahabad, his father would feel better, since there was a real doctor here to prescribe medicine and family to make sure that he followed doctor's orders, took his medicine and avoided sweet food. Back in Vrindavan, his condition would always worsen.

A few weeks ago, he had become visibly frail. His second son Anandkumar, who also lived in Vrindavan, happened to be abroad on tour at the time, so Premkumar took his father and Mataji to Allahabad. He was taken to the intensive care ward, where he died early the next morning. He was cremated the same day.

It all happened so fast that hardly anyone was there except Mataji, Premkumar and his family. Premkumar called me the next day. The wider family had set out for Amta, their ancestral village, where Vidur Mallik had been born and where his last rites would be performed.

Every time I looked out of the train compartment's darkened window, I saw high water, standing in the trenches at the side of the tracks, scummed over, yellowish-green. When the train stopped in a small town called Chaprakacheri, I got out to buy biscuits and fetch some water. It was only five in the morning, the sun was only just over the horizon but its heat was already fierce. If the train kept to its timetable I would be in Darbhanga some time in the evening, I thought; someone from the family would be there to meet me and I might reach the village the same night.

Meanwhile, the compartment was filling up with passengers. They relayed news and jokes to one another from one compartment to the next, their voices raised, their main concern being money and the various ways it might be got. I kept seeing ruins outside the window, half-finished houses with iron rods sticking out from cement pillars; they had not even been fully built but were already going to wrack and ruin. A wooden pole on a temple roof held a bundle of straw and a broken clay pot.

Some of the young men who had boarded the train worked in the law courts and wore white barristers' bands at their throats. In loud voices they told one another of the cases they had on the go; they smelt of betel and lime. Hours later, the Ganga glided past below us, vast and yellow. The landscape beyond our window barely changed; a broad plain, lonely trees, fields always full of people, water buffaloes in the ponds.

By now my fellow passengers had become interested in where I was bound. I told them that I was heading to Darbhanga and thence onward to the village. They laughed. There would be a lot of water there, they reckoned, we had not yet reached the main flooding. None of them had a clear idea of what it might be like in those parts. We were already late, the train was rolling forward at walking pace by now. No one knew how many hours we may still have to travel.

Ghataro Gram—the village where the Malliks' ancestors had once lived—is near Hajipur, the town we had just passed. It is a satisthan. A small stone pillar in the village square shows the goddess in a wreath of flames. Her forehead has been brushed with red powder, flowers and ashes of incense sticks lie all around—showing that rites are still celebrated here. One of the Mallik ancestors had become sati in Ghataro Gram by climbing onto her dead husband's pyre and placing his head in her lap to burn together with him.

For the Malliks, the sati was a fixed point in their lives. They believed unquestioningly that she heard their prayers. The story went that before the flames devoured her, the sati had prayed that musicians be born to her family in every generation. This had held true right down to Vidur Mallik's grandchildren. The children were already musicians when they were born. A few years before, I had seen one of Vidur Mallik's daughters arrive at her brother's house in Allahabad with a little bundle in her arms, wrapped up in a blanket; only the face peered out from beneath a woolly hat tied under the chin. When she told me that this child, who might have been all of two years old, could sing, I assumed that this was a proud mother exaggerating the truth. The child seemed to have no desire to sing at all but simply made little complaining sounds when the mother tickled it under the chin and urged over and over again, 'Gao, gao!—Sing, sing!' At last, he gave in to her demands, and sang—an entire song, line for line, word for word. The voice of course was that of an infant but the text and the melody were clear and easy to understand. Everyone in the family knew this song. If I had not heard it and seen it myself, I would never have believed it. It was as though the music were passed on as part of their genetic code.

The family originally came from Rajasthan, where the cult of sati survives to this day. Certainly, the burning of widows had been forbidden in 1829 by British governor general William Bentinck, who called it an 'inhuman and impious rite', but the British had not managed to quench the belief in a sati's powers. Only a few years before, an eighteen-year-old girl had been burnt on her husband's pyre in a village in Rajasthan. Rumour had it that she had been drugged and that her in-laws had pushed her back into the flames three times as she tried to escape. Supposedly, they had hoped that sati pilgrimage might be a lucrative business, tempting pilgrims to the village. It was certainly plausible. When the news spread, thousands of peasants from the district poured into the village and tried to build a temple. The circumstances were never entirely cleared up.

The Malliks knew the story of course. It was certainly possible that the villagers had murdered that girl but, in their view, that had nothing to do with sati. Their ancestress had been a true sati, their family history was the proof. The sign of a true sati was that the fire would ignite itself, as in her case. Her family had locked her up in a hut to prevent her suicide but suddenly, the thatch had burst into flames and she emerged, her eyes shining like those of the mother goddess. I heard the story again and again of how the fire had started at the sati's right toe as she brought down the blessing of perpetual music for her family. At the beginning of the last century, the princely printing house of Darbhanga Raj Press had published a verse chronicle of the family, which began with an invocation to the sati.

In Hajipur I bought a copy of *India Today*. 'What's Wrong with the Weather?' asked the front-page headline. Two-thirds of India were suffering from drought because the monsoon had not come, it said, and the ever-increasing temperatures threatened to dry the Ganga at its source. By contrast, eastern Bihar had had twice the usual rainfall and was flooded. 'Weather Forecasts Go Crazy: Drought Approaches Hundred-Year Record', ran a subtitle. The article predicted the consequences of climate change: the Himalayan glaciers would melt by 2020, so that, after initial disastrous floods, nothing but desert would remain. In the next decade, rice and grain harvests would drop by 15 per cent and the climate would breed a wave of epidemics such as dengue. The predictions were anything but restrained. The rest of the world had hardly noticed the current catastrophe, a mix of floods and drought, and the author had taken the opportunity to throw together all the predictions he could find on the subject. By 2015, parts of Bombay would be submerged by the rising sea level, he wrote, Bangladesh would be completely gone, and the US would be transformed into a parched desert. 'Is Sex OK?' asked the next page. 'India's film industry is trying to free itself from the clutches of a prudish and archaic censorship, but the government is still putting up a fight.' The culture pages reported on a concert in Delhi where more than forty musicians had played instruments that seemed doomed to vanish—rudra-veena, sarangi, pakhwaj and many others which young people were no longer learning because they offered little profit. 'I can't bear the thought that in future, Indians might have to learn the rudra-veena from foreigners, an instrument that has been played in India for thousands of years,' complained Asad Ali Khan. 'Isn't it scandalous?'

The current Patna edition of the *Times of India* gave more precise information about the situation in the north of Bihar—more dams had broken, the situation was getting worse. People were sitting on the roofs of their houses or in trees and they would have to stay there until the waters receded, since there were no boats. People who had fled for higher ground with their herds had not had anything to eat for days. In a town called Rosera, convicts had been moved to the upper storeys of the prison but now the building was unreachable and they were in danger of drowning. The report ended by declaring that the fury of the waters was so great that the authorities had been forced to suspend all relief measures for the time being.

Around noon, a group of soldiers entered the carriage, armed with automatic weapons which they leant on the seats. The gun barrels gleamed with many years' use. What had they seen, these weapons, where had their muzzles been pointed? The soldiers didn't ponder such questions but sat cracking peanuts, handing out a few nuts to a blind beggar who was wandering through the carriage singing a prayer, led by a child. The soldiers were the bodyguards for a politician who was sitting in the next compartment.

They brought along a *Hindustan Times* which had some more precise information: at least a hundred and fifty-seven had drowned in Bihar, including twenty-eight dead in Madhubani district, north of Darbhanga; twenty-one districts in all were affected by the floods; six thousand, one hundred and forty-five villages were underwater. Soon, it was reported, the army would intervene.

In the afternoon it began to rain. A wet water buffalo stood stoically in a field, while three white herons stalked sedately through the puddles. As the hours went by, the rain became heavier. A storm came on, the wind tearing at the branches of trees bowing down beneath the driving downpour. Wet dogs and cows swept past

our windows. People were cowering on a station platform, their trousers, shirts and coats soaked. Umbrellas
flapped in the storm and turned inside-out.

In the twilight, huts glided past the train windows,
scanty shelters built of stacked mud brick. They were
covered over with sheets of plastic and with sacking,
weighed down by wooden planks. The sheets were
rattling under the rain and the paths had become
quagmires.

THE RAINMAKERS

Darbhanga, 1788

Not a cloud could be seen in the sky as the two brothers sat down in the square in front of the Kali temple. The heavens groaned. The rivers, the canals, the waterways, the streams and ponds had all dried up long ago and the wells yielded not a drop of water. The soil was parched like the cracked skin on a starving body. The people were crying out for water. The bazaar had become a ghost town, the hot wind blew dust across the broad square by the empty ditch where, earlier, crops had grown.

The famine of 1770 was the worst in Tirhut in living memory. In Tirhut—the land of herdsmen—peasant farmers lived alongside their livestock. Water buffaloes and cows provided them with milk and they cooked their meals over the dried dung. The cattle ploughed their fields, pulled their carts and brought up water from their wells. But now the region between the Bagmati, Gandaki, Kamala and Kosi rivers was utterly laid waste. Now the Kosi was called the 'River of Tears'. Thousands of square miles that had previously been under the plough lay abandoned. Hunger and thirst had killed half the population and the other half had fled. Birds of prey wheeled above this wilderness looking for carrion but finding only bones. Hordes of wild elephants rampaged through the land, with no one left to stop the havoc they wrought. Bandits robbed anyone who dared to travel the land. The moneylenders mercilessly demanded payment of their debts. The seed set aside for the next planting season had long been devoured. The East India Company's tax collectors only made the situation worse. The farmers usually paid half of their harvest, eight annas in a rupee. One rupee was sixteen annas back then. Anna also meant a meal and one rupee could mean sixteen meals. Now the oppressors were demanding nine annas from the farmers.

'As far as the eye can see, there is only waste land,' a local judge observed in 1781. There were no longer any farmers who could be taxed. In 1783, the tax collector in charge of Tirhut suggested that farmers could be fetched from the realm of the wazir of Awadh to repopulate the abandoned lands. But there was no rain in the next two years either. News came that even in Lucknow, the fabulously wealthy capital of Awadh, which once had been the Pearl of the Orient, the starving citizens were stripping bark from the trees that shaded the boulevards of their city.

A huge crowd had gathered to listen to the two miracle-working singers who had come from Awadh. The maharaja sat not on his throne but on a carpet spread out on the ground, his courtiers gathered round him; all were equal before the goddess. Maharaja Madhav Singh had called all the pandits of Mithila; he had ordered the brahmins to perform the Vedic sacrifices and to implore the rain god Indra's help. He had asked the aid of tantriks, sadhus, fakirs and magicians; he himself had prayed for rain for his suffering people—but no rain came.

The brothers Radhakrishna and Kartaram were said to have learnt the siddhi of rain-making, the magical power contained in Megh—one of the six wonder-working ragas of the fathers. There were only six such ragas that were said to have special powers. Musicians said that Bhairav held the power to set a pestle grinding in a mortar on its own; Malkauns could melt stones; Hindol could raise a wind; Shri caused flower buds to burst into bloom; Dipak could light the wicks of oil lamps; and Megh brought the rain.

To attain siddhi required not merely musical perfection but spiritual practice. First of all, the acolyte had to renounce all property and worldly ties to devote his strengths entirely to serving the holy music. Their teacher had told Radhakrishna and Kartaram that to attain siddhi they must spend seven nights meditating at a cremation ground. They must see within their hearts the image of a jewelled island in a sea of nectar. Among the parijat trees growing on the island, they would find a temple built of ornate stone and within the temple the kalpadruma, the miraculous tree. Beneath this tree they would find Shiva, sitting with the goddess at his right hand in the form of the holy syllable Om. They must descend through the hole in the crown of his skull and meditate until from the very centre of that syllable, the bindu, a stream of sound would pour out into their hearts, following the path of the sushumna, the second of the three channels in the human body. This ritual was called 'the inward bath' and was simply the first of many. It must not be revealed to the common crowd, whom Shiva in the Guptasadhana Tantra called cattle, telling the goddess that she must not reveal this mystery he had taught her to the profane, any more than she would bare her yoni in front of strangers. In truth, he told her in this esoteric text that she herself was the secret and that he was nothing but an ignorant fool.

These were deep mysteries and it required many years of practice to understand the teachings. Radhakrishna and Kartaram lived as fakirs, attaining the bodies of yogis, the spirits of shishyas, the voices of gandharvas. Their guru whispered the rain-making mantra into their ears on the banks of the Ganga in a sacred spot that magnified its magical power ten thousand times.

His name was Bhupat Khan. They studied with him for twenty-two years—twenty-two, the number of the shrutis, the microtones described in the ancient texts. Bhupat Khan belonged to a magical tradition which taught the siddhis to awaken the miraculous powers of the ragas. His mother was a descendant of Tansen, the arch-mage and musician, one of the nine jewels of Emperor Akbar's court. His splendour outshone that of everyone else, even if the old musicians knew the names of all those on whose shoulders Tansen had stood— above all, his guru Swami Haridas who lived as a hermit in the forest of Vrindavan. Emperor Akbar had wished to hear him sing but could only fulfil his wish by approaching the hermitage incognito, disguised as his court musician's groom. The emperor asked the singer why he could not sing as beautifully as his teacher in the wilderness on the banks of the Yamuna. Tansen answered that his guru sang not for a mere emperor but for God.

When Radhakrishna and Kartaram asked for permission to return to their home village after twenty-two years of study, their teacher Bhupat Khan told them to sing to his mother, their guruma. This descendant of the great Tansen, in whose veins the miracle-worker's blood flowed, decided that they had to study for another six months, and so they learnt even more than the twenty-two shrutis that the wise know of. Another version says that there are not twenty-two shrutis but an infinite number—as many as there are emotions in the sea of human feeling. No one could ever reach the further shore of this ocean of sound. As one of the dhruvapadas puts it: 'The knowledge of sound is endless; musicians, saints and even the gods have tried to find its furthest shore, but none have ever reached it. They sang and they sang, and at last they became weary.'

But Radhakrishna and Kartaram could not tire. They knew how hard a task the maharaja had set them and for a long time they had hesitated to answer his entreaty. Finally, they agreed to sing because they saw the despair and misery of his people.

They asked the maharaja for a secluded room where they could prepare for their task. After a ritual purification, they entered the chamber, sat down and lighted the lamps and incense before praying for the mother goddess' blessing. No one else was allowed to enter. After seven hours, they emerged. The family legend says that they had prayed with their eyes closed and, suddenly, it was as though a hand had touched them. Someone was standing behind them, a hand on each head. They opened their eyes but could see no one. The mother goddess herself had touched them. Shakti had given them a sign that their song would be heeded.

They thanked the goddess and strode out towards the Kali temple, where a crowd awaited them. The residents of this dusty town, the farmers from the parched land, all crowded round Maharaja Madhav Singh and his courtiers. More and more people streamed into the square in front of the temple, watching with burning curiosity as the two singers prostrated themselves before the goddess. Their faces gleamed, reflecting an unearthly light, their eyes were as dark and deep as wells. The watching crowd turned their gaze away, hardly daring to look at them. Only the children still stared, wide-eyed. Radhakrishna, the elder brother, seemed like a god to them; black locks flowed down past his shoulders, the brahmin's sacred thread was tied about his torso and he glowed like a hero warrior from the great battle in the Mahabharata. Kartaram, the younger, was no less than his brother, just as Lakshmana had been the equal of his brother Rama.

The sun beat down on the heads of the crowd and bathed the temple square in a livid, glistening light. Not the least scrap of cloud was to be seen anywhere in the sky. The heavens were completely clear.

Silence fell. The two brothers, orange cloths wound about their waists, sat with their heads bent, praying. A gentle murmur could be heard; even the priests could not follow the words, for this prayer was spoken only for the mother goddess.

A sigh went up as the elder brother took the first breath of the long journey which lay before them. Kartaram joined in and the two raised their voices together. Every breath sent a new lament to the heavens for the pitiful state of the earth, for the suffering of the men and animals who must live there and yet died. At first, there were only single notes, drawn out, sustained, but soon the voices began to pulse in the rhythm of the blood flowing in the singers' veins. The sound became more urgent, as though they had mounted horses that were flying up to the skies. They sang the sthayi, then the antara and the sanchari.

When the brothers had reached the abhog, the fourth and final part, a tiny white cloud appeared on the eastern horizon. The listeners watched with astonishment. Slowly the cloud drew closer, driven by a wind that sprang up from the north, where the Himalayas stand. It spread and grew. Dust scurried upward and grains of sand scoured the farmers' burning skin as they stood staring open-mouthed first at the sky and then at the two singers whose saffron raiment fluttered in the wind.

They sang on, untroubled, utterly submerged in their devotions. The brothers had their eyes closed and thus could not see what was happening round them. The first drops fell even before they had finished their song. The people gaped incredulously at dark spots marking the sand the colour of blood.

A cold breeze sprang up and soon the wind, whipping the rain across the open square, rattled at the temple doors. Birds screeched, shrill, fearful; the storm snatched straw from the rooftops and drove sharp-edged palm leaves across the square, torn from the trees. The earthen wall of a hut collapsed, water flooded the field. The farmers had cowered down onto the ground but now they got to their feet, fearful, and ran.

The courtiers tried in vain to protect the maharaja. They tried to hold a cloth over him but the wind tore it from their hands. They looked at him imploringly. Still, the two brothers sat in the middle of the field, their eyes closed, and seemed not to have noticed the tempest.

Crouched over, fighting to make his way against the storm, the maharaja crept towards the two brothers on his knees. The storm lashed down at him and water dripped from his locks. Streams of water were flowing down the singers' shoulders. The maharaja could no longer see the ground. As he remembered it later, they seemed shrouded in water right up to their chests. He bent down, plunged his hands into the water that gurgled and lapped about the singers and touched their feet. He implored Radhakrishna and Kartaram to end their song, to put a stop to the storm.

Thus he broke their meditation and the thunderstorm too came to an end.

III

Samastipur, Thursday, 1 August 2002

The *Shaheed Express* finally arrived around midnight, having stopped on the tracks several times along the way, sometimes for hours in the middle of nowhere. Samastipur turned out to be its final stop on this journey. It was another twenty-four miles from Samastipur to Dar-bhanga but word had it that the lines were underwater all the way. A bridge had gone down and the train could not go on.

How long would it take for normal service to be resumed? Perhaps a week or two, my fellow passengers thought, or perhaps longer, no one could say for sure. Perhaps, they told me as they went their way, there were boats that could take me across the river where the railway bridge had gone down, but to get that far I would have to wade through the flood water for at least six miles. In some places it was chest-high and I would have to carry my suitcase on my head. They shouldered their own luggage, then left the compartment and vanished into the night.

I asked round for alternatives. The only train going anywhere beyond Samastipur had set out from Howrah Station in Calcutta and went onward to Raxaul, the Nepali border station. Perhaps I would be able to get to Amta via Nepal; after all, it was only twenty miles from the border to the village. Granted, there was no official border crossing on the way to Amta but I knew that Indian pilgrims could cross the border to get to Janakpur, home of Janaka, king and god, and his daughter Sita. The holy town is on the Nepalese side but pilgrims can cross the border without showing a passport. I thought I could persuade a border official that I was a pilgrim.

They told me that the rails were clear as far as Raxaul and the journey would take about five hours. Water was gushing down the deforested slopes of the Himalayas, which could no longer stop the rain. The Terai, the plains at the foot of the mountains stretching from Nepal to India, were also flooded with water that had burst the dams and was rushing down into India but it might be possible to find a car in Raxaul. In which case, I could reach the Darbhanga district by going along parallel to the border. Admittedly, it was a detour of several hundred miles but it seemed the only possibility to get there. It was shortly after midnight and the *Mithila Express* to Raxaul was due at 4.08 that morning.

The land was already called Mithila before the maharajas made Darbhanga their capital. They had not conquered the land but held it as a grant from the Mughal emperors, not for their military service—as was usual— but for their great learning. Customs were said to have survived in Mithila that had long died out elsewhere. The brahmins still scrupulously fulfilled their forefathers' ancestral duties, going back centuries; their rites took longer and were different from those in other regions. The farmers' wives in Madhubani painted pictures on the mud walls of their huts that were a counterpart to their husbands' deep knowledge of the sacred texts. In Mithila, the saying went, even the parrots spoke Sanskrit.

That was long ago though. Mithila is the border region in northern Bihar. Decades ago, the Indian press had decided that the whole province was a realm of darkness and paid almost no attention to it any more. Bihar is the poorest state in India. Almost the entire population lives off the land, the only industry worth mentioning is the illegal manufacture of firearms. The government is even more corrupt than that of the other Indian states. The former chief minister was a notorious villain who stayed in power thanks to crooked deals with the rich landowners who really ruled the state. Right now he was no longer in power but before he went to prison for his crimes, he had helped his wife to take over his job. Be all that as it may, the two of them barely had any influence outside the capital Patna.

Conditions were worst round Patna. The country was run by rival landowners who controlled private armies. Whole villages were burnt down when the landless labourers who made up one-third of the population dared to exercise their right to vote.

Conditions got steadily worse. A land reform had been launched all of forty years ago but the government had purchased less than 1 per cent of state territory for proposed redistribution and only a fraction of this had actually changed hands. The Dalits—whose civil rights were mere fiction—continued to live as little more than slaves. Things are not quite as bad in northern Bihar but even here the illiteracy level is one of the highest in India. Three-quarters of the population can neither read nor write, nor do the universities function properly; the infrastructure is falling apart.

I knew all this as an eyewitness. Ramkumar, the eldest of Vidur Mallik's three sons, held a post as professor of music at the Sanskrit University housed in the last maharaja's palace at Darbhanga. He had taken over the position on the death of his uncle, Ram Chatur Mallik, but hardly ever lectured or gave classes. The university only existed on paper. Most of the time it was on strike for some reason or other and the professors had not been paid a salary for ages.

At last, I found someone on the platform who was willing to open the first-floor waiting room for me. After he had unfastened the padlock, he led me back downstairs to the stationmaster's office to go through the formalities required before I could spend the night. The door was open. A light bulb dangled from the ceiling and a huge book lay open but the chap in charge was not to be seen.

My rescuer assured me that he would certainly turn up soon. He went off looking for him but came back alone after a quarter of an hour. A microphone hung on a wooden board on the wall. He switched it on and mumbled hoarsely into it incomprehensible words that boomed up and down the empty platform in a tinny echo.

Nothing happened. After another ten minutes, he repeated the whole procedure. At last, a tousled man in uniform turned up, rubbing sleep off his eyes. He leafed ostentatiously through the huge book, examined my ticket and copied the information into the columns on the page. I had to pay a few rupees and sign, then I could go and sleep for a while.

Wooden bunks stood in the flickering neon light; the beds had patched old sheets and pillows flattened from much use. Mosquito nets hung from the bedposts, torn and dark with age; given that they had huge holes, they clearly no longer served their purpose. I lay down beneath the fan that wafted the hot air across the ceiling. It was midnight but still much too hot to sleep. My head ached. I tried to plan how I might reach the village. A little later, the power went off. The neon lights flickered and died, the fan groaned and went round one last time.

Why couldn't the Malliks get themselves a telephone? After all, there was a connection to the village. There were three brick houses in Amta, with tiled roofs, although the rest were built of mud brick and thatched with straw. One of these brick houses had belonged to Ram Chatur Mallik, the family patriarch and court singer to the last maharaja; he had died more than ten years ago. The second belonged to his great-nephew and disciple, Abhay Narayan Mallik, who now lived in Delhi, and the third belonged to Vidur Mallik. There was certainly a dusty, old black telephone standing in Ram Chatur Mallik's house but it had already stopped working by the time I first visited Amta twenty years ago. There was vague talk of having it re-connected and a sum of money had even been set aside for the purpose but the plan was never carried out. When he had called me a few days ago from Allahabad, Premkumar Mallik had told me that there was a telephone in the next village, Gangadah. The family had just been getting ready to travel to Amta.

It was a sizeable family—Vidur Mallik had three sons and three daughters and between them they had nearly twenty children. Then there were the other aunts, uncles, nephews and nieces on his father's and mother's sides. Most of them no longer lived in the village but were scattered across North India. In addition, the villagers from all round the neighbourhood were also to be fed, the count going on to three thousand people.

As far as I knew, this was going to happen the next day. I estimated that I might, perhaps, be able to make it to Darbhanga by the evening. It would have been good to be able to call, to find out how or whether I could reach Amta at all but Premkumar Mallik had forgotten to give me the number for that telephone in Gangadah.

The darkness didn't last long. Every few minutes the neon tube and the fan would come back to life, only to wheeze and die again almost immediately. An entire family, with children and luggage, trooped through the room to wash in the lavatory next door. The stationmaster ran after them, trying to shoo them out, but the wife had already bolted the bathroom door on herself. I heard water rattling into the bucket which she then poured over herself. One by one, all the family members took their turn.

By the time they had made themselves scarce, a man had lain down on the bed next to mine and was snoring. Outside in the night, the locomotives shrieked like wild birds.

Bihar, May 1984

Main phir dil vahin laya hun

—someone had carefully painted on the partition behind the driver, high above the passengers' heads, so that they had a good view of the curling calligraphy, framed with hearts: 'Hither I carry my heart once more.'

On the right side of the bus, an aeroplane swooped above a landscape with lakes, while on the left, gazelles leapt through snowy mountains; garlands of hearts and roses swathed the whole vehicle. On the rear bumper dangled a black tin cutout, a frightful face meant to ward off the evil eye.

We were driving north. The bus bumped across the concrete ridges of a newly erected bridge but there was no water to be seen. To the right and left of the road we could see a dry, dirt-coloured landscape, until we crossed the Ganga, now a mere trickle. It was early May and the dry season had just begun.

I didn't know where I was carrying my heart but I was curious as to what awaited me in Amta. Vidur Mallik, sleeping next to me with his arms folded across his chest and his head tipped over to the side, was my guru. I was studying singing with him but there was no excessive formality between us. A year ago, he had taken over the music school in Vrindavan, the gurukul where we had lived together since. His eldest son Ramkumar was looking after the family lands back in the village but Vidur Mallik had to keep an eye on things and a visit was long overdue.

He had been speaking of it for weeks but Vidur Mallik was not a man to make decisions quickly. He was the kind of person who prefers to set off quite suddenly on a momentary impulse and to tackle problems only when they absolutely cannot be put off any longer. In India, you are supposed to reserve a seat if you want to travel on the night train and since these seat tickets are rare, you really need to turn up at the station a day or two beforehand. Vidur Mallik had been unable to decide, though, when he wanted to travel and so at the very last moment we had squeezed onto the *Ganga Yamuna Express* running east from Mathura. We spent the night stretched out side by side on a single-plank bed that a friendly conductor had found for us, for a consideration of ten rupees. In the morning we had changed in Patna, boarding the bus which would take us to Darbhanga.

A roadblock came into view. Two men were posted to the left and right and as the bus came closer they tugged on a rope weighted down with dangling stones, blocking the way. The driver had to stop, and they collected their toll.

As the bus set off again, I nodded off to sleep. In a half-doze I noticed that the buses coming the other way were slowing down, the drivers calling hints and news to one another in hoarse voices.

The next barrier approached. This time, a timber beam blocked the road but in the meantime, our driver had thought up a trick to save paying the toll. At first, he slowed down and acted as though he wanted to stop but as soon as the men at the roadside lifted their beam, he stepped on the accelerator and slipped through. The bus lurched but none of the passengers batted an eyelid.

A rattling woke me. The vehicle was groaning, the worn tyres complaining as the driver turned off the tarmac highway onto a dirt road through sandy scrubland, dotted with a few sparse shrubs. Apparently, there was no other way to avoid the next road block. Wrenching wildly at his wheel, our driver was taking us over a ploughed field which only oxcarts could properly cross. We wallowed through potholes, climbed hillocks, swaying dangerously on the embankments. As we got back on the highway at the next village, the bus tore a lump from the leaf roof of one of the huts at the roadside and took it along.

The passengers laughed. One of them told me that the bus had no travel certificate and shouldn't even be on the road. This was why the tickets were cheaper by a few rupees. They had chosen this bus because it was cheap. It didn't matter that the journey would take a little longer, we'd arrive sometime, and what were a few hours here or there?

It was dark in Laheriaserai, the Darbhanga suburb where we got off the bus. Only a few gas lanterns were shimmering in the distance. We followed the lanterns and Vidur Mallik stopped in front of a wooden shed. In the darkness I could make out the form of a man stretched out on a table. Vidur Mallik called something, the man leapt up, bent down and touched his guru's feet in ceremonial greeting. He was Vidur Mallik's student and played the flute. By day he ran a 'hotel', or what was called a hotel in this part of the world—a wooden shed with sacking stretched across to shelter customers from the sun, where he served tea. At night he lay down to sleep on the only table in the place.

The two men led me through the darkened streets to the hut where I was to sleep. By the light of the kerosene lantern I saw a bed, a chair, a few old clothes, a bookshelf.

Vidur Mallik pointed to the sign that hung over the door, 'Pandit Sukhdev Mallik Sangeet Mahavidyalaya'. He explained, 'This is the music school that I opened in my father's name. I lived in this room for two years.'

A mosquito net hung over the bed, black with smoke. As usual, it was tattered and full of holes. The windows were shut and barred but the mosquitoes made their way in and found my blood even in the dark.

We set off for Amta in the early hours. In the morning light we found a bus at the station which was so full that we had to climb onto the roof. The vehicle set off, juddering and shaking. The passengers drew their heads in away from dangling power cables; a little later, we had to duck beneath the branches of a palm tree that stretched across the road. The leaves were enormous, their thorny edges razor-sharp; they could easily have decapitated a man. The people sitting round me ducked nimbly, while I involuntarily flattened myself out on the roof to avoid the branches, as much as I could amid the luggage and the suitcases. My neighbours laughed at my efforts.

They were in a good mood. It was a clear morning, the wind of our motion cooled us as the day's heat gradually increased. From where I sat on the roof I could see all across the flat countryside. Fields stretched out left and right, interrupted by palms and mango groves. Poplars and the scaly olive trunks of the eucalyptus trees lined our road. We overtook oxcarts and bicycles, huts whizzed past, people at the roadside dodged out of our path, children ran and tried to follow the bus, dogs ran after us for a while and then were left behind, barking. The earth was brick-red, sandy, the ditches still full of the last monsoon's rain, the plants luxuriantly green. Northern Bihar is one of India's most fertile regions—properly irrigated, the soil can give three or even four crops in a year. Shrubs at the road-side were hung with the upside-down white datura blossoms, while tendrils of violet-blue morning glory wound round branches and gateposts. In the distance, long columns of smoke hung above the chimneys of a brickworks.

Whole thickets of ganja grew in the ditches at the side of the road. The local hashish is not smoked but ground in mortars and made into a tasty drink with sugar and almonds, sometimes with poppy seed, and served in the evening as a cooling and relaxing drink called thandai, whereas the green stuff got from the dried and pounded leaves is called bhang. Round Darbhanga it is so popular that a folk etymology derives the name of the district from the phrase gate—dar—to bhang.

Taken as a drink, bhang will cool, but hashish, which is smoked, heats the body. Sadhus smoke hashish to dry out their bodies and sit in front of burning fires, while bhang is the drug of choice for the responsible paterfamilias. A miniature painting in the Prince of Wales Museum in Bombay shows Shiva sieving the drink with its crushed leaves through a cloth, surrounded by his family. His wife Parvati holds their little son Ganesha in her lap while Ganesha's steed, the rat, nibbles at a sweetmeat; his brother Kartikeya feeds grass to the bull Nandi, who is lying placidly, content. They look expectantly at the pot in which their father is mixing the green treat. Under the picture we read, 'The Holy Family'.

Baheri, the station where we climbed down from the roof of the bus around noon, is the Bihari equivalent of a village from a Western film. On either side of a dusty street stand thatched huts and little shops made of wooden posts, metal sheeting and sacking. The only brick house, a one-storey building with a tiled roof, belonged to the local country doctor, who played the sitar and had studied under Vidur Mallik. We rang the doorbell. Vidur Mallik wanted to pay his respects but the doctor was out on call.

A little way down the street was the police station and a hut with a public address system. Horses were tied up in front of the hut, carts were parked at the side of the road with their shafts resting in the dust, while a tractor chugged its motor next to them. Chickens clucked across the street, cows, donkeys and goats grazed among the huts. The shops were selling food and sweets. A man sitting behind a woodfire fished out the sweet, sticky brown rings of jalebi from the hot oil bubbling in his rusty cauldron. He poured us little clay cups of tea that tasted of smoke.

There was a bar as well. Clay pots and bottles lying about on the ground in front of the thatched hut showed that it sold tadi, a rather foul-smelling palm toddy. Drive an axe into the trunk of a palm tree and during the course of the day, the sap will run from the scar into the pots you have tied to the trunk. It will ferment under the hot sun and in the evening, it will be ready to drink.

We set off on foot for the village, having hired a rickshaw driver to carry our luggage. He walked behind us, pushing his vehicle across the field. There was no point even thinking of riding. After a few hundred yards, the dirt road tailed off onto a muddy track across the fields, through deep holes, across ditches and slumped and broken bridges.

After a good half hour, Vidur Mallik stopped and pointed to a white dome in the distance, looming from the dark green stand of trees.

'Look, that is the temple that my father built!'

Only the temple roof could be seen above the sea of foliage. The village of Amta lay hidden among the trees of the mango grove that gave the village its name; Amta is a continuation of am, mango. As we neared the little wood, men ran towards us across the fields, waving their arms. 'Malik! Malik!' they called, even while they were a good way off. Mallik was Vidur's family name. It is close to 'malik' which means lord or master. Possibly, the family adopted the surname Mallik when the maharaja made his gift of land to them. The word malik arrived in India with the Arabic-speaking merchants and the soldiers who served in the Mughal army; among its other uses, it is also one of the ninety-nine names of God mentioned in the Koran. Gradually, the word had become the family name, even though they had remained Hindus like their princely patrons in Darbhanga.

This was unusual for Indian musicians. Most had become Muslim thanks to their close association with the Mughal courts. It was enough if a musician chewed the betel leaf that a prince had handed him—a sign of favour which could not be refused—for people of his religion to regard him as contaminated, a person that must be shunned.

The men in the village called me mehman, guest, and kept using this name for the next few weeks. This society worked with clearly defined roles; by using this appellation they reminded me that I was a guest, someone who was welcomed but who would not stay.

The farmhands surrounded Vidur Mallik and asked him the news, while he handed out bidis, little Indian cigarettes, a few crumbs of tobacco rolled in the leaf of the tendu tree. He gave me one too, drawing it from the colourful paper packaging showing a solemn face, the founder of the bidi company. 'My father smoked bidis as well,' he said as he shook it out. 'Earlier, brahmins used to breathe fire, now they just breathe smoke!' Laughing, rather proud of his father's joke, he told me the story, which went all the way back to the times of the Angrez Raj, the British rule in India. His father had come up with this bon mot when soldiers had demanded to know why he did not take the bidi off his mouth when a British officer went past. The soldiers had laughed at his joke and let him go his way.

Vidur Mallik often spoke of his father. I had never known him but his portrait hung on the outside wall of Vidur Mallik's house in Amta. It was a glass painting in the naive style, showing head and shoulders of a man with a white beard, surrounded by a wreath of red roses. The sky behind him glowed light blue, and the man was clad in the saffron kurta of a sadhu. A red shawl draped round his shoulders, he looked at the viewer pensively.

Pandit Sukhdev Mallik had not been part of the royal court, a circumstance which determined the course of his son Vidur's life as well. From the beginning, the family's history had been dominated by the argument about whether it was better to live on one's own land and holdings or whether to follow the maharaja to his

court at the capital. At first, Radhakrishna and Kartaram had not wanted to accept the extensive estate which
the maharaja had offered them as a reward for conjur-
ing the rain. Maharaja Madhav Singh had to try his
suasions on the brothers for almost a week until they
finally accepted. They came from far-away Awadh;
the maharaja wanted to have them living nearby but
Radhakrishna and Kartaram refused. They saw themselves as fakirs, as sadhus, and wanted to serve only
music. They knew that owning land could do nothing
to them but they feared that it may distract their descendants from music, so that the spirit of serving the goddess, of concentrating on one thing alone, would vanish
from their family.

The family had split into two factions, divided
between life at court in the capital and life on the land.
The division survives to this day. Vidur Mallik was
descended from the elder of the two brothers, while
Ram Chatur Mallik—older than him and more highly
regarded—was descended from the younger. But the
line of division did not run cleanly between descendants
of these two forefathers: over the course of many generations, the split had led to rapprochements and then
to new breaks and new names had come into the family
by intermarriage with other great musical dynasties.

The story of two brothers was told over and again, in
new variations, in the Mallik family; in the grandfathers' time two sons were born to Sukhdev Mallik—
Chandradev was born first, little Chandrabhushan
eighteen years later. Bachchaji, as Chandradev was

called, turned out to be an ornament to the village, a charming and likeable soul, good-looking, an excellent harmonium player, blessed with a wonderful voice and, on top of all this, he was an exceptional pupil when for the village it was unusual to go to school at all. The villagers always asked his advice if they had a difficult decision to make.

Apparently, the perfection of his qualities made the gods jealous. When he was twenty, a sickness claimed him quite suddenly, in a few hours, on the day before the tilak ceremony which was to mark his engagement to his beautiful young bride.

People avoided naming the illness aloud, so as not to give it more power than it had already shown. Later, they said that an ill wind had blown through the village. His father, warned by a foreboding, had forbidden Bachchaji to visit his friends in the village but the young man had pleaded with him. The father relented since it was the eve of his son's engagement and he didn't want to spoil his fun.

But in the night, the ill wind blew even into Bachchaji's ear. Streaming with sweat, shivaering with fever, supported by his friends, he came home. He was dead before sunrise.

It went so fast that no one understood what had happened but Sukhdev Mallik reproached himself bitterly. It was the greatest imaginable misfortune and after that night, he never sang again.

In Amta, no holiday, no wedding, no puja went without singing. Even the farmhands spun out the gamak, the deep rumbling lines of song, brought up from the depths of the diaphragm, that reminded them of their buffaloes, as they pushed the ploughshare in the fields. Life in the village was a tapestry of sounds, syllables, words, cries woven together anew each day, building to ever higher cascades of melody, accompanied by the beating of drums.

The old dhrupads created by the forefathers were recited on auspicious days at court, verses which invoked the majesty of the gods. Other, simpler, songs were part of the village festivals, a different song for every season, sung spontaneously at gatherings by the light of an oil lamp under the star-filled skies. Sukhdev Mallik had been one of the pillars of the tradition, a learned man, who, like all musicians of his generation, had studied with the great Kshitipal Mallik, an ornament of the court at Dumraon. But after the night Bachchaji died, Sukhdev Mallik never sang.

It was not that he fell silent entirely. Every evening he sat in front of the temple for the goddess which he had built beside his house—the temple whose dome I had seen through the trees—and recited the names of Sita and Rama; but he did not sing very loudly, only for himself and for the gods. He formed the syllables with his lips, over and over, faster and faster, countless times, until his voice was chirring like the cicadas that rubbed their legs against chitinous breastplates in the twilight of the fields round the village.

His grandson Ramkumar told me how their grand-father had called him and his brothers to his house one day when they were little and invited them to do as he did, to invoke the divine names over and over until the names began to sparkle and gleam like heavenly cicadas.

'Jhingur,' said Ramkumar, showing me with thumb and forefinger the length of the insects he was talking about. 'Jhingur.'

I liked the word, its unusual sound, beginning with the *jha* which has to be drawn up from deep in the chest and ending with that rolling *gur*. Gur on its own would mean the tasty brown jaggery, pressed out from the sugar cane and cooked.

Ramkumar's gesture was inseparable from the word. His hands spoke a language which was part and parcel of his talk. He had a whole gamut of such gestures—not only Ramkumar but everyone here had them—a sort of sign language which was unmistakable, and cried out to be learnt.

At first it felt strange repeating with my hands what I had already said with my mouth. Why, if I was talking about the fish in the pond in front of the house, did I have to measure out the length of a fish every time on my forearm? And what did that gesture of the index finger looping upward round the right ear mean? Simple—I have to use the toilet! When a brahmin squats to clear his bowels, he winds the sacred thread round his right ear so that it does not touch anything unclean. By using the corresponding hand movement, you don't even need to say where you are going.

At first, I didn't understand these gestures; they seemed funny, almost childish, but once I started to repeat them—first as a joke, then methodically—I began to understand how useful it was to have this extra level of communication. Nor are only the hands used; the expression on your face, the raising of the eyebrows and the glance are all part of this system. The Malliks used this level of communication most fully on stage; they are actors and their song is a sacred performance.

'Jhingur,' I repeated, raising my right hand, measuring the cicada's length with my forefinger and thumb and shaking it in front of his eyes to show Ramkumar the chirring sound. I beamed at him and he grinned back.

'Laughter is important,' he said. 'If you don't have a good laugh at least once or twice every day, you get sick.'

He had listened to music even in the womb. In the *Sangeet Ratnakara* we read how in the seventh month the embryo 'hides the hollows of its ears between its thighs, while the jiva within remembers the terrors of earlier births and, self-sustaining, contemplates the possibility of liberation'. The children in the family heard the old songs as soon as their ears were formed; a garland of breath, a chaplet to welcome and crown each new generation. These wreaths of sound were woven differently from the different stems of song but always round the same ancient core.

The surviving brother Chandrabhushan was renamed since his name reminded the family of his dead brother. With the appropriate brahminic ceremony, he was born again with the name Vidur. His father found the name fitting, since in the Mahabharata, Vidur is able, by righteous living, to escape the curse laid on him at birth by a sage.

Young Vidur had an ear for music too. He drank in the endless mantras that his father sang on the temple steps each day. Having lost his elder son, the father never let the younger boy out of his sight. Why send him to school? What would it help him to learn things that he, Sukhdev, had never needed in life? He could teach the boy himself everything that he would need to live here in the country.

Sukhdev Mallik regarded the court with the habitual suspicion of a conservative brahmin. Everyone knew that courtiers drank alcohol, that they ate fish and chicken, that they had easy habits to say the least. Ram Chatur Mallik turned up at Sukhdev's door one day, word of the boy's talents having reached him, offering to take his son Vidur along to the city, to teach him and help him on in his career; the father refused.

He didn't think well of court life. His son would forget his dharma and begin to drink alcohol and eat eggs—the very worst excesses that Sukhdev could imagine. Rumour had it that after his feasts, the maharaja would have the dancers line up on the steps to his bedchambers and would run his hand over their breasts as he mounted the stairs. Sukhdev Mallik reckoned the princely court a den of playboys and he wanted his son to have nothing to do with them. He had heard that dreadful things happened at court.

On one occasion, the maharaja had buzzed his singer's home village in his private aeroplane, flying close above the rooftops to startle the simple villagers. Kameshwar Singh had a weakness for flying and had assembled a fleet of private aircraft to satisfy it. A man in the village pointed out for me the path, skimming the tops of the mango trees, that the aeroplane had flown, with the maharaja and the singer riding inside. It had been almost seventy years ago but the event stuck in the collective memory of the village.

Vidur Mallik grew up in his dead brother's shadow. From love or from fear, his father kept him in the village, but the villagers never thought that there was anything special in store for Vidur anyway. He began to play the tabla. There was nothing disreputable in this, all the Malliks knew how to play the tabla or had at least an idea of how it was done, but it was simply an accompanying instrument, not one of the trademarks of a court musician. The city branch of the family looked down on their country cousins and liked to quote the founding fathers, who had supposedly predicted that they would turn into simpletons if they lived out there in the country. Murkh, the city slickers called them—silly fools.

But Vidur Mallik's passion did not flag. He learnt the songs that he heard from his father, his uncle, his grandfathers and all the family; he got hold of the books which Pandit Bhatkhande had written back at the beginning of the century and which formed the syllabus at the music colleges. He befriended a pakhwaj player who lived next door. Ramashish was the son of the incomparable sitar player Rameshwar Pathak, of whom it was said that birds flew down to perch on his instrument when he played it, in a style of unsurpassed sweetness which is lost today. Vidur sang with the drummer for ten years until the villagers became used to the sound coming from that hut night after night.

His father had declined an invitation to play on the radio. What could a radio broadcast mean for the songs which Sukhdev Mallik sang for the gods in the temple? He suspected that they would be heard in the bazaar and even in worse places, which he didn't want to think about. Ram Chatur Mallik was invited too, back in 1952 when the radio station was newly founded, and soon enough he could be heard all across the country, playing on the National Programme.

Vidur Mallik had no such reputation. He had no guru to promote him and had to make his way on his own merit. He underwent the obligatory auditions for All India Radio, so that once a month he could go to Darbhanga and sit himself down for an hour in front of the microphone at the local radio station. He and the pakhwaj player were invited to festivals, they went to Muzaffarpur, to Samastipur, as far as Patna, he played concerts in villages and in small towns, at weddings and in temples. He was also invited to Kathmandu, where his father and his grandfather had sung. The first thing he did when he got there was to make the pilgrimage to the Pashupatinath Temple where, to his consternation, a bull gobbled up the prasad that he had wanted to offer to the god. A priest reassured him that this was a good sign, that Shiva had accepted his gift, but that night he dreamt that his mother was calling him home and he left Nepal in a hurry. He found her on her deathbed; he had come home just in time to say goodbye.

Vidur Mallik's first performance outside Bihar was in 1975. I heard him, together with his teenage sons, at the Dhrupad Mela on Tulsi Ghat in Benares. It took a good while before I dared to speak to him but over the years, we became much closer. In 1983, the family came to Europe for the first time. When he came back home, Vidur Mallik used the money that he had earned in the West to build a little temple, right next to his father's temple which I had seen shining forth from among the treetops. He had prayed that he might be allowed to follow music. No one in the village had believed that he would manage it, but he had reached his goal. The temple was a sign that he had followed in his forefathers' footsteps.

Mataji was waiting for us on the veranda in front of the house. When she saw him, she drew her sari over her head, then bent down to touch his feet. He put his hand on her head. Chairs were brought out, one for him, one for me, and we sat down. Then he turned to his son Ramkumar and tousled the hair of his grandson Santosh and the twins, Samit and Sahit. Villagers squatted on the ground round the chairs, gazing at me in silence.

A long line of visitors turned up—relatives, tenant farmers, the cattleman who milked the water buffaloes. The villagers in Amta are Hindu, though the tailor who came from the next village to measure for the kurtas for the approaching wedding was a Muslim. An interreligious dialogue unfurled; the men talked for hours about when the world would end and what Hindus and Muslims variously expected for the event. They reached a common conclusion: quite soon. Times were bad, even if you were an Indian musician who owned some few acres of land.

When the founding fathers had ended the drought with the rain raga, Maharaja Madhav Singh had given them the neighbouring villages of Gangadah and Narain along with Amta and surrounding lands, but that was more than two hundred years ago. The family had grown and ramified, the land had passed through countless hands and been parcelled up again and again.

The family no longer owned the other two villages. Amta was the last one left to them but even in Amta they now owned only a fraction of the fields. Vidur Mallik's land lay directly behind his house, eight hundred bighas where rice and wheat was cultivated. The hands who worked the fields lived in the thatched huts of the village and took half the crop. Vidur Mallik's two younger sons had left the village and handed their shares of the land over to their elder brother Ramkumar, but it was not enough to feed him and his six children.

The women slept inside the house, the men out on the veranda thatched with palm leaves. Bamboo rods dangled from the wooden beams, carved with ornate patterns now filled with dust. The rods had water pots fixed to the end; with these yokes the boys had fetched the sacred water of the Ganga from a distant temple. Wooden pegs on the wall held all sorts of housewares and the tools for working the fields.

A dull thud woke me. A hollowed-out log, a yard long, used to divert water from the irrigation ditches out on the fields, had crashed down onto the wooden floor right by Vidur Mallik's head as he lay there. The thin sisal twine that held the log in place had frayed, and it had missed him by a hair's breadth. Perturbed, I looked at him but without saying a word he simply looked at the frayed ends, knotted the string back together, got up and hung the thing back on the same hook from which it had fallen—with the same air of calm as when he corrected a student who had skipped an important line in a dhrupad. Tradition needed no new twine, the old strings were good enough and would be used and used again for as long as possible.

Cicadas chirred and dogs barked in the distance. Then I heard a scuttling right by my head. I switched on my pocket torch. There was no electric light in Amta, everyone carried a torch round after dark.

Next to me sat a rat—not one of those grey monsters that race through the city sewers but a trim little brown country rat, with a glossy, dark brown coat. Its whiskers twitched in the lamplight. It seemed not at all disturbed by my torch but quite calmly dipped its little snout into the pot of water I had set down before sleeping.

As I took a stroll through the fields behind the house the next morning, I could see a man approaching from some way off, carrying a large wooden box on his back. When he had come closer, he put his case down, cranked at a handle set in the side and had me look through a lens.

I saw India's wonders: the Taj Mahal, the Gateway of India, that huge arch on the Bombay waterfront, the tall Qutb Minar and the Delhi Parliament building. There was only one battery-powered black-and-white television set in Amta, which a Yadav herdsman had bought when he grew rich, and the village children still got to see the world through such magic-lantern shows, popular since early in the previous century.

Vidur Mallik had a fishpond in front of his house. At dusk, fireflies glimmered as they flitted to and fro above the water and in the skies above the stars twinkled in the hot night air. After sunset, village life was lived in silhouette. The only lights cutting through the dark were probing torch beams or the flickering wicks of oil lamps.

A beam of torchlight drew its circle round Suresh Pankaj's smiling face. Suresh was an itinerant singer who had been drawn here by a wedding but he had arrived a day too late. He didn't demur for long when we asked him to sing for us.

A harmonium was fetched, and his fingers glided over the keys, striking a chord while he pumped the bellows with his other hand, and settled into his rhythm. He hawked deeply and spat sideways.

'There was a beginning and there also will be an end—all men will return whence they came, one day!' Like a soul singer, he began at the peak of ecstasy, then dropped his voice and left it hanging, questioningly, in the air. 'Why are you so proud, you dolls of clay?'

Another passage played on the harmonium, then the answer. 'God called Father Adam to life from a clod

of clay and from his rib made Mother Eve. One by one, he made all things that live.'

Suresh's songs spoke to the Bihari villagers' hearts. He sang of the glass bangles that women wore round their wrists when they are married and that shatter as easily as marital bliss; he lamented the passage of time, when the mother goddess' photograph is replaced by a portrait of the film star Hema Malini.

'He made Krishna from clay, Radha from clay, he made Rama from clay, Sita from clay,' Suresh sang. His songs transcended barriers of religion, death makes us all equal. The temple walls and the minarets on the mosque—are they not all built of clay? 'Raja, praja aur fakir'—the king, the subject and the beggar, all were made from clay and to clay they shall return, just like all the heroes, the emperors, the famous lovers who came before.

'All things return thither,' Suresh sang in a hoarse, cracked voice, 'Some by water and some by fire. Whether sunk in the water or burnt by the flames—one day all men return to clay. None have stayed and none shall stay!'

The next day we walked across the muddy fields, Suresh looking natty in sharply tailored narrow trousers and a colourful shirt, Ramkumar in his scrupulously folded dhoti and freshly ironed kurta. Ramesh, his cousin from next door, had brought along a tabla An old man whom one and all called Master Sahel turned up with a little box containing a harmoniur

with a bakelite keyboard, the bellows pasted together with coloured paper. At first, they did not want me to come along; Ramkumar warned me that it was a long trek but I was curious about this trip and why they were all dressed up to the nines. We crossed the fields in the growing heat of the day. Master Saheb had packed up all the instruments onto his bicycle and shoved it along through the furrows; the box with his harmonium, the tabla in its bag, my sarangi.

After a couple of hours, we could see a crowd. Tents had been pitched on an open field, while water buffaloes bathed in the muddy irrigation ditch round its edge. A thatched walkway surrounded the ceremonial altar on which a fire burnt and a large crowd of bucolic types walked round this temporary cloister, circumambulating the holy fire. It was a village celebrating its Vedic sacrifice. News of the event had spread for many miles and visitors from all round had come to join in the rite.

A man led us towards one of the tents where we asked for water. 'Wait, there will be sherbet for you!' he proclaimed, wanting to give us a special treat. He took sugar by the fistful, shovelled it into a cloth of no particular colour, knotted everything together into a bundle and swirled it round and round in the tub that stood in front of him. Then he took the cloth out and served us the sticky, sweet water in metal goblets.

He had been apprised of our arrival; we were the musicians booked to give a concert. The stage was a heap of earth piled up beneath mighty trees at the side of the field. In the evening, we took our seats there, surrounded by farmers who squatted all over the field.

Ramkumar and Suresh sang, the cousin played the tabla, Master Saheb's fingers flew across the keys of his harmonium, while I did my best to keep up with the melodies on my sarangi. The ritual fire glowed in the distance, the stars shone above; from the other side of the field, I heard distorted sounds like those of an electric guitar.

In fact, it was an electric guitar. A travelling theatre had set up their show on the other side of the field and were competing for our audience. They had a lot to offer; as there was no electricity, they were giving a live re-eanactment of Indian films. The audience gathered in front of their heap of earth was much larger than ours since the performance promised to be a sensation.

An orchestra had taken its place in front of the stage. The band leader stood at an antique harmonium—not one of the neat little boxes which you can place on your lap, as Master Saheb did with his, but an upright model, with a little bench for the old fellow who sat working the bellows with his feet. A young man of about fifteen years was giving his best with a rudimentary drumkit, while another teenager wearing cowboy boots was twanging away on the electric guitar, its amplification powered by a car battery.

The guitarist was also the master of ceremonies. He gave a short speech announcing the title of the film which we would see, and then, holding his nose, gave a splendid imitation of a shehnai. He droned and hooted, reproducing the sound perfectly while the audience laughed and applauded.

The backdrop for the first scene was unrolled from bamboo poles planted in the soil at the back of the stage. By the light of the oil lamps, we saw a snowy mountain landscape, made all the more magical by the moonlight that lay across the whole stage. A little stream bubbled up from between verdant trees, while the figure of Shiva, floating in the sky above, water streaming from his locks, indicated that we were at the source of the Ganga.

The troupe was about to perform a film which had recently hit the screens in all the big Indian cities. *Ram Teri Ganga Maili*—Ram, your Ganga has been tainted—was the latest blockbuster by Raj Kapoor, who owed his success to his ability to bait and tease the Indian film censorship board by keeping within their regulations but going well beyond the bounds of the permissible. First of all, he had put a starlet into a bathing costume and then this shrank into a bikini. In a previous hit, Zeenat Aman had appeared in a mini-sari. But the heroine of his new movie, Ganga, trumped all of this by dancing under a waterfall in the opening scene, clad in a soaking-wet white sari which clung to every contour of her admirable breasts.

The bespectacled girl playing the part of Ganga was not, however, going to bare any skin. The spectators out here in this field in deepest Bihar got to see a more sober version of the celluloid spectacle. The actress set down the copper vessel of water from the Ganga that showed that she was the goddess of the river—as the river is feminine in India—settled her glasses back on her nose, leafed through the notebook in which she had her songs' lyrics jotted down and struck a pose. The audience sat in silent anticipation.

'I am Ganga,' she announced to the onlookers—rather superfluously, since everyone knew who she was, but that was the dialogue from the film; those were the words from the cassette tapes sold in all the bazaars. 'Tujhe bulayen yeh meri baahein,' she sang. 'These arms of mine are calling out for you.'

'Aah yahan—Come!' answered the young man in cowboy boots, who had left his place in the orchestra, and began to dance with the girl, twitching his shoulders suggestively before the backdrop of the mountains. The other musicians sang the chorus.

The spectators were still cheering when a low rumbling growl from the bass drum broke in. Torches were swung behind the scenes and three young men with kerchiefs tied across their faces ran across the stage. The girl fled, pulling the boy along with her. The two of them scurried to and fro, hither and yon, about the bare earth stage, pursued by the three men; wild shrieks, then it fell dark and we heard the snare drum crush.

The live performance skipped over what happened next, but the audience knew the story. The ingenuous young man was the son of a corrupt Calcutta politician, who had come to the Himalayan source of Mother Ganga seeking the clean air of righteousness that he could not find down in the corrupted sink at the river mouth. Ganga took pity on him and assumed the form of a blue-eyed village beauty. Love at first darshan. She gave ear to his yearning in a rude hut on the mountainside, but a vengeful ex-fiancé and his friends sought the young couple out with mischief in mind. The young bride's brother had taken it upon himself to protect her, as village custom demanded, but—and this was what the snare drum had just announced—the bad guys shot him.

The girl appeared onstage again—she really did have blue eyes—and leafed through her notebook, then launched into the next song. 'You have given me the jewel of your love!' she sang, lovingly placing her hand on her midriff, so that the audience knew that the encounter had led to something. She was pregnant, her lover had gone back to Calcutta. End of act one.

The rest of the story is soon told. The young man returned to Calcutta only to discover that his father had already arranged his marriage to a suitable bride, with an advantageous family alliance. The village girl followed him, along the course of the river whose name she bears. In Benares, she was kidnapped by villains and sold into a brothel. The setting for the next scene was a party on a luxury houseboat on the Ganga. It offered a painted version of the night sky, bestrewn with stars, even more impressive than the real night sky up above the stage and the painted flats; and then the sumptuous fabrics of the houseboat where the maiden danced, singing of her plight.

A scheming brahmin sold her on to Calcutta. The film is full of allusions to hypocritical priests and corrupt industrialists, who conspire to pollute Mother Ganga. As fate would have it, she ended up dancing at her lover's wedding, a hired nautch girl, and found herself face to face with his new bride. She sang 'Ek Radha

Ek Mira', the hit of the cinema season. The scenery was then changed again for the third act, when both women confronted the hero and he had to choose the right one—which he duly did.

The same story has been told in India for thousands of years, of a young and somewhat naive prince who leaves his city and is beglamoured in the wilderness by a goddess of supernatural beauty. King Shantanu had such an affair with Ganga, incarnated as a beautiful woman, in the Mahabharata, which dates back to the second or third century before Christ; six hundred years later, Kalidasa used the motif in his *Abhijnana-shakuntalam*, the most famous of all Indian plays, which also inspired the great German playwright Goethe. This wandering troupe of players in the field were bringing the newest version of the story to life before our eyes, merely the latest and by no means the last link in a chain that stretches back throughout Indian history.

We awoke from our own enchantment with a shock the next day, when the rite of sacrifice was over and the crowd had dispersed from the field. The organizers vanished as well, although they had promised us a fee. They waved to us from their jeep as they left, smiling and promising that they would send a car or a cart to take us to their village where all arrangements would be made but it grew darker and darker and no one came.

We spent the night with the rest of the actors and orchestra, who were in the same sort of mess, waiting for transportation, for their manager had absconded with all the takings. The ground was damp, so we used the rolled-up scenery as cushions. The actors explained that they were from Calcutta, only the heroine was from Nepal—it would be unthinkable for Indian girls to perform in public in the sort of story we'd seen.

No one turned up the next morning. We were running out of drinking water and it was getting ever hotter. Ramkumar reckoned that the organizers would turn up soon but I was running out of patience, as was Suresh. Together we set off for the nearest road. The singer knew this area from his wanderings and had a rough idea of how we could get back to Amta by bus.

We found the road but there was no bus. The fields were utterly deserted. A couple of farmers passed by in the afternoon and told us that there would be no more buses that day, as the drivers hereabouts were on strike after a bus had run over a child in a nearby village. The villagers had beaten up the driver, possibly even hanged him, and since then all the buses had stopped running.

So we sat in the shade of a tree by the roadside and Suresh dictated to me the text of the song that he had sung so often in the past few days.

'Listen, you who think yourself wise, listen to the names of those who have become clay! Alexander the Great became clay, the great Tamberlane became clay, Akbar, Shah Jahan and Alamgir, all became clay. Kings, subjects and beggars, all ended as clay.

'Ask the clay what the minarets are made of, and ask the clay how the walls of the temples were built! The clay has seen prophets and saints, the clay has seen

Rama and Hanuman. Here on this earth men throw bombs and men fire cannons, yet the earth has such a great heart that she will take them all back to her bosom. All who have lived here on this earth, all will return to her!'

A jeep took us along to the next village, where we bumped into the manager of the travelling theatre. I told him how much I had enjoyed his troupe's show. He beamed with pleasure and explained that he was just getting ready to collect his performers from the field, he only had to organize transport.

I gave him fifty rupees for the guitarist, inam, as it is called in India. These gifts to musicians who have played particularly well form a goodly part of their income and I had enjoyed hearing an electric guitar out there under Bihar's wide skies. He had even let me play a little, handing it over so that I could riff out a few chords like John Lee Hooker.

'You should never have given him the fifty rupees!' Ramkumar declared, when I told him about this later back in Amta. 'He'll give five to the boy with the guitar, and keep the rest for himself.'

He told me what had been going on in the village while I was away.

'The old man has arrived,' Ramkumar reported. While we were hiking across to the Vedic ceremony, Ram Chatur Mallik had arrived in Amta. He was the oldest musician in the family and the villagers duly called him buddhou, the old man.

Ram Chatur Mallik sat on the veranda in front of his house. He peered at me through the thick, dusty lenses of his spectacles when he heard my voice. He could hardly see but he was much pleased when I asked whether he could teach me more about his music.

'Come with me to Darbhanga and I will tell you everything!'

IV

Samastipur, Thursday, 1 August 2002

I staggered out onto the station platform at about half past three in the morning, not having slept a wink. The train was due just after four o'clock. The loudspeaker rattled, announcing a delay of one hour. Once this term had expired, the delay was extended to one and a half hours and finally to two.

In the meantime, dawn had broken. At six o'clock, a train crept into the station and came to a standstill by the platform, groaning. Clusters of men with orange scarves wound about their heads were hanging from the open doors of the compartments; they let go of the door handles and the footboards and jumped down onto the platform before the train came to a halt.

It was like an invasion. In the blink of an eye, they had occupied the platform. The orange cloths bound about their waists showed that they were pilgrims. Almost all were barefoot. Invocations in praise of Shiva were printed on the cloths in large red letters. Some wore leopard-print T-shirts while others had colourful paper hats perched on their heads. Once the men had jumped down onto the platform, excited to have arrived, the women followed. They had very little luggage other than their staffs and urns—bundles of blankets, a few small bags. Plastic sheets were spread out on the ground and little knots of people gathered on each. They were still in high spirits from the excitement of the pilgrimage and the young men kept calling out, 'Hara Hara Mahadev!' It was Shiva's war cry, and his trident was printed on their lungis and T-shirts.

Across their shoulders they carried long bamboo poles decorated with orange flowers and gold and silver bands, water jugs hanging from each end. Mostly these were plastic bottles but here and there I saw an old copper urn. These containers were all protected by a sort of wicker cage that prevented them from touching the ground. Inside was holy water, fetched all the way from the Ganga. It had to be taken to the Vaidyanath Temple. A ritual took place there in the month of Sawan, when this sacred water was poured over the lingam. They were on their way back to their villages and because of the floods this train was their only means of transport.

Strictly speaking, this pilgrimage should be taken on foot, at a quick march and as far as possible without stopping. Things became critical when the man carrying the water had to pee. Since the water must not touch his body while he did this, he had to set the contrivance down and purify himself before picking it up again.

Several such bamboo yoke poles, covered in dust, hung from the rafters of Vidur Mallik's veranda; his sons had carried them from the Ganga, several hundred miles away. They had told me the story behind this water-carrying ritual. The Shivalingam, the sacred stone at the centre of the Vaidyanath Temple, had been brought thither by the demon king Ravana. I heard how Ravana had once tried to carry Kailasha, the holy mountain, home of Shiva, from the Himalayas down to his homeland Lanka, in order to spare his mother the pilgrimage. Of course the plan didn't work. Shiva stretched out a single toe and knocked him down but he gave the demon a magical lingam—with the warning that the lingam would stop fast in the first place where the demon set it down.

The rest of the gods had a plan to prevent the gift. Varuna, god of water, entered Ravana's body and filled his bladder, so that he felt the irresistible urge to pass water. Vishnu offered to hold the holy stone for him but as soon as it was given to him, he threw it to the ground and straight away the Shivalingam put down roots. Ravana tried in vain to lift it again. As a sign of his remorse, he cut off his own heads, all nine of them, but Shiva returned him to life by setting each head back on his shoulders. This was a healer's deed and thus the temple was called Vaidyanath, 'Lord of Healers'.

This story of the lingam's magical powers was the reason one must not set down the urns of holy water— just as the lingam itself was fixed immovably, so too would the water transfer its magical powers to the earth once set down.

Mithila Express, *Thursday, 1 August 2002*

The Bengali conductor looked at me pityingly through his gold-rimmed spectacles when I asked whether there were any onward connections from Raxaul. Difficult, he declared. Certainly, there was the passenger train, a narrow-gauge railway, but that track might well have been flooded out too. He had only heard about the narrow-gauge, it was not listed in his timetable. The mere mention of it made his lips twitch in a sympathetic smile. He didn't want to discourage me though. Perhaps I could find a taxi that might take me onward. Certainly, there would be no buses running at the moment since a general strike had been declared throughout Bihar just the day before. The state government had tripled the road tolls from one day to the next and since then, bus and freight transport was at a standstill. Any private cars that ventured out on the roads risked being pelted with stones by roaming gangs or set on fire.

I enjoyed my train ride since I knew that the luxury of an air- conditioned carriage would not last long. Outside the window, a flat landscape dotted with single trees went past, in harsh sunlight. There was a lot of water about; the irrigation ditches were all full, some overflowing, but it didn't quite look like a flood.

Raxaul, *Thursday, 1 August 2002*

Raxaul station was a double-headed terminus. At the front, trains reached the end of their lines from Howrah in Calcutta, while behind the station building I found a goods yard where huge bales were piled up. The platform was empty. A lonely dog panted in the blazing noontide heat in front of the narrow-gauge lines but there was no train in sight.

The passengers waiting for the narrow-gauge were all crowded into the ticket hall on the other side of the station. It was jammed full, the queues in front of each window stretched out through the whole hall. On the plastic-sheet encampments, little forts had sprung up built of sacks, milk pails and packets tied in twine, where groups sat and waited, having sent their people to the windows to fight for tickets.

Among all these, the pilgrims with their orange headscarves whom I had already seen at Samastipur moved here and there. They nervously clasped their poles with the jugs of water to their shoulders, called their slogans and tried to find a place in the many-armed snaking line that grew and spilt out over the steps in front of the ticket hall.

By the look of it, the train they were waiting for must be days overdue. The ticket windows were barred and had boards nailed across them for good measure. Far more people were waiting here than could ever possibly fit on one small train. They looked ready to fight for every last seat.

I found a rickshaw driver in front of the station entrance who wiped the sweat from his brow with the end of his lungi when I asked him about a hotel. There was no one at that station whom I could have asked about transport to Darbhanga, so perhaps I would find things out more quickly in a hotel.

Yes, he said, beaming, there was a hotel hereabouts. He would take me to Nepal Hotel, best in town. The sun beat down upon us as he toiled along with his rickshaw, through the potholes on the street that led into town. The water was spilling out from the ditches at the roadside and overflowed the street in many places, forcing us into detours.

He turned onto a side street with his vehicle, motioned that I should wait and disappeared round the corner. A little later, a young man with a roguish expression appeared, beckoning that I should follow.

He led me to a door with a sign hanging above it that proclaimed the Nepal Hotel. The hotel was a garage, with one room to its interior. The door to the reception stood ajar. The man lounging about behind a table was clearly the boss. He had gathered his cronies round him in two rows of sagging chairs, to his left and right.

They looked at me curiously, then sent the rickshaw driver off to fetch tea for everyone. I asked the young man behind the table whether there was any way to hire a car to take me to Darbhanga.

'No problem!' he declared. 'Granted, there is a total boycott on the roads and on top of that, the road surfaces may not be in any condition to speak of since Raxaul district has been underwater for several days, but you're in luck! I'll help you. I'll fix you a car to get you as far as Sitamarhi.'

Sitarmarhi was about halfway to Darbhanga.

'The driver knows all the short cuts, nothing will happen to you, for sure!'

He talked over the situation with his friends on the sagging chairs while we all drank more tea.

Since I had first met the Malliks almost thirty years ago, I had learnt the broad Bihari dialect and so I could follow the discussion that unfolded over the next half hour. I wasn't sure that the plan the boss had worked out was at all realistic. The narrow-gauge train was due to leave at three. I told him that I'd like to be sure in good time whether he could really get hold of a car for me.

'You certainly can't go on the passenger train!' the young men said, in chorus. 'Absolutely impossible, much better with a car!'

The boss remembered that he could call his friend in the next village to find out how the roads were over there. The telephone was kept in a wooden box in front of him on the table, locked away with a padlock, but the key was missing. One of the men was sent off to find it. After he had finally opened the box, taken the telephone out and tried and failed several times to get a connection, his friend at the other end finally picked up and the boss mumbled something into the mouthpiece.

'Road's clear at least as far as my friend!' he said, beaming. 'And there may even be a bus from Sitamarhi. I'll send you off there with a taxi, which will get you as far as Darbhanga if you need it to. This whole thing will cost three thousand rupees but you just pay fifteen hundred up front, I'll take care of everything else.'

I gave him the money, he made another call, hung up and then fell silent. I asked him whether the transport strike would not be a problem.

'The driver knows all the short cuts out of Raxaul and the country people are quite peaceful,' he replied, incensed. 'There are no thieves here, as you have in Delhi!'

He began to tell his friends a story about how once, in Delhi, his belt had been stolen as he took a nap somewhere. To act out the incident, he jumped upon the table, unbuckled his belt and imitated a hand sneaking his belt out of its loops furtively from behind. Since he had unbuttoned the top of his trousers beforehand, they slipped right down to his sandals and his grey underwear was there for all to see. His friends clapped enthusiastically and laughed at the wonderful performance.

The telephone rang again. It wasn't good news. All the roads round Raxaul were underwater and there was no getting through. I asked the boss what was happening with the train; after all, the scheduled departure time was long past. He suggested that we send the rickshaw driver to the station to find out what was going on—he had joined the little council and was following the discussion in silence.

When I asked whether the train would not have left already, he reassured me. 'Surely, the scheduled time of departure has passed but the train is always late, two hours at least. We can certainly all enjoy another cup of tea.'

The rickshaw driver in his red shirt and chequered lungi was sent off on his errand but came back shaking his head. They were certainly expecting the train but there would be absolutely no chance of getting a seat.

'I'll soon fix that,' the chief assured me. He claimed to know someone at the station who could take care of everything. I was after all on my way to my guru's last puja. Since it was such a noble mission, he would charge me only five hundred rupees for the journey and the rickshaw driver would accompany me and make sure that I got a seat.

I asked him whether I couldn't manage that on my own.

'No chance,' he retorted. 'You'll never get a seat without a fixer! When you both reach Darbhanga, you just buy him a ticket back here. If there are any unexpected problems, he'll even take you as far as the village.'

He took the money I had given him from his shirt pocket and counted out a thousand rupees back into my hand. Then he told the rickshaw driver what his part in the plan would be. It didn't seem to impress him much that he had been chosen to accompany me for the next twenty-four hours, under almost impossible conditions, to a village which may or may not have vanished underwater.

He nodded impassively, as if this sort of thing happened every day, then bent down and heaved up my suitcase onto his rickshaw. I wanted to follow him but the others kept me back. They scoffed that we had at least an hour, if we got to the railway station by five o'clock, there would be plenty of time.

While I had been away, the crowd at the station had tripled in size and was in a feverish anticipation for the arrival of the narrow-gauge.

The charge for the doors got underway even before the train came to a halt. Someone in the crush pushed a piece of paper into my hand, folded about the train tickets. The boss from Nepal Hotel and his friends had come along with me to the station and now they shoved me through the throng towards a wagon, telling me once more how sorry they were that they had not been able to get me a taxi.

I recognized the rickshaw driver behind one of the barred windows, clinging onto the handle of my suitcase and pointing to the carriage door with his other hand. Clusters of people hung onto the door, all pushing to get in together. The only way to board the wagon was brute force. Since there was no way I wanted to let the rickshaw driver travel to Darbhanga on his own with my suitcase, I threw myself into the fray.

The wagon was as narrow as its gauge suggested and, inside, it was only equipped with the most rudimentary necessities. Planks had been laid across wooden supports to serve as seats, shifting as the crowd scrambled over them. People clung onto the metal frames which had, at some earlier point, held the overhead luggage nets. I managed to worm my way through to my new friend in the chequered lungi. Clinging onto his seat with one hand, he yanked me towards himself with the other and quickly got up to push me onto the window seat where he had been sitting a moment before. At least a dozen people were squeezed onto the wooden plank which normally seated four, their feet on the luggage that covered the entire carriage floor.

More and more people packed into the carriage, clinging onto the iron skeletons of the luggage nets, pulling themselves upright, or lay down across sitting passengers' knees, until every cubic foot of the carriage seemed full.

The windows darkened. Outside, people were busy lashing motorbikes, bicycles, huge milk churns, bales of fabric and luggage onto the bars across the windows. This was all in a day's work for them; they knew how to jam a bicycle's pedal and handlebars into the iron bars with such practised ease that there was no need to tie it on. Then, having done this little task outside the carriage, they were pulled into the compartment, right over the heads of those already there.

Passenger Train, Thursday, 1 August 2002

As soon as the train left the station, I saw the water. The railway was raised up on its embankment barely a yard above the water, which stretched away to the horizon left and right. Treetops rose above the surface here and there, sometimes even a house roof or a brickworks' chimney; otherwise, it was a lone and level waste of water.

I could only peer out through a chink since the window was covered by people and objects. The view of the sunset just beginning over this huge open expanse took my breath away. It was as though an ocean had unexpectedly spread out on dry land.

My view was blocked by the skinny backside of a peasant woman wrapped in a threadbare sari, swaying right before my face. It was not unpleasant; everyone here was caught up in some unwonted proximity to someone else. She was trying to get to the window to get some air but she could only pant and gasp. It was so crammed in this oven of a train carriage that there was hardly air to breathe among all the packed bodies.

'Ha! Ha!' the passengers called, as the train got moving again and a faint breeze blew in through the windows. Then conversation died down. Everyone was utterly preoccupied with how to last out the hours until this rolling time machine disgorged them. It made the present last for an eternity and stretched the future into immensity.

The train crept over rails at walking pace. The only sound was the squeal of iron wheels on hot steel. The rails groaned, as though melting in the mounting heat, beneath the weight of tonnes of railway wagons crammed full with people. Not that these people's weight would count for much, I thought, despite their numbers. They seemed light as feathers, short, fine-boned, with delicate limbs.

It began to grow dark outside. Black clouds of smoke from the locomotive chimney drifted past the window and flecks of soot flew into the compartment.

Then the darkness spread within the wagon as well. First the light bulbs on the ceiling diminished to a red flicker, once or twice; finally they gave up altogether.

The train stopped again and again, in the middle of nowhere, while men with lanterns paced past the windows and checked whether the stretch ahead was passable. The passengers waited, silent and supplicant, for the steam whistle to hoot and announce that we would be moving on.

At last, the lamps went dark. I could peer through between the people blocking most of the window and saw trees standing as shadows in front of a dark unending stretch of water which mirrored the stars. The shapes dissolved in the night like an old photograph slowly fading in the sunlight. No one said a word. I felt that the wagon was rolling, with all its passengers, into the realm of shadows but these were other shadows than those which cling stubbornly to people in the sharp daylight. The hard edges flowed, shapes dissolved. The shadows took over.

The wheels rattled their hypnotic song while the wagon rolled onward into a world ruled by the deepest black. It drew me into the darkness, I had become a shadow myself.

In Sitamarhi, halfway to Darbhanga, there was a power cut. Not a single lamp was lit at the station. Most of the passengers left the compartment. They vanished quickly into the thickening darkness, where only the outlines of a few lighter objects could be vaguely recognized. Those left behind stretched their limbs luxuriantly, and as joints loosened, so tongues. Soon everyone knew everyone else's business, where they came from, where they were headed. No one had even heard of

Amta, but the prevailing opinion was that Darbhanga itself was not flooded since the town stands a little above the surrounding plain.

Darbhanga, Friday, 2 August 2002

It was well after midnight when we arrived. A few dim bulbs lit the empty station hall. Along with my companion in his red shirt and lungi, I took a turn round the building to see if there was any sign of the Malliks. We had agreed that Ramkumar's twenty-one-year-old son Prashant would wait for me at the station but it was now two and a half days after the agreed rendezvous. In the meantime he must have heard that no more trains were coming in from Delhi and, I assumed, had gone back to the village.

A neon tube was flickering in the square in front of the station but otherwise it was dark and silent. A few jeeps stood by the front door, their drivers stretched out to sleep on roofs or back seats. At last we managed to wake one. We asked whether he could take us to a hotel. He didn't answer but bent down and got to work on his ancient vehicle's engine, pulling out wires and knotting them together. Only the most vital parts were left and the handles and flanges had been touched by so many hands over the years that they gleamed in the neon light as though polished.

The jeep grumbled into life. Its frame jumped and trembled like a tractor, and I had to hold on tight to avoid being thrown from the front seat. We drove, without lights, through the narrow, muddy streets, flanked left and right by shuttered shops and houses. The only living things were the furiously barking dogs. At last we stopped in the darkness before an iron gate. The driver hammered on the door again and again until an angry voice began hurling curses at us. He shouted back but the door would not open. At this hour of night, all doors in Dar-bhanga were closed.

I hardly recognized the town in the darkness. Last time I came here, I had arrived by bus, and I had no idea where the railway station was. I thought of the lodgings I had taken the first time I came here, over twenty years ago. The place had been called Arvind Hotel and was the town's top hotel. We found it, a forbidding fortress of bare cement, but events unfolded just as before; endless hammering on a metal gate, an invisible voice shouting back at us, furious about the noise. When no one opened up, we drove back to the station and tried to bed down on the platform.

Darbhanga is a district capital, so the station was equipped with a waiting room but since no more trains were expected for the night, it was locked up. The staff had all gone off to sleep and would only reappear in the grey light of dawn, when the narrow-gauge train would be readied for its journey back to Raxaul.

My companion said his goodbyes, since we had seen those jeeps waiting by the entrance, the sleeping drivers waiting for me to hire them for a ride into the village. I bought him a ticket, pressed a few banknotes into his hand and asked him to pass on my heartiest thanks to everyone back at Nepal Hotel.

THE EMPEROR OF DHRUPAD

Darbhanga, May 1983

The maharaja's guest house, once an architectural jewel, was now just a ruin.

In better days, Raj Atithi Nivas, as it was officially known, had welcomed prominent guests. Maharaja Kameshwar Singh invited the cream of Indian and British society for polo matches, elephant rides and tiger hunts; famous film stars, musicians and dancing girls would often spend months at his court. The guests, reeling home a little tipsy from one of the splendid parties that he gave in the nearby palace, would have steered themselves by the towers and battlements of the guest house; these could still be seen from afar but the roof was now full of holes. The plaster was crumbling, the gate would no longer shut, the two side doors hung askew on their hinges.

The building consisted of two low octagonal towers, connected by a central hall. After the maharaja's death, the right wing was converted into a police station, while the court singer occupied the left wing. Ram Chatur Mallik had lived in this house for thirty years, whenever he was in Darbhanga. He spent part of his time in his home village, otherwise he was on pilgrimage or on concert tours. Despite his advanced age, he still took every possible opportunity to travel—he was a wandering singer, a lover of life, always pleased to be invited to sing at a mela or at a wedding.

His lodgings in the guest house consisted of a single octagonal chamber with a small pantry and a lavatory attached at the back. In summer, a boy from the village cooked meals on the veranda by the front door while in winter, the fire was brought inside to the hearth. Pale channels trickling down through the black soot left on the walls showed the passing of each rainy season. It must have been decades since the walls were last plastered and painted, probably in Kameshwar Singh's day.

The maharaja's singer had cast his spell over me when I first heard him at Tulsi Ghat in Benares in 1975 but it was no simple matter to make his acquaintance. The Mallik dynasty of musicians had split into two branches right at the beginning of their history and, over the centuries, a certain animosity had developed between the clans. There were disagreements about the interpretation of certain ancient ragas, about the wording of texts, perhaps there were other squabbles too of which I knew nothing. Members of the two factions treated one another with cool politeness but even though they belonged to the same tradition, they never sat on stage together. The lines were firmly drawn.

Ram Chatur Mallik, the last of this large and ramified dynasty to have served at court, was the elder statesman of the family and—as far as I could judge—had the greatest repertoire. His only student, Abhay

Narayan Mallik, had taken a university post in a distant part of India and no longer lived in Bihar and the worry was that a great part of the old singer's knowledge might be lost since he was getting on in years. It seemed that he took the same view; once, when he was invited to Vrindavan, I heard him ask the priest to send him a young man from the temple to learn from him. He was looking for someone to whom he could pass on his knowledge, but Bihar was a long way from Vrindavan, some six hundred miles, and who wanted to go to Bihar? No Vrindavan temple singer had ever found his way to Darbhanga, nor had any Western ethnomusicologist. As far as the outside world was concerned, it was terra incognita.

When I arrived in Darbhanga, I stayed at Arvind Hotel, a colourless concrete monstrosity behind an iron gate on one of the main streets. The hotel was frequented by those few businessmen and government officials who had to come to Darbhanga for whatever reason; most of the rooms were empty at any given moment. An ancient in a crumpled dhoti would turn up in the mornings to serve tea but other than that the guests had to fend for themselves. There were power cuts at unpredictable intervals and at nightfall swarms of mosquitoes appeared from the darkness. The nets hanging from the bedposts were full of holes and offered little protection. I had to take a rickshaw to get from Arvind Hotel to Raj Atithi Nivas, because in the rainy season the streets became quagmires. Black sewage ran knee-high in the streets and myriad mosquitoes bred in these conditions. In places, it was impossible to get through on foot.

The singer gave me a warm reception. He was happy that someone who had come all the way from Europe was interested in his songs and he wanted to find out what had happened since his last visit there, about thirty years back. I, on the other hand, wanted to learn more of his strange life story, of which I had only heard hints and allusions. He took me on as his student. Days stretched into months until the daily journey from Arvind Hotel became too much trouble and I moved in with the old singer in his guesthouse.

The princely courts had come to an end when India gained independence, but Ram Chatur Mallik still had the aura of the court about him. This was shown not least by the way he had his own court gathered round. One of the first things I learnt about him was that he had never in his life cleaned his lota—the little metal pot with which traditional Indians wash after they have moved their bowels. It had long fallen into desuetude in the cities, since wherever there was mains water, you would find a pot or a tin can standing by the toilet to use instead. In the countryside though, everyone still carried their own lota about with them. Properly, one would clean the lota oneself by scouring it with a mixture of soil, ash and water after use. It is lowly work since it reminds a person of his bodily functions and to perform the task for another puts one in a state of ritual impurity, but the court singer's status was evident from the fact that Ram Chatur Mallik had a servant whose responsibility this was.

Everyone called the white-haired old man, well over seventy, Kali-babu; I never found out his full name. Kali-babu was a brahmin and thus wore the distinctive topknot on the crown of his head. Once he had been a wealthy man and he still owned a little bit of land near Darbhanga. One morning, he disappeared to take a look at his mango trees, the next day he reappeared, black and blue from bruises all over—a band of goondas had taken the harvest while he was away and had beaten him up when he protested the theft.

Kali-babu, who had spent most of his life serving the court singer, was not one to complain though. I learnt that he had originally come to learn music from Ram Chatur Mallik but for some reason this had never happened. Kali-babu stayed on and became his valet. He had spent more than forty years at his side when I met the two of them. Kali-babu had the honour of cleaning Ram Chatur Mallik's lota; he accompanied him to the toilet, massaged him with mustard oil and served him his food at mealtimes.

Whenever Ram Chatur Mallik was not round to hear, people called him buddhou, the old man, otherwise he was called babu. When the singer had a visitor, Kali-babu would tug a shirt down over the old man's head, over his long face with its large ears. A white lock of hair would always spring up above his brow and Kali-babu would solicitously comb it down into a neat side parting.

Apart from this hairdo, Ram Chatur Mallik bore a striking resemblance to Charlie Patton. There's only a single, grainy photograph of this first great singer of

Mississippi Delta blues, from which Robert Crumb drew a picture—the same long thin face, the same ears, the same mouth. The resemblance was even stronger in his portrait. The parallels between the king of Delta blues and the emperor of dhrupad ran deeper than mere appearance though. Both were legends in their lifetimes and both singers could conjure up the spirit of a river and its landscape. There seemed to be some inner kinship between the Mississippi delta and the Gangetic plain; the river rolling along through the flat land round about, the poverty of the workers in the sugar fields. I imagined I could see cotton plantations just behind the rice fields; the oppressive heat too was the same, wrapping everything in a flickering haze. Even their voices were alike. Patton's rough baritone, the result of a lifetime of hard work in the fields and hard drinking in the shebeens, seemed to echo in the Indian singer's grainy tones, furred by eighty years of dust and heat. Ram Chatur Mallik's voice was still capable of soaring passages of youthful exuberance. Even after a stroke and partial paralysis, the full, sonorous tones from deep within his powerful ribcage made microphones unnecessary, just as legend had it that Patton's voice could be heard quite clearly five hundred yards away.

Patton died in 1934. He had been a restless, solitary soul, a ladies' man, a drinker, model for many bluesmen and rock singers later on. He was the first to play a guitar behind his back, which Jimi Hendrix imitated. Patton's character flummoxed people. A record company issued a shellac disc where, instead of his name, they printed 'The Masked Marvel' on the label. They promised another disc to whoever could guess the singer's name.

For me, Ram Chatur Mallik was a masked marvel too, a mystery. I could still recognize what a fine figure of a man he had been in earlier years. People round would always remark on how well his name suited him; chatur means clever, cunning or sly. He still had the charm that must have blazed at full strength when he was in the prime of his life. In the maharaja's day, the court singer had been a well-known figure, with his heroic and rather roguish good looks and a voice that could convey, just as needed, manly defiance or seductive charm.

He had been born in 1902 in Amta, the musicians' village where his ancestors had always dwelt, and was brought to the court in 1924, aged twenty-two, by his father, who had a post as najib. He married young but his wife died a little afterwards and he never married again. He didn't need to. Women pursued him, for he had a magnetic personality which could still be felt, especially when he sang thumris, the romantic love songs that tell of utter devotion to the beloved; his audience would still sigh and swoon, even in his old age, as he sang these.

Kali-babu told me how crazy Siddheshwari Devi had been about Ram Chatur Mallik and his thumris. She was one of the queens of the genre, causing a furore in Benares in the thirties and forties. The queen of thumri and the charismatic court singer had re-enacted the story of Yussuf and Zuleikha, as told in the Koran and hinted at in the Bible. In the Old Testament, Yussuf is called Joseph, though Zuleikha, wife of Potiphar, the governor of Egypt, has no name. When Yussuf rebuffs Zuleikha's advances and she accuses him of attempting rape, his shirt is examined and found to be torn at the back, not the front, thus proving that he had been running away and she had been clinging onto him.

Kali-babu told me how Siddheshwari Devi had tried to force Ram Chatur Mallik to teach her one of his songs.

'When he came to Benares to give a concert once, she ran after him and tried to make him stop so that she could hear again the words and music of a thumri that he had just performed,' he said, laughing. It was a happy memory. 'She clung onto the hem of his kurta!'

He grabbed hold of the hem of his own shirt, at the back, to show me how Potiphar's wife had grabbed Joseph.

'But he wasn't having any of it, he ran off, escaping her, and that's how she tore his shirt!'

He laughed out loud.

'She wasn't just after the song, she wanted the singer as well!'

Most of the day was spent outside on the guesthouse terrace. Every morning the woven mattress where the old man lay would be taken out and put in front of the door. The day began with a lengthy ritual in which Kali-babu would take Ram Chatur Mallik out to the front garden and pour a bucket of water over him, then wrap a fresh dhoti about him and hang up the old one to dry on the garden fence. When he had lain down on the terrace, his servant would rub the old man's body with sharply odoured mustard oil, after which it was time for puja. The singer would unwrap the red cloth with its golden tassels from the picture of the goddess and set the picture in front of him. Kali-babu set the bottle of water from the Ganga within reach. Ram Chatur Mallik prayed every morning, murmuring mantras and forming complex mudras with his fingers. He would finish by sprinkling water from the bottle onto the holy items and putting the red tika on his forehead.

His breakfast was a dish of sattu, a porridge of chickpea flour, to help his stomach. He groaned. He could move only with difficulty and had trouble with his digestion but the mind inside this frail old body was lively, alert and curious. He yearned for a good meal, often enquiring about the food in Europe. He had sattu for breakfast; at lunchtime and in the evening, the cook prepared dal, chapati, rice and vegetables, the usual Hindu diet. Some mornings a woman would come, carrying a basket of fish balanced on her head. She would kneel down and spread out her wares before the old man. They would haggle over the price for an age and then the fish would be chopped into small slices, cooked and served in a curry, complete with head.

The terrace overlooked a little front garden which the police officers from the station next door used for their morning work-out. The rest of the time, they were on duty at the bus station nearby, a wide bustling square where people welcomed new arrivals or milled about looking for a bus that would take them where they wanted to go.

The drivers blared and honked their horns to drum up trade until late into the night. The driver's mate would hang out of the front door, chanting the names of their destinations and beating his hand on the door panel. The noisy machines would turn onto the road that ran in front of the guesthouse, their motors screaming, and leave us shrouded in sooty, black diesel fumes.

Whenever there was a few minutes' peace I tried to persuade Ram Chatur Mallik to sing. His visitors often made much of his great reputation as a singer but none of them were particularly interested in actually hearing him sing. He had few opportunities, other than occasional concerts and a monthly visit to the local All India Radio station, when Kali-babu would help him into the studio and see that he was sat down, and Ram Chatur Mallik would bring out some of the songs from the storehouse of his memory. When I asked about his songs, I would bring out my cassette recorder and note down the lyrics, and this was a welcome opportunity for the old man to consult his memory and give his best—but such opportunities were few and far between and often interrupted.

Visitors began to appear early in the morning, needing this or that favour or piece of advice. Mostly they came from Amta, young people and old, squatting by his woven mattress or sitting in the visitor's chair according to their rank. They would ask after his health, bring some village news and then say what it was that they needed. It was nearly always money. The patriarch's earnings from concerts and the radio supported an impressive number of people. His only son worked for the railways far away in Ranchi and never sent word; both his grandsons lived in Patna.

Once a week Ram Chatur Mallik set off for a tour of town, on which he would visit his doctor, the radio station and the dignitaries at the local university. A rickshaw was ordered, Kali-babu helped his master into his black overcoat, combed his hair and set the black wool cap on his head. He would look appraisingly at the thick, dusty lenses before settling the spectacles onto the old man's ears but Kali-babu himself didn't have very good eyes either. The two old men didn't set much store by appearances anyway. Every morning Kali-babu would change Ram Chatur Mallik's dhoti but the sattu stains after each mealtime didn't bother him much. The master only wore a fresh shirt if Kali-babu put it on him. Probably he had decided to pay no more heed to such matters when the local raj came to an end. His forefathers too had dressed like sadhus; a certain modesty of appearance was so to speak family tradition and he simply slipped back into these habits.

The boy would bring the rickshaw up to the steps that led down from the terrace and we would all help the old man up onto the seat, where he would collapse with a sigh. Even with his spectacles perched on his nose, he could see very little through the lenses.

'Come, sit with me!' he would call, looking uncertainly in my direction. 'You are a very smart man! Tell me, do you have a moustache?'

The palace garden began behind a wrought-iron fence across the street, collapsed in places so that passers-by could simply step through the gaps to take a short cut, not needing to go all the way to the main gate which we passed in our rickshaw. The rusted gate had stood stuck open for years now, still displaying the maharaja's faded coat of arms, ubiquitous in Darbhanga—a dolphin inside a six-pointed star.

The foot traffic had worn a path across the park lawns, crossing a majestic avenue of palms running up to Kameshwar Singh's palace. Before the gate sat a white marble statue of his ancestor, enthroned—the bearded Maharaja Lakshmishwar Singh, who had built this extensive palace. He gazed out over your head as you looked up at him, his cloak thrown back and his hand resting on the hilt of his sword, the turban on his head plumed with a proud feather. He had called his work Lakshmishwar Vilas, though his descendants renamed it Anand Bagh, the Garden of Joy.

A tall bell tower dominated the grand building while the white stone window-frames, oriels and balustrades contrasted pleasingly with the red sandstone walls. Shortly before he died, the last maharaja had donated the palace to the university, which accordingly was now called the Kameshwar Singh Sanskrit University.

The university music department was housed in a building where musical and dramatic performances had entertained state guests. It was a pretty little building in Indian art deco style, gently crumbling in the park a little away from the palace. It was named Saraswati Bhavan, for the goddess of music and scholarship.

Ram Chatur Mallik held a post as professor at the university. Even though he was well past pensionable age, he regarded it his duty to call in on the music department once a month. There were no classes or lectures; possibly it had always been intended this way and his position was merely formal recognition for a lifetime as court singer but perhaps he gave no classes simply because the music department had no students. The only person we ever met in the Saraswati Bhavan was the director, who welcomed us heartily and shuffled the papers that lay before him on his desk. Tea was served, we exchanged pleasantries and gossip and then we left.

Our next stop was the vice chancellor's residence, where the old gentleman happily answered my question when I asked whether the university had any documents about musicians at the princely court.

'Of course, but naturally!' he said emphatically. 'We administer the princely archives!'

He furrowed his brow and a pensive smile spread across his face. 'Well, it may not in truth be the entire archive but we certainly have a part of it,' he added. 'I don't know whether that will include documentation about the court musicians. It's in a side-wing.'

The entrance to the archives was in the shadow of the building, where the dark red sandstone lent it a rather melancholy air. The dolphin, emblem of the raj, and the last maharaja's initials were marked on the red background. I knocked and went in.

In the twilight I saw a room where the walls were covered with tall dark wooden shelves. A whole row of further rooms could just be seen through a door in the back wall and they all seemed to be furnished much the same, though only faintly visible in outline. A damp, mildewed smell lay in the air. In the middle of the room, a man clad in red dhoti lay stretched out on a table. My knocking had evidently startled him; he rubbed his eyes reluctantly and stood up.

The shelves were divided into uniform cubbyholes, each one crammed full with bundles of paper tied up with red string, most of these many tiers deep. The paper was dark brown and falling to pieces, the edges of the wrinkled pages crumbling and tattered. Many of the heaps were stuck together so that I could not tell whether there was one sheaf of paper or several. They would fall to pieces at the slightest touch. Since the princely court was abolished, no one had laid a finger on these relics of the Darbhanga raj. The bitterness that had undoubtedly been in the air when the princely state came to an end had given way to sheer indifference.

It looked as though the old man who watched over this room had spent the last few decades asleep in this forgotten archive. When the university took over the palace, someone must have decided that an archivist had to be appointed, but since then no one seemed to have bothered him.

He looked at me mistrustfully.

'Is this all the documentation that you have here?' I asked.

'No,' he replied. 'This is just what we need for our day-to-day requirements!'

He didn't bat an eyelid. It was impossible to tell whether he was being serious or just making a very dry joke. I looked at him sceptically but he had wrapped himself in his shawl to fend off further questions.

He shook his head reluctantly when I tried to discover details of the archive's activities. I had come some decades too late; the documents were visibly crumbling in the damp tropical air. When the university had taken over the princely archives, there had been no such thing as air conditioning. The papers had fallen to pieces in the damp heat of the tropics and after that no one had given a thought to how the documents might be preserved.

The vice chancellor had told me that the library was on the terrace on the former palace's top floor. I went there via a roof garden, with a view over the ornamental lake that stretched out into the parkland behind the building. The domes of the Kali temple at the other end of the palace gardens reared up behind the trees. I could imagine the open square among the domes, fringed with banyan trees, where Radhakrishna and Kartaram had sung their magical rain raga all those years ago.

The library doors were closed. I put my hand on the pane of glass and peered inside. A pleasant little hall filled with bookshelves revealed itself. A few men were gathered round a table at the back wall, some sitting on chairs, others squatting on the floor. They were hearkening to a man sitting behind the table, who was reading aloud from a newspaper spread out in front of him. I knocked but the men were so engrossed in the reading that they didn't hear me.

I rattled the door. The reader looked up reluctantly, set his news-paper aside and signalled at one of the listeners to go and see what I might want. The door opened a crack and a face appeared.

The man told me that the library was closed, the staff were on strike.

I asked whether he couldn't make an exception for me; after all, I had travelled thousands of miles to visit the library. The face vanished while he went for advice to the man who had been reading from the newspaper. When he reappeared, he shook his head.

'No,' he said. 'Unfortunately, that is not possible.'

The vice chancellor had nodded in a friendly fashion at my interest in the history of the court musicians. He had promised me his help and support, so I set off to find him in his office in another wing of the palace. The secretary in the waiting room showed me to a chair and a little later, the vice chancellor himself appeared. He recognized me, smiled and assured me that I was certainly entitled to use the library. To emphasize that mine was an official request, he gave me one of his staff to smooth the way.

We climbed back up to the rooftop together. On recognizing their colleague, the librarians opened the door and let us in. Everything seemed in order and my companion left, but the men then sat down and paid me no attention at all, listening to their ringleader reading aloud. Obviously I was an uninvited interloper.

I cleared my throat but none of them deigned even to glance at me.

'I would like to see a book!' I declared in a forceful tone that they could not possibly ignore. Irritated, the reader put his newspaper aside. Clearly he held it against me that I had interrupted his reading a second time.

'That's impossible! I can't simply hand out books to strangers, surely you realize that?' he asked. Despite his rudeness, he used the formal Hindi mode of address.

'The vice chancellor has sent me to you,' I retorted, equally politely.

'That's as may be, but you need permission in writing to use the library and we issue that, not the vice chancellor.'

'Wonderful!' I said. 'What must I do to obtain permission?'

'You'll need a written letter of recommendation from the vice chancellor,' the librarian answered and turned back to his newspaper.

I wasn't giving up. I tried to persuade him that it would be in his own best interests to help me spread the word abroad about Mithila's glorious history and its princes.

'Aha!' he said emphatically. 'You are a foreigner! Foreigners are not entitled to use the library.'

I shrugged and set out once more for the vice chancellor's office. In the waiting room, I was told that he was in a meeting and there was no telling now long it might continue. It would be best if I came back the next day. I plucked up my courage, knocked on the door to the vice chancellor's office and opened it without waiting for the receptionist's approval. A group of distinguished-looking gents was sitting about him; he beckoned me in with a gesture that spoke of mild impatience. I told him what the trouble was and he sighed, picked up a ball-point pen and scribbled a few words on a strip of paper.

Triumphantly, I held this paper under the head librarian's nose. He examined it suspiciously, then bent down and fished out a huge, shabby tome from the depths of his desk drawers. He opened it up in front of me and I filled out the required information and signed, at which he went back to his newspaper.

'Now I would like to see a book,' I said, to the newspaper.

'Which book?' said the voice behind the broadsheet pages.

I had heard of a book documenting the consequences of the earthquake that struck northern Bihar in 1934, when the Darbhanga district had been worst affected. Temples had collapsed, the palaces had suffered damage, a large part of the town was simply razed to the ground. Someone had told me that the book had photographs of all the buildings and an extensive commentary, but so far no one had been able to show me a copy. Since it had been published by the Darbhanga Raj Press, I assumed that it must be in the library.

The librarian looked at me expressionlessly but I could see that he was prodding his foot about beneath the table. We heard a yelp of pain. A young man climbed out from under the table, where he had evidently been sleeping unremarked until that moment. The librarian had kicked him in the ribs as a sign to wake up. The boy rubbed sleep from his eyes and looked at the librarian, who still said nothing but lifted his head and jerked his chin towards me in command.

I told the young man what I wanted. He could neither read nor write and had no idea what books were in the library, but he led me through the room and I browsed the shelves quite peacefully. Cobwebs hung across the glass panes of the bookcases but I could make out a few titles. It looked as though this really had been the maharaja's library. He had the complete run of *Sacred Books of the East*, yellowing English novels and works on religion, economics and politics.

I also found the book about the earthquake, a whole pile of them. There must have been more than a hundred copies, bound in dark red marbled paper. A golden dolphin decorated the cover and beneath it the title, *The Bihar Earthquake and the Darbhanga Raj*. The pile was tied together with twine, suggesting that most of the print run had been placed on this shelf straight from the press.

I would have liked to look through a copy but the glass doors of the bookcase were padlocked. I asked the boy for the key and he sent me back to the librarian.

'Very difficult,' he pronounced, wagging his head pensively. 'A colleague of mine is in charge of the key but he has had to go back to his village on important family business.'

'When will he be back?' I asked.

He would certainly be back in a week or two, the librarian declared. It would be better if I could call in then.

On the way back down to the ground floor I passed a gallery of dusty, broken windows halfway down, that pointed not outward but into the palace. Curious, I opened one of them. The passage I was walking along turned out to be a balustrade overlooking a wide hall from above. It was the throne room, where the official audiences had taken place.

Light seeping through the coloured panes of the dim windows shrouded the room in a mysterious, twilit atmosphere. The double doors down at ground level were closed, the exterior windows barred, the only light in the room came in from above. Doves fluttered about when the light fell upon them from my open window.

Their calls echoed in the twilight of the hall as they flew up and perched on what was left of the chandeliers that hung from the ceiling. Once my eyes had grown accustomed to the dark, I could see the golden ropes that held together the tattered, faded remains of dark red brocade curtains. The floor had once been covered by a carpet but I could only guess at what colour it had been beneath the dust and the dove droppings.

At the head of the hall, askew on a single nail, hung the dolphin, the princely coat of arms, faded, and beneath it on a marble pedestal with chipped and broken corners, the remnants of a throne in the Louis XIV style. The velvet upholstery was torn and the gold on the arms, legs and back had worn thin. Sawdust shavings burst from the cushions, while other, similarly shabby chairs stood in rows at the wall. Above the throne hung the remains of a dusty canopy where the doves had built their nests.

Vaidyanath Dham, Holi, February 1985

One day, Ram Chatur Mallik told me that one of his students lived in Vaidyanath Dham and had a music school there; it was one of the places that he regularly visited. Holi, the spring festival, was approaching, and they celebrated it in their own way in Vaidyanath Dham, so this was another reason to visit the holy site.

The four of us set off—the singer, over eighty years old, his valet Kali-babu, only a few years younger but still robust, next in the entourage the teenager from the village and I. The boy's job was to cook and do the heavy lifting; during the months I stayed with Ram Chatur Mallik and Kali-babu, several of these youngsters had turned up and then left again. It was demanding work and none of them lasted long with the two ancients.

Deogarh, the nearest town to the temple of Vaidyanath Dham, is a rustic little place where cows wander across the streets. Ram Chatur Mallik had painted an enthralling picture of the music school with his words, and when we reached it the hand-painted sign outside bore a long Sanskrit inscription worthy of a university but inside was simply one large empty room with a few tanpuras and tablas hanging on the walls and a harmonium. His student, an old man himself, received us. In place of mattresses he simply shook bundles of straw onto the bare floor for us to lie down on. This was the usual practice; we had come as pilgrims to take part in the rituals celebrated in Vaidyanath Dham.

The word dham indicates a place of pilgrimage. Vrindavan too is a dham, a holy place, but Vrindavan is dedicated not to Shiva but to Krishna. Encounters between the two gods follow a strict etiquette. When Shiva wanted to watch Krishna dancing with the gopis on the banks of the Yamuna—at least this is how they tell it in Vrindavan—he had to transform into a milkmaid himself, for only women or those in woman's form may approach Krishna.

At Holi though, this protocol was set aside and the two gods met and mingled freely at Vaidyanath Dham. Kali-babu told me how the priests would place a golden statue of Krishna on the lingam in the inner chamber of their temple—a unique ritual performed nowhere else.

Hundreds of pilgrims thronged the narrow doorway that led to the room where the theophany would take place, a chamber of only a few square yards. At the centre of the room was the lingam, surrounded by a low balustrade. It took the form of a roughly dressed block of stone, since the lingam had broken when the demon king Ravana dropped it. This stone, named for Vaidyanath, Lord of Healers, is one of the twelve jyotir-lingams, lingams of light, scattered all across India. They were not made by the hand of man but by Shiva himself and are believed to have unusual powers. The pilgrims in the room prostrated themselves and tried to touch the stone with their hands, clinging onto the balusters while others surged in behind them.

Nor did Ram Chatur Mallik want to miss this darshan, the sacred sight of the two gods meeting. He could only walk a few paces on his own and that too only when leaning on his stick, but the fracas at the doorway was far too lively. Kali-babu grabbed him under one shoulder and I took hold of the other and the two of us shoved and pushed the old man, wrapped in his dhoti, through the crowd. He had bared his torso, as was the custom, to be able to bathe in the sacred radiance of the jyotirlingam. When we got in, the little low chamber was in uproar, with the pilgrims swarming cheek by jowl. Coloured powder was scattered hither and yon, water was squirted all around, shouts and songs filled the air.

The pilgrims behind us shoved for all they were worth to touch the sacred stone where Krishna's statue stood. Ram Chatur Mallik too sank to the ground, wanting at least to press his brow to the balustrade round the lingam. People pushing from behind lurched over him and someone stumbled. For a moment it looked as though we would be crushed by those behind us, then we had him by the arms and were fighting our way out. We breathed a sigh of relief once we were out in the open air.

That evening a crowd of people awaited us on the terrace surrounding the temple. A concert had been announced and a cloth had been spread out to mark where the musicians would sit. We took our places, someone pressed a tanpura into Kali-babu's hand and the old man who had greeted us at the music school tuned his tabla.

Ram Chatur Mallik sang until late into the night. Just as his fore-fathers had done before him, he began with one of the old dhrupads that were still known and loved hereabouts. The old man sang his way with great dignity through the traditional raga sequences, lending each one a new splendour, matching the splendour of the god whom the songs described. Perhaps audiences in the big cities had forgotten about him but here in the quiet of rural Bihar, his old art was not yet out of fashion.

The moon shone through the branches of a tree on the temple roof, bathing the faces of those who sat in a massed circle round the singer, listening with delight. They wanted to hear more and more, asking for the old songs that were only ever sung at this mela, at this place.

Ram Chatur Mallik knew them all—a seemingly endless chain of melody, compositions that I hadn't heard before, songs telling how Shiva and Krishna met to play Holi on the heights of Mount Kailasha, spraying one another with coloured water.

'Do you hear that?' whispered the old man sitting next to me. There were tears in his eyes. 'He is the dhrupad samrat, the emperor of dhrupad! No one who comes after him will be able to take his place.'

Darbhanga, 1986

*The Last Maharaja of Darbhanga Indeed Memories of
the Princely Days, with all their Good and Evil twin
[sic] into Nostalgia for the Vanished Past*

—read the little man with the glasses and the clever
face. His hair was thinning and his English was quaint.
He wore a white kurta. I had been sent to him because
I was looking for eyewitnesses to princely history. He
lived near the guesthouse and I took a rickshaw to meet
him. Amar Kant Mishra sat across from me on the
wooden platform outside his front door. He had been
the last maharaja's private secretary and still respect-
fully spoke of him as 'Maharajadhiraj' and took care
to add a string of letters after his name.

'What do those mean?' I asked.

'Maharajadhiraj Dr Sir Raja Bahadur Kameshwar
Singh, G. C. I. E., D. Litt., LL. D.,' he said. 'Grand
Commander of the Indian Empire—it was an order
founded in 1877 conjunct to the Star of India. The
maharaja was a member of the Order, first class.'

His knowledge was encyclopaedic. Safely stored in
his memory, he had a list of the buildings the maharaja
had owned, including the country house in Cornwall
which was still tangled up in ownership disputes. He
knew the temples which the maharaja had sponsored,
the number of elephants (over a hundred) and all their
names, the aeroplanes that the maharaja had loved to
collect (more than a dozen). The largest was an
American Douglas 47/Dakota IV, the famous 'Gooney
Bird'; a special model, the C-47B, had been built for

Himalayan goods freight and Kameshwar Singh used it to transport whole parties of guests. He also had a Tiger Moth in his fleet, nicknamed 'Tiggie', and a Lockheed. In 1945 he added a Beechcraft Cargo Twin Bonanza, the same model that crashed in 1959, killing Buddy Holly and the Crickets.

Amar Kant Mishra had seen the maharaja every day, had dealt with his correspondence, organized his travel and taken part in the parties, the festivals, sporting jaunts and court hunts. Kameshwar Singh's father had been president of the All India Landholders' Association, the son was the largest landholder in India. He died in 1962 leaving no heir and the private secretary saw the estates fall into ruin before his eyes. He told me that he had begun to write his memoirs, the story of the man he had served for two decades.

I asked him to tell me a little about the musical soirées at the court and he opened to the chapter in which he described the great darbar, the state reception given to mark the auspicious date of Dussehra, celebrating Rama's defeat of Ravana's demon army. He began by describing the palace where the darbar took place.

'Anand Bagh was the only palace that remained untouched by the ravages of the earthquake when it destroyed all the other majestic buildings,' Amar Kant Mishra recited, reading gravely from a manuscript bound between purple boards. He fitted his voice nicely to the weighty matters he was describing. 'Temples, hospital, stable, library and officers' bungalows collapsed in a couple of seconds that fateful noon of January 15th in 1934: but the palace was untouched, barring its long tower, the massive redstone structure fitted with the giant clock manufactured by Benson of England in the nineteenth century, that fell on the ground. In his book *Darbhanga Raj and the Earthquake*, Kumar Ganganand Singh says that "Fact looked like fiction," referring to the escape unhurt of the two-year-old baby, the Senior Rajkumar Jiveshwar Singh, son of the late Raja Bahadur Vishweshwar Singh of Rajnagar, who was playing with his hostess in the first floor of Anand Bagh that fateful day.

'No sooner did the young rajkumar and hostess get in the car near the portico than the big massive clock tower fell to the ground. Had they been late even by a second the result would have been disastrous. They were driven to a safe place in the field by the attending nurse Mrs Hear White, who, though injured by a falling brick, did not lose her presence of mind or her sense of duty. The rest of the members of the royal house were in Calcutta.

'Built for nine lakhs of rupees a hundred years ago, this palace was used for state ceremonies. Every year, on the last day of Ashwin Navratra, the Vijaya Dashami, a royal darbar was held in the evening in the famous Darbar Hall of Anand Bagh.'

As the secretary read, I saw with my mind's eye the throne room that I had found in the university, which had once been the Garden of Joy.

'On this day, the traditional throne of gold and silver with multicoloured satin canopy, heavily studded with the jewelleries, used to be placed at one end of mirrored wall of the hall. Here sat the Mithilesh, sporting his traditional brocade achkan, complete with diamond buttons, and crown with sashes and furs, and royal sword with ivory handle tied at his waist.

'The darbar took place in the evening, at the time appointed by the raj pandit, after going round the capital in a big glittering procession headed by the maharaja on a gold and silver chariot drawn by a couple of tuskers, the last being his favourite elephant Moti Prasad, followed by the cavalcade of elephants and horses carrying the raj officials, the personal staff and the distinguished dignitaries. On their arrival back at the altar of Lakshmishwar Vilas, the bugler would take the position and sounded the grand arrival with its flute pipe. The chobdars shouted, "Rooh-barooh—Maharajadhiraja Bahadur ki salamat!" and the drummer announced the order with beating the gold drum.

'The maharaja would enter the hall with attendance of his aides and royal escorts and made to sit on the decorated dais over a raised platform covered with velvets on the bejewelled throne beneath the canopy. A senior officer of the raj secretariat conducted the proceddings [sic], by which he would announce, "By the command of His Highness, the darbar is declared to be opened," and would read from a glossy foolscap sheet that he handled, the names of the persons or groups in accordance with the order of precedence, to come one by one and present his salaam to the Mithilesh.

'To start with the pandits, who would come in a group headed by the raj pandit and offer a pair of coconuts, chanting the richas of the Vedas in chorus, and return back to their prospective seats. The next to follow used to be the nearest of kin to the throne, the last being Raja Bahadur of Rajnagar, Vishweshwar Singh, the second son of the late maharaja Rameshwar Singh, who offered gold mohurs as a salaam to the crown, then would follow the babuahs, the nearest of kin of the royal lineage, and then the chief manager, the private secretary to the maharajadhiraj, officials of the raj secretariat, the personal staff officers and the gentry, doctors, lawyers and state guests.

'After all these settle down, the secretary of the chief manager, the last being Sri S. R. Maitra, a beautiful lovable personality, announced the names in the same order to come to the throne and receive the bira of paan (betel), the most auspicious ingredient of Mithila's cultural heritage, prepared with gold and silver tobacco which the maharaja would pick up from a silver casket nearby, having been helped by a liveried attendant, and gave it to the persons on queue in accordance with the warrant of precedence, who received it as a token of the love and blessings of the reigning Mithilesh on this happy and auspicious occasion. After these formalities, the officer on duty, donning the churidar and an achkan with the colourful safa, the traditional turban of the darbar, also announced any award, promotion, relief to the tenants, donation and other jahgirs, before it dispersed with his mighty tone of winding up saying, "By the command of His Highness, the darbar is declared to be closed."

'After spending two hours in the Darbar Hall, the Maharaja would move upstairs to his private drawing room where his engagement awaited a colourful schedule—a cocktail dominated by French champagne, with ice cubes floating over the goblets, and the bara pegs of Scotch, jingling in the hands of the royal guests whom the liveried butlers served with snacks, gravy and epicurean delicacies, followed by music and dance presented by the court musicians and dancing girls imported from Lucknow, Benares and Jaipur.

'When the evening crossed its youth and entered in its adulthood, the gracious night started advancing with all its wings of darkness and innocent calmness, pierced by the light in thousands of candle power that dominated the hall of Lakshmishwar Vilas, and the rhythm of thumri, melody of heart-touching songs and the tinkle of ghunghroos, followed by the colourful tuning of vibrating performance, amidst aroma of cigars and fragrance of lavender-soaked cosmetics sending up spirals on incense kept that affluent crowd of El Dorado spellbound. A sweet damsel welcoming the night sang, "Jeevan bhar bhor na ho sajni, sada rajni hi rahe, yahi man bhawat hai"—All my life, may it never be dawn, dear friend, may night remain always, this is the thought in my mind; another finkin lass, with liqueur brandy in her right rosy hands, seated in the centre surrounded by the solo stalwarts, robbed the attention of the people there, who heard her rendering ghazals that echoed elastically in the affluent assembly set in session there.

'Among many great ghazal singers of India, K. L. Saigal and Begam Akhtar, who spent most of their time here in the company of Raja Bahadur Vishweshwar Singh, who was himself a lover of music and veteran harmonium wizard of the era, also graced such occasions with their presence. These ghazal wizards were found well imbibing the spirit of the ghazals before singing them. The splendid feast to the ears established that the persons assembled there, it seems, were taking away the nectar from the vast ocean of music, for the sweetness, the soulfulness and the respectability escorted the way of the Indian character. With such ecstasy and glamour of passing time, not as a bit of history frozen into bricks, but as a living legend, stands today the Lakshmishwar Vilas!'

With a sigh, the secretary shut the cover on his manuscript.

Ram Chatur Mallik was the first singer from the family to travel to Europe. For Mithila brahmins it was a sacrilege to cross the kala pani, the black water of the Indian Ocean, which brought about a state of impurity that could only be cleansed—if at all—by complex rituals. When the maharaja announced in 1932 that he would fly to London for the round table conference on the future of India, the conservative pandits of Mithila protested furiously; but the twenty-five-year-old Mithilesh had his way. He reassured the brahmins that he would be taking enough water from the Ganga with him for himself and his entourage to drink, so that they would not defile themselves with the black water of foreign lands, and had two sterling silver tanks made for the purpose to hold thousands of gallons apiece. While these were being taken overland to Bombay, he sat himself at the joystick of his Dakota and flew on ahead. His court singer was among the entourage who took ship to London.

Once in London, they took an entire floor in the Savoy, where the prince practised his golf strokes on the roof, sometimes sending the balls into the Thames. When there was not enough water from the Ganga left to wash with, the hotel's hot-water pipes served the purpose, each one gilded and as thick as a man's arm. Even today, in nostalgic TV documentaries the Savoy happily remembers how these could fill a bathtub in fourteen seconds. When the prince grew bored with the politicking, he would fill an aeroplane with his friends and spend the weekend in Paris, at the Moulin Rouge.

'For he was a jolly good fellow, for he was a jolly good fellow,' sang Ram Chatur Mallik, remembering the old English glees he had learnt in London and waving his arms to the beat as though dancing as he sang, 'For he was a jolly good fellow, and nob'dy can deny!' He still had a moth-eaten dinner jacket hidden away in the chest under his bed in the guesthouse, left over from those days.

'Give me champagne! Give me champagne!' the ladies would call; he pointed to his cheek, showing me where they had kissed him when he was in Europe as a courtier.

'Whatever Ram Chatur-ji has told you—it's all true!' Professor Das' voice was quite emphatic.

'He doesn't make things up!' he insisted. 'The Malliks aren't city folk. City musicians are real rogues, I tell you, but the Malliks are village people. Furthermore, they are brahmins. It's true that Ram Chatur-ji drinks alcohol but that comes from having lived at the court—an inevitable consequence of being so close to the maharaja.'

Professor C. L. Das had a passion for music. For decades, he had reviewed the Indian National Programme radio broadcasts in the Patna newspapers. He was the son of a small zamindar who owned some land in Nepal, though the family originally came from Mithila. He had known Ram Chatur Mallik even as a boy and some of his ancestors had served Rameshwar Singh when he built his palace in Rajnagar at the end of the nineteenth century. The enormous Naulakha Palace, in a Saracen Gothic style, was a wonder that could compare with Bombay's Victoria Terminus. When his father died, Kameshwar Singh kept only the Darbhanga palaces and generously left the Rajnagar district to his younger brother Vishweshwar, settling upon him an annuity of six to eight lakh rupees, enough to live quite comfortably. The prince was mad for music and became bosom friends with the singer. They ate together, drank together and sang together. The singer performed every night at court, and together they enjoyed the last sunset of imperial India.

'I grew up in Rajnagar, very near the court,' Professor Das told me. 'Raja Bahadur was very easy-going with Ram Chatur-ji, treating him like one of the family, and I would say that Ram Chatur-ji was even more easy-going.'

The professor shook his head and adjusted his spectacles.

'The idea that a man from a dhrupad dynasty could sing such moving thumris was quite out of the ordinary!' He smiled at the memory. 'Raja Bahadur used to tease him about that. "Your dhrupad is too solemn for my tastes," he would tell Ram Chatur-ji, "Dhrupad is such a cold, mathematical business! Where is the fire, the emotion?" Raja Bahadur was a musician himself. There was a famous harmonium player in Benares, Soni-babu, who could cast a spell on his listeners when he sang thumris with such feeling and spirit. Didn't sing other styles, of course, only thumri, which—as you know—needs emotion more than anything else. Raja Bahadur invited Soni-babu to Rajnagar for six months, to learn a little from watching him play the harmonium. He challenged Ram Chatur-ji to match Soni-babu's artistry.'

'Sarkar!' Ram Chatur Mallik had answered. 'Your Highness! We dhrupad singers have spent years learning our art and we have such a mastery of music that we can sing and play in whatever style you please! Why does Your Highness talk of Soni-babu? I can sing for you every one of his songs and I can sing them the way they really should be sung!'

Raja Bahadur gave him six months, the professor recalled. 'Ram Chatur-ji had never sung thumri before in his life but over the next few months, he took over Soni-babu's whole repertoire and sang it for Raja Bahadur. Once he had heard all the songs, the prince acknowledged that Ram Chatur-ji was indeed a master of thumri, but there was much more to follow—the whole country went crazy for Ram Chatur Mallik's thumri singing and all the music lovers of North India agreed that he was a wonder.'

'He's a person with a phenomenal memory,' Professor Das continued. 'Countless musicians have come and gone in this house but no one made such an impression on me.'

The professor took off his eye-glasses and twirled them thoughtfully in his fingers.

'You know, Ram Chatur Mallik has a dual nature, a split personality almost. Only those who are close to him know his true inner nature. He has such incredible depths. It is a very personal matter, something quite unique. He's a sport of nature! A very unusual man. I tell you, soon enough people like him will be nothing but legends!'

In Ram Chatur Mallik's grandson's house, in Patna, stood the harmonium which the prince had played to accompany his friend's singing. It was a small chest equipped with keyboard and bellows. The prince had bequeathed it to his singer on his death.

Kali-babu knocked on the instrument's lid, then pointed to the keyhole with its ivory surround. 'He gave the strongroom key to his servant but he always carried the harmonium key round with him!' he told me. 'So do I!' He held out to me the guesthouse key, which he had knotted into his brahmin's thread so that he would never be at a loss to find it.

Ram Chatur Mallik too carried a key tied to the thread which hung about his shoulders, the thread which was ritually changed once a year. This key opened the padlocked chest containing his most precious possessions, hidden under his bed.

The most important object in this chest was a book which, like the portrait of the goddess and the objects which Ram Chatur Mallik used for daily puja, was wrapped in a red cloth. The singer had inherited this handwritten manuscript from his father and it contained the texts of all the songs passed down in the family—hundreds and hundreds of verses, the oldest dating back to the great Tansen at Emperor Akbar's court. It also contained a disquisition on the meaning of the ragas and mysterious diagrams showing the possible combinations of various notes and their ornamentation.

Sometimes Ram Chatur Mallik needed to see this book to reread a verse. Opening the book required elaborate ceremony. Kali-babu pulled the metal trunk out from under the bed; the old man then had to bend very low so that the key he carried on his thread could reach the padlock. Then Ram Chatur Mallik would lift out the book wrapped in its red cloth but before unwrapping it, he would murmur a few mantras and touch the bundle to his brow several times. The book he then took out from its red cover had evidently been much used over the decades. Within their cardboard covers, some of the folio pages were torn and the title page was only half there, showing what remained of an ornate calligraphy—lines of script making a portrait of the monkey god Hanuman, holding a flag in one hand, a mace in the other. The old singer fumbled as he tried to turn the pages and tore them further.

Darbhanga, January 1988

The rickshaw turned towards the lion-crowned gate that led to Ram Bagh, the older and more decayed part of the palace grounds in another part of the city. We crossed a broad square to reach the house where the prince's son lived. The maharaja had had several wives but left no heirs. His younger brother's sons therefore stood to inherit but the family relations were tangled. The elder son lived in a little bungalow near the radio station, where it was said that he had devoted himself entirely to tantra, following his grandfather's example, and was never seen in public. Rajkumar Sabeshwar Singh, who lived here in the house in the grounds of the old Ram Bagh palace, counted as the official heir, even if there was no court to honour him as such. Ram Chatur Mallik had announced that he had invited us to hear him sing.

A group of raffish-looking, ancient, toothless figures clad in rags was squatting at the gate in the wall round the palace precinct. When they saw the old singer arriving on his rickshaw, they clambered laboriously to their feet and hobbled towards the vehicle, using their canes. He called out to them and one of these ancients leant close to the seat, fished the singer's shawl from his shoulders with a stick and wrapped it about himself. It was an act of rough-and-ready camaraderie, such as I could only assume had been the order of the day among the courtiers.

Rather unnerved by the encounter, I shrank to one side but Ram Chatur Mallik laughed out loud. 'These are the wrestlers!' he called to me. 'You see here the maharaja's bodyguard! You can't imagine what fine figures of men they used to be! These were the heroes who cast down all our enemies!'

The prince's bodyguards accompanied us, on their canes, into the house, where we sat in the audience room. The prince's son appeared, a well-fed, bearded man of middle age. He emphasized to me how close his father had been to Ram Chatur Mallik, how they had eaten, drunk and caroused together, how the prince had treated him like one of the family. He himself continued the tradition. The table was set for the family and Ram Chatur Mallik and I were invited to partake of the meal, while Kali-babu was served in another room. Raja Vishweshwar's son brought the food to the table himself, including a tasty leaf dish that I hadn't eaten before, an uncommon water plant that only grew here in Darbhanga's ponds.

Traditionally, at a house concert, dinner is taken only after the performance but here we followed princely etiquette, which dictated that the maharaja's heir would only turn to the pleasures of music once he had eaten. We sang; I was invited to sing a dhrupad too, since our host was eager to hear what the court singer had been able to teach me. At the close of the concert, we were given the traditional court gifts—a sum of money, a dhoti and a portion of betel.

We planned to travel to Patna in the next few days and the prince's son asked us to pass on his greetings to Arun, Ram Chatur Mallik's grandson, who worked as a watchman for the newspaper which the last maharaja had founded in Patna and which his nephew had inherited. The Hindi newspaper was called *Aryavart* while the English edition was the *Indian Nation*. The singer had been part of his father's court and the prince's son saw it as his duty to provide for the singer's family too.

Patna, February 1988

When I told Indian acquaintances in Delhi or Bombay that I was studying dhrupad, and in Bihar at that, they would raise their eyebrows in amazement. Dhrupad? What was that? Most of them had never heard of it. Anyone who was actually interested in their country's classical music knew instead about the contemporary sitar stars or the sarod or tabla players.

India had long forgotten Ram Chatur Mallik. He was part of a past that survived only in the remote districts. Hardly anyone outside Bihar knew that he was alive and even within Bihar, only a few knew his name— some of them musicians or the surviving members of the court, a few old men in distant temples, members of his large and ramified family.

'He was at all the weddings celebrated in my family, and in the holidays we used to visit him in Darbhanga,' Dubey-ji told me. 'It is a great personal happiness to me that I have such a man as my guardian! My father was a dhrupad singer too. When I was eight or nine, I sang to Ram Chatur-ji a melody that my father had taught me. He was so pleased that he gave me his pocket watch. I still have it. Many people have Ram Chatur Mallik to thank for the happy lives that they lead today!'

His full name was Chandra Prasad Dubey. Earlier he had been the rector of a school in the Patna district where he lived, though by now he was retired. I was staying with Dubey-ji, since Ram Chatur Mallik was staying with his grandson Arun and there was no room for another guest there. Not long before, the two-roomed house had been hit by a flood. There was still a streak of mud a yard high up the walls, showing where the water had filled the house. Arun said that there was no point repainting. There would be another flood soon for sure and he would be happy if he could just save up enough money to send his son to school.

There was not much space in Dubey-ji's house either. We slept in the same room, each under a net to keep off the swarms of mosquitoes that invaded the room at night. I listened to Dubey-ji's voice for hours in the darkness, as he conjured up pictures of the past.

'Ram Chatur-ji never had any worries,' Dubey-ji's voice said from beneath the net on his side of the room, 'No material worries, nor in any other regard. Not his whole life long, nor today, may God be thanked! Of all Raja Bahadur's courtiers, he was by far the most talented, which is why he was also the most respected.'

The maharaja was reckoned to have been the wealthiest zamindar in all of British India. Darbhanga was not a native state governed by rulers by right of conquest but was actually held as an estate. The zamindari system had been introduced by the East India Company and originally the landholders acted as tax collectors for the British. To start with, they held the land on five- or ten-year leases. It was Lord Cornwallis who made the zamindars the permanent rulers of the land and allowed them to bequeath titles to their descendants.

There were dozens of zamindars in Bihar and every one of them had an estate of some size and a corresponding court. They regarded it as a privilege to be able to keep musicians, and many of them were themselves musicians.

'Kumar Shyamanad Singh of Banaili was an exceptional singer; the very best musicians would meet at his court,' came Dubey-ji's voice from the darkness. 'Lakshmi Narayan Singh of Panchgachiya was famous throughout the land as a patron of music; Shatrunjay Prasad Singh of Jamila, near Ara, whom they called Lallan-ji, was an incredible player of the pakhwaj. Govind-babu in Gaya learnt harmonium from Babu Soni Singh and played every night. He was mad about music! They say that for many decades he never slept at night.' Dubey-ji rattled off a seemingly endless string of names.

'It was a real challenge for any musician to play for these zamindars,' said the voice in the half-darkness, lit by a neon light from the street. 'Ram Chatur-ji was a court musician of the very first rank. He could go wherever he chose, he was always welcome not only in Bihar but in all North India. His close friendship with Raja Bahadur made him not merely a courtier but one of the family. He and Raja Bahadur were inseparable, the raja took him along everywhere, even to the native states. The raja of Bikaner, the raja of Jaipur, the maharaja of Kashmir—they all became friends.'

'Also the maharajas of Bettiah—you will play for them next week—they had their own tradition of dhrupad as well, as you will hear.' I had told Dubey-ji that we were travelling to Bettiah for a dhrupad festival organized by the Music Academy of Bihar.

'When you set off, you must stop by here,' Dubey-ji concluded. 'I would like to say goodbye to Ram Chatur-ji. I have so much more to thank him for than I can ever tell you!'

For days I had been hearing about a ceremony where Ram Chatur Mallik would receive an order. The next morning he was helped into his sherwani, the mid-length black coat that he had worn in his great days as a courtier, and Kali-babu carefully combed his hair and set on his head the black cap saved for official occasions. The whole family got going, the grandson taking his wife and children on the motor scooter, grandfather, Kali-babu and I on a rickshaw.

The Krishna Memorial Hall where the occasion was to take place was the size of an indoor-sports stadium. The hall staff took charge of us and the old singer was helped up onto the stage where he sat on one of the chairs standing on a worn carpet, ready for him and the others who would be inducted into the order, the Gaurav Puraskar, which a patriotic society awards to distinguished citizens. Ram Chatur Mallik had put on his spectacles and was peering about with great interest. Next to him sat a Madhubani peasant woman who had become famous for her traditional painting and on the other side, a young man who had won a pole-vaulting championship. The list of decorated persons was extensive. The patriotic society's eminent members made speeches in praise of the recipients gathered onstage, then placed garlands of flowers and sandalwood round their necks, pinned outsize decorations onto them and presented the trophies that went with the award.

Hardly anyone in the audience, though, was paying any attention to what was happening on the stage. The hall was restless, there was an air of anticipation that I simply couldn't explain. For a good quarter of an hour nothing at all happened. The speeches had all been held but the audience sat there stubbornly. Then a murmur ran through the crowd. A knot of people moved through the hall towards the stage, then a figure in a glittering blue silk suit stepped out from their midst and took the speaker's podium. A fiery-red scarf thrown over his shoulders reached to the ground.

A roar went up from the crowd. 'Shotgun Sinha!' they called, adoringly. Shatrughan Sinha was by far the most famous actor ever to come out of Bihar. His nickname 'Shotgun' referred to the way he had made his name playing villains. Shotgun Sinha stretched out his arms and calmed the crowd and then launched into an impassioned speech in which he conjured up a glorious future for Patna's film industry, painting the rosiest of pictures. Bombay, he told his listeners, was fabulously wealthy but a long way away; Patna had to have its own film studios, the film industry was a matter of national importance which must not be monopolized by individual cities. In all the years that he had spent in distant Bombay, he had never forgotten his home and its image had never faded from his heart.

It hardly mattered what he said, though; it was far more important that he gave his audience the chance to see him, that he gave them the darshan that a god gives his worshippers in the moment of theophany. The hall was full to the brim, they had all come to see Shotgun Sinha. People hung on his lips as though bewitched, but they still seemed to be waiting for something. They didn't merely want to see him but to touch him as well. I should have expected it but I was utterly taken aback when, as soon as the film star had finished his speech, the crowd rose to their feet as one and mobbed the stage.

I looked at the stage. Ram Chatur Mallik was still sitting on his chair; the other dignitaries had been listening to the film star speak but had made themselves scarce when the crowd rushed to the stage and surged over the row of chairs. Ram Chatur Mallik's head disappeared as though under water. It looked as though the horde of people who were all trying get close to their idol would simply bury the old man. Since he could no longer stand up unaided, he was entirely helpless in such a situation. I ran to the stage. His eyeglasses had fallen off and he was fumbling for them and peering about short-sightedly for a familiar face. I grabbed other people by the hand who had also realized the danger the old man was in. We formed a ring round him, and a push from behind almost sent us face down on top of him; but as suddenly as it had begun, the terrifying moment passed.

In the last few days I spent with my guru in Patna, we were on our own. The grandson and his wife had been invited to a wedding in another town, while Kali-babu had to look after affairs in Darbhanga. Only the six-year-old great-grandson was left behind, so I too stayed in the house in those nights.

The wooden bed where the old man slept stood next to me. I lay on a mat on the floor, looking up at him. In the flickering neon light, his chest rose and fell peacefully. It was entirely silent except for his breathing and the whining mosquitoes. On the other side of the mat lay the great-grandson, snuggled up to me in his sleep. I felt myself to be a link in the chain of generations, as I never had before. Now I helped the great-grandfather when he had to go to the toilet at night and I cleaned his lota. His skin was rough and cracked like an old elephant's. I was surprised at how cold his body felt when I massaged him with mustard oil.

Berlin, September 2005

'Don't go out these days, prefer not to,' Huzur Biswambhar Roy tells the moneylender Mahim, who has come to invite him to a musical soirée. Roy is a zamindar, a great landlord, but the Ganga has flooded his estates and also taken his wife and son, who drowned during the storm that devastated his land. In one scene in the film *Jalsaghar*, Huzur Biswambhar Roy carries his dead son in his arms. He bears the guilt for the deaths since although the storm was brewing, he called his wife and child back from a journey to attend a mehfil, a courtly entertainment that is to take place in his jalsaghar, the music room he loves above all else.

Bengali director Satyajit Ray made the film in 1958, as a story of the Indian aristocracy's disproportionate and extravagant love of music and dance in the thirties. It shows the last years and weeks in the life of a landlord grandee who is, in the end, driven from his home by a parvenu from the village. I knew the music from cassette tapes but I did not see the film until September 2005 while I was writing down my memoirs of life with Ram Chatur Mallik. In 1958, there was still no stereo recording and the monophonic soundtrack sounds as though it too came from a cassette player or even from one of the wire-spool recordings stored in the archive of the Santiniketan university which preserve Rabindranath Tagore's singing. Ironically, such steel-wire recordings sound much clearer than early cassettes or shellac records but the system has been so long out of use that there are hardly any machines capable of playback except in the archives themselves.

Fuzzy sound spills from my television set; sometimes you can hardly hear a thing, sometimes the notes sound loud and clear and sometimes they flutter and whoosh as though run through the wrong system at post-production. This contrast between the decaying soundtrack and the wonderful clarity of the black-and-white images merely underlines the whole film's theme, for it is a deeply melancholy eulogy to a form of musical appreciation that simply no longer exists.

In a key scene, the impoverished zamindar stands on the roof of his decaying palace, which looms above the muddy plain of the flooded Ganga. Curious sounds can be heard from the other side of the village that had been his, sounds such as he has never heard. We see the landlord's stooped figure hurrying across the rooftops, his posture shows the strain of trying to place this strange noise. It is the rattling of a generator, his servant tells him. The arriviste moneylender has brought electric current to the village, to make his festivities more brilliant than the zamindar ever could. From now on, the generator is part of life, and the village will never be the same. This moment has decided the future. Man has lost his accustomed peace and quiet, electricity has come to claim the soundscape and he will never again be able to hear music without the machines competing somehow.

'Washed out, everything is washed out!' the landlord says to Ananta, his last remaining servant, when the ground has been snatched away from under his feet. He turns down the moneylender's invitation but can't get over the thought that Mahim is trying to outshine him. He knocks his cane against the glass-and-crystal chandelier where candles once shone, now hung with cobwebs. From outside, we hear the plangent tones of Bismillah Khan's shehnai. The zamindar looks in the mirror and touches his face, as though astonished to find that he is still alive, still flesh and blood.

'How much is Krishnabai taking?' he asks his servant. He is prepared to spend the very last of his money to give one final splendid soirée, to which he invites Mahim, his enemy. The servant has never refused his master's command but points out that the dancer's fee will cost the last of his gold. The landlord glares, silencing him. Only the costliest dancing girl is good enough for his purposes and there is no question but that he will pay the fee. Once more, the mirror is polished and cleaned, the candles lit.

'Tell me, how will the thing go?' Mahim asks a fellow guest, puffing at his cigarette in perplexity. 'It looked a bit queer to me!' The mood is driven, haunted. The singer lifts his voice and the sarangi joins in, the dance begins. 'How do you like it, grandpa?' the moneylender asks his grandee neighbour, smirking solicitously. For one last time, the soundtrack reveals what the musicians could offer their noble patrons, exquisite phrasing, masterful improvisations. At the climax, the dancing girl's feet skip and stamp with breathtaking speed. As we watch, the scene seems to stretch out endlessly, a living, lasting rhythm brought into this world by the sitar master Imrat Khan. The zamindar and the moneylender together watch her feet move across the richly embroidered carpet, astonished. The dance finally ends in a tihai, the triple repetition that closes a composition in the Indian classical repertoire.

'Well done, Baiji! Well done!' Mahim calls to the dancer, clapping, but the zamindar stops his hand with his cane. 'The master of the house reserves the right of paying inam first!' he declares, throwing to the dancing girl a purse filled with his very last coins. When the last guests have left, the old man stays behind in the darkened music room. 'Failed! Couldn't do it!' he chuckles, satisfied, as his servant pours him the last of the brandy. 'Couldn't do it! The son of a moneylender! What cheek! What tomfoolery! A moth trying to reach the stars. But failed, failed! Do you know why he failed?' he asks, turning to his servant. 'Blood! The blood in my veins!' Until this moment he has spoken Bengali but now he repeats that last sentence in English, leading his servant through the portrait gallery of his ancestors, naming each of them.

His father's name had been Rameshwar, like the father of the maharaja of Darbhanga whom Ram Chatur Mallik served. He was one of the last witnesses to a world which this film shows disappearing, a world where music was still appreciated by connoisseurs, not by the ignorant nouveau riche. In Darbhanga, I had plucked a thread from the hem of a dying tradition and now I sit in front of my television in Berlin and contemplate the thread that I hold in my hand.

There are further parallels between Satyajit Ray's film and Ram Chatur Mallik's life. His son too died, tragically, before his father. For a Hindu, this is the greatest imaginable tragedy—that his progeny will not be there to light the sacred flame of his funeral pyre. As I watch the film I feel it again, this unending sadness, the loneliness that I felt the first time I heard the disc of dhrupad singers. The singers have grown tired. No one now wants to listen any more to their complex arts. When music and electricity formed that new alliance, the ragas lost their magical power. The film, made in 1958, is a prescient work, containing everything that I have experienced since I first came to India.

The film's central theme is not nostalgia but a sober appraisal of tragic decline. Ray was anything but a conservative and was attacked in India for his 'Western tendencies'. *Jalsaghar* was supposed to be a commercial film, after his previous self-funded films, *Pather Panchali* and *Aparajito* had not been as successful as hoped. It could have been an early precursor of today's Bollywood productions but during scriptwriting the originally entertaining story by Tarashankar Bandyopadhyay became a tragedy, for which Ray recruited some of the finest musicians of the day—Vilayat Khan, Ashish Kumar, Robin Majumdar, Bismillah Khan, Dakshina Mohan Tagore, one of the last to play the dilruba, the stringed instrument that the zamindar is shown playing in the film. The instrument's name means 'weeping heart' and it was invented in the late nineteenth or possibly the early twentieth century. The film does not conjure the Mughal inheritance; rather, it is entirely a twentieth-century story.

'To you, my noble ancestors! To you!' Huzur Biswambhar Roy toasts, lifting his glass to the family portraits. Then he comes at last to his own portrait. 'And to you, my noble self!' he calls. Who is he, though? An old man who has overestimated his strength? Or the last of a noble breed, who even with his last breath upholds the values of a dying culture? A black spider crawls across his portrait and settles on the elegant riding breeches he wears. He tries to sweep it away from the picture with his cane, then lifts his glass again. The flickering candles of the chandelier are reflected in his drink, though in future, they will be replaced by electric bulbs. Breathless string music is heard, which seems to presage electronic music, announcing the new age and its sound. The grandee sees the ghosts of the past flare in these lights, until the candles die.

'Ananta!' he calls to his servant, falling to the floor. 'All lights gone! All lights are out!'

'Of course,' his servant answers. 'The candles are burnt, my lord! It's nearly dawn, the sun will rise!' He opens the shutters, the harsh rays of the morning sun light up the scene; the old man calls for his horse and gallops to his death.

Bettiah, March 1988

'This is my waistcoat and I'll do what I like with it!' shouted Ram Chatur Mallik, outraged. 'You beggars! And my dhrupads belong to me as well, just like this waistcoat! And I'll do what I like with those too!'

It must have been a turbulent scene in the room the day after Ram Chatur Mallik's concert in Bettiah.

Kali-babu told me about it later. I was not there myself but I was the focus of attention.

The secretary of the music academy had turned up in Arun's house in Patna to invite us to the dhrupad mela that would take place in Bettiah.

'Peter Saheb, those are gold mohurs you have in your pocket!' he had told me, when he saw the cassette recorder running while Ram Chatur Mallik sang, lying on his bed. 'Gold coins! Every song is a coin!'

Bettiah is a small town in the Motihari district, the former seat of a small principality. The maharajas of Bettiah had worshipped Kali and were famous for the dhrupads they sang in praise of their goddess. Their lineage still survived, as did the Kali temples, although the palace had crumbled away. The secretary had invited us to the dhrupad mela in Bettiah and welcomed us in front of the comfortable though old-fashioned guesthouse left over from British times, standing amid carefully tended beds of roses in a large park. For the three days that the mela would last, several dozen dhrupadiyas lived in this house. It was a state-wide festival and all the great names of the tradition had been invited.

In the afternoon, while I was taking a little time to sightsee, the secretary of the music academy had turned up in Ram Chatur Mallik's room, so Kali-babu told me later. He began to upbraid the old singer for teaching a foreigner. The real bone of contention was that Ram Chatur Mallik had given me his family manuscript.

'A foreigner! He will sell that book in the West and make thousands of dollars!' shouted the secretary.

'India's heritage is being squandered! How could you do such a thing? We won't allow it!'

I had in fact only photographed the manuscript; the original was still wrapped in red cloth in the chest which the singer always had with him, even on his travels. Granted, I had opened the book in the sunlight in Arun's front courtyard in Patna and photographed each page as I turned it, and apparently word had got round. 'Thousands of eyes are watching you,' as they say in India.

Ram Chatur Mallik sat up in bed, unbuttoned his waistcoat and held it under the secretary's nose. 'If I gave you my forefathers' book, it would be eaten by ants! If I give it to Peter, he will take care of it, it will live on, when you are all gone and forgotten!'

On our way back, the secretary gave us a lift as far as the crossroads where our roads diverged. He had to go back to Patna, while we were returning to Darbhanga. He let us out and then pointed to the old singer sitting on his metal trunk next to the car. 'Take him with you,' he said to me in farewell. 'Take him wherever you want.'

'When you go back to Germany, best not stop in Patna,' Kali-babu commented. 'Best not even get off the train.' He raised his arms and thrashed the air to indicate what might happen to me. 'They're dangerous, these people! Whatever you do, don't get off at Patna!'

Germany, January 1990

'Now I turn away from this and give myself wholly to the other,' the voice told me. I heard the voice in a dream and I knew that Ram Chatur Mallik had died.

I had gone back to Germany three years before, after many years in India, when a combination of malaria, dysentery and typhus almost killed me while I was on holiday in Manali. For several weeks, I lay helpless in a mountain hut. I couldn't stand. Next to my bed was a pail, full of the blood that had surged out of me. The farmer whose hut it was, fearing that I would die, fetched the doctor from Manali, who gave me a handful of antibiotics. With the last of my strength, I made it as far as Frankfurt, where an ambulance sped me to the nearest hospital. It was tropical malaria. In the first night, I received an injection every fifteen minutes since my blood was already collapsing. Every hour, the orderlies changed my sheets, which dripped with sweat. Four weeks later I was discharged. I took a house in a small village in the Taunus Hills, where I could live modestly. I weighed only eight and a half stone and it took me several years to recover fully.

In September 1988, I heard that Darbhanga had been been struck by another earthquake. The shock, measuring 6.7 on the Richter scale, had run through the Himalayan tectonic plate upon which the town stands, the worst quake since 1934. The epicentre lay less than fifty miles north of Darbhanga. I read in the *Hindustan Times* that after sixty seconds, it looked as though the town had suffered a blitzkrieg. 'It was like the climax of a horror film,' was how one of the surviving Darbhanga residents had described his experience. 'A beam came crashing down from the ceiling right onto me. Before I even realized that it was an earthquake, I lost consciousness.' An entire class of schoolchildren died—they had been staying overnight in their madrasa for the Muharram procession the next day. One hundred and fifty thousand houses were affected and one-quarter of these had to be torn down.

The villagers were the worst affected but help reached them last of all. Rescue efforts took days to start since the four army helicopters were being used by Prime Minister Rajiv Gandhi and rival political magnificos. The opposition hauled the government over the coals because the chief ministers of Haryana and Andhra Pradesh had not been received with the appropriate state protocol, which was apparently an insult to the people of these states. The victims of the earthquake were supposed to be paid a sum of two hundred and fifty rupees but they received only fifty or hundred, with the rest vanishing. The *Hindustan Times* also printed a picture of the collapsed tower of the Naulakha Palace in Rajnagar, where Raja Bahadur had dwelt. The maharaja's guest house in Darbhanga, where the last of the court singers had lived for fifty years, had also collapsed. 'Raj Atithi Nivas is nothing but a pile of rubble,' Ram Chatur Mallik wrote to me. 'It is a miracle that I escaped the destruction with only a few cuts and bruises. I have had to move into a hotel. My house in Amta also has cracks in the walls. I am going to Patna until I find a new home in Darbhanga.'

Then I learnt that he was ill. First he had an operation on his eyes, though he hoped to recover from that. He wrote to me every month. 'I hope that you recover soon,' I read in the letters that he had dictated to a scribe who put it down on paper for him. 'A life of struggle is better than a life that simply glides on quietly in its course. Such a life offers little adventure, little joy. God has granted that I recover my health but I do not feel well when you are away. When you were here I sang a great deal but now that no one sees to it that I practise, I never find the time. The music-conference season is beginning now in India. If you were here, we could make a good dhrupadiya of you!' I heard from Arun that he gave concerts and travelled about the place but then he was admitted to hospital in Patna with heart problems.

In the second week of January, *India Week* reported, 'He continues to try to sing but he can only gasp. Sometimes he can make his voice heard but it is only a shadow of what it was. Then comes a painful racking cough, which throws him out of bed, struggling for breath. The eighty-seven-year-old Ram Chatur Mallik, the last surviving doyen of the Bihari dhrupadiyas, is lying on his deathbed in a room in the Patna College Medical Hospital, according to doctors.'

A few days after the dream in which I had heard his voice, I received the black-edged invitation to his funeral rites. 'Grandfather expired on 11.1.1990. Programme of Last Riot: 20.1.–22.1.1990' Arun had written in English on the card, which was printed in Hindi.

A few weeks later, I had another dream. Here I saw that I had been carrying my guru's body round with me for several weeks, wrapped in a violet cloth. It was already very small, perhaps sixteen inches, as shrivelled as a mummy. I unwrapped the cloth. The skin on his face was dark as leather and his nostrils were sealed.

Then I held a wooden rod in my hand with a needle at its end. I thrust the needle into the parchment-like skin, opening his nostrils. In my dream, I was happy that he had visited me one last time. Whatever it was that blocked his path to liberation—I had done what I could to free him.

V

Darbhanga, Friday, 2 August 2002

He couldn't drive me, the driver told me when I woke him. Not only was there a transport strike but there was also a chronic shortage of petrol. On top of which, the name Amta meant nothing at all to him. I remembered that the road to Amta branched at a place called Baheri; Baheri was a bus station, and this gave the man enough to know the direction I wanted to go in.

I asked him how much the ride would cost but he didn't answer. He didn't even look at me but just stared off into space. I offered him more money, since we were at least agreed on a destination. When I asked him whether he was worried about the transport strike, I touched a sore spot. He snorted scornfully at the question, lifted the heavy bonnet of his car and poured water into the radiator. He lashed a bucket to the back of the car, bent down beneath the bonnet and pulled on a few loose cables. After a few false starts, the engine sprang to life. I sat next to the driver and the jeep jolted off and away. There was a crack in the windscreen, the side doors had long gone and the wind of our passage cooled my face pleasantly as we turned the first corner. I began to exult in the triumphant feeling of being, finally, on the road to Amta, after all the obstacles I had overcome on my journey and in such a sturdy, well-ventilated vehicle to boot.

Yet, after only a couple of hundred yards, the jeep came to a stop. At the edge of the road two youngsters peered from behind an oily wooden trestle covered with bottles full of a dark fluid.

'Petrol,' the driver murmured. We needed fuel but the two children didn't want to sell us any. They were worried that if they were found out as strike-breakers, their shop would be burnt down.

We took a turn round town to try all the other fuel shops. I knew that there was a filling station in Darbhanga but even when there was no transport strike, it was always besieged by long queues of men with buckets and jerrycans. Now it was closed.

We had no luck with the next three roadside sellers either. At last the driver turned the jeep onto a narrow alleyway and stopped by a back door hidden by a bush. He knocked, the door opened, a man handed out two old whisky bottles filled with fuel. The driver held them to his nose for a moment, testing, and then tipped them into his tank.

I tried to work things out. It must be a good twenty miles, twenty-five even, to Amta. When I had lived in Darbhanga with Ram Chatur Mallik, the villagers had come all the way into town on bicycles, which took them the whole day. There couldn't be more than two litres in those two bottles and given how much fuel a jeep needs, that would never be enough. The driver, though, waved away my objections. We'd be sure to find some more on the way—and off we went.

I knew that the road was in a bad state. The asphalt surface was constantly interrupted by miles of rubble, landslips and huge potholes. There were a few stretches of asphalt stitching the road together, in between the stretches where we slithered across mud and bare dirt, but the road surface stopped abruptly after each such section. In many places it lurched downward a whole yard, only to end directly in front of a mud wall, at the top of which the asphalt resumed. It was astonishing what the jeep could manage. Sometimes, the driver could steer round these earthworks, with the jeep tipping precariously to the side all the while, but in other places, ditches filled with water at the side of the road made any such manoeuvre impossible. Somehow the driver always managed to wrestle the jeep back upright when it began to tip and to urge it over seemingly insuperable sheer slopes. My head knocked with some force against the bars that held up the canvas roofing but what was a little pain compared to the knowledge that I was on my way?

The road was utterly deserted because of the transport strike. Clay pots hanging on poles in front of a hut showed where tadi was sold. We spent a good part of the morning hunting for more bottles of petrol in the roadside villages. The engine kept overheating. The driver would stop to scoop up water from the ponds and puddles, to top up his radiator and tip a bucket of water over the engine block. We sat at the side of the road and waited for the engine to cool down.

Around noon we rolled into Baheri. The sun was directly overhead. It was unbearably hot. Waves of baking heat struck me in the face now that the wind of our passage had died down. We drove through the little town, which still looked like the set of a Western film, and turned onto the dirt track towards Amta, branching off from the road. As we left town, we found a concrete pipe lying across our road. It was supposed to help vehicles over a ditch, but the rains had washed the road away on either side. A few bricks had been piled up hastily to help oxcarts to climb over the pipe but they would almost certainly give way beneath the weight of a jeep. The driver switched off his engine and looked at me. He wanted to turn back.

We had agreed that he would take me as far as the village, which was still two and a half miles ahead. I hadn't yet paid him the balance of the agreed fare and I was able to persuade him to give it one more try.

On the track across the fields we crossed more such improvised bridges. We passed a temple, mango groves, the brick building with its bare courtyard where Vidur Mallik's sons had gone to school. I couldn't quite remember any longer where exactly the turn for the village was, we might even have missed our turn. The driver stopped the jeep next to a man who sat at the roadside in the shade of a tree. Yes, he'd heard that they had held a wake over in the next village. He pointed onward, the way we were going.

Then I saw the spire of the temple looming up from the green sea of treetops in the distance. I recognized the banyan grove in whose shadow the Monday market took place, which I used to visit with Vidur Mallik's sons. The track led across the fields towards the village. At the first mud hut, we turned onto a narrow brick-laid footpath. Children ran after us and women looked out of the huts, pulling their saris over their heads when they saw the jeep. I remembered that the pond which Vidur Mallik had got dug for his house ran behind these huts. The path was so narrow that it would have been impossible to turn round, but the children nodded and pointed in the direction we were headed. We rolled slowly into the courtyard of the big house and the jeep stopped.

The sun stood at the zenith. All colours were washed out, as though the heat had bleached everything. The sand in the courtyard, the stalks and husks lying on the ground, the lime-washed wall—all seemed the same colour as the sky. Paler yet were the shaven heads of the men who sat on the veranda in front of the house. I recognized the brothers, Ramkumar and Premkumar. They stood up as the jeep came to a halt, came towards me and looked at me as though I were a ghost.

Yet they looked like ghosts themselves. They had shaved their heads, as is customary in India when a close relation dies. Instead of their usual topknots, there was a shining waxy expanse above their brows, lighter than their faces. A blue stubble of hair was beginning to grow back on their scalps and their faces beneath were exhausted, with dark rings round the eyes. They looked at least as worn out as I felt. We embraced wordlessly. Ramkumar pointed at the picture of his father which now hung on the veranda, at the place where the glass painting of Pandit Sukhdev Mallik had been.

This time Mataji was not standing on the veranda. She was crouched in the inner courtyard, as small and hunched as a child. Mataji was only a little younger than her husband, her eyes had always lit up when she looked at him. Now she was sunken and crushed, lying on the earth in the inner courtyard surrounded by the women of her family, unable even to sob. 'I will never be happy again in my life,' she stammered, when I took her hand.

They were all utterly exhausted. Vidur Mallik had been cremated in Allahabad on the evening of the day he died. In fact, it is the eldest son's task to light the pyre, but Ramkumar, who lived in the village, was not in Allahabad, so it was Premkumar who had to give him the mukhagni, setting alight the corpse by putting fire in the mouth. Anandkumar would not have been allowed to do it since these last rites were forbidden to a middle son; only an eldest or youngest son could perform the act. It was the last blessing that Premkumar had from his father.

'He died at five o'clock in the morning,' Prashant reported. The twenty-one-year-old grandson was the last to see his grandfather alive. The doctor had reassured the family and sent them home, but Prashant had slept in front of the sick man's door and found him dead in his room the next morning. 'He never wanted anyone to worry about him. He didn't want to go to hospital, he didn't even want us to buy him medicine. We had to think up pretexts as to why he should take it. Sometimes we managed to, sometimes not. All he wanted was to live quite unselfishly in Vrindavan, like a sadhu. He never wanted to take anything from anyone, he just wanted to give.'

The pujas which must be performed on the death of a brahmin are complex and time-consuming. In principle, they could also have been performed in Allahabad, but it was a given that the family would gather in Amta, home to all of them save for the youngest grandchildren who had been born in the city. Not least, the villagers and the locals had to be involved. It would have been impossible to pass them over. They had to take part in the old man's death, taste it on their tongues, not simply hear the news from elsewhere. Premkumar explained that the family would have lost standing if they had neglected to hold a great feast to mark the death.

'When a dead man's soul sees that the ones he has left behind are eating and are happy, then he too is happy and can prepare for a rebirth at least as good as the last one. This feast is a way to say farewell. It would be enough if only three or maybe five people ate, but we knew that our father wanted us to invite the villagers from Amta and from all round to take this last meal.' He showed me the square in front of the house, where three thousand people had sat down to eat. Huge iron cauldrons still stood here and there, while dogs foraged in the heaps of discarded leaf plates on which the food had been served. The family had served the food themselves, Premkumar told me, and mimed how they had gone up and down the rows of guests for hours, making sure that everyone had enough to eat, that they were as full and happy as Indian custom demands on such occasions.

He too had slept little over the last few days. Since his father had died, he had hardly rested. Mataji was not well, and he had to make sure that the family all arrived from Allahabad. The pujas had lasted thirteen days.

'We believe that the dead man's soul hovers round for thirteen days,' he told me. The person who had given the mukhagni was most at risk. He had to stay apart from others and in order to keep the threatening shade away, he had to always carry some iron object in his hand. Two or three others had to be with him while he slept, to watch over him.

'While we were in Allahabad, my father always slept in my room,' Prashant explained. 'I felt the old man's presence the whole time but I was never scared. He was almost a saint.'

I knew Prashant's room up on the rooftop terrace. I had slept there myself when I was in Allahabad, and I also knew that the fear of being visited by a dead man's shade was something to be taken seriously. On my last visit, I had been carrying with me in my luggage the ashes of a friend, given to me by his wife back in Germany, since he wished to be scattered in the Ganga. The thirteen days had long passed and at that time I knew nothing of the Indian custom. The family had asked whether I wanted Prashant to sleep with me in the room but I had declined.

The ashes were in my suitcase, in a plastic bag. I lay down to sleep but after a little while I woke up. The suitcase was behind my head, on the other side of the room, and all at once I felt that a grey mass was moving towards me. It was nothing human, an inchoate form, an oozing grey emanation coming towards me. For a moment, I was overwhelmed by panic. The door was bolted on the inside to deter thieves but the thing that I had to face was here in the room with me.

I got up, switched on the light, opened the door and went out to the rooftop terrace. I wondered whether to wake up the family sleeping downstairs. It was long past midnight and I hesitated to shake anyone awake at this hour of the night. Seen soberly, the whole thing seemed ridiculous, but I went to my suitcase and snapped shut all its three locks before I lay down on the bed again.

Shortly after I turned off the light, the grey mass was back. It was moving towards me again, and again I felt that fear. A glimmer of light came from behind a curtain in the corner of the room where the family altar stood; Premkumar came here every morning, drew back the curtain and performed puja. A little red light bulb glowed there night and day.

I had never entered the shrine but now I drew the curtain aside and sat down where I had always seen Premkumar sit. I saw a whole gallery of gods before my eyes, the mother goddess in the middle, surrounded by the pantheon. I saw Lakshmi, Ganesha, Radha and Krishna, ancient statues, the murtis that Premkumar had inherited from his father, perhaps his grandfather. When I saw them, the dread that I had felt melted away and I breathed freely again. I sat and looked at the family of gods for a long time. They seemed to laugh at me, not with mockery but with benevolence. Why are you afraid? they asked. What can the ghost of a dead man do if we are with you?

Next morning at breakfast, I told the family what had happened to me that night. They looked at me, concerned, and reminded me that Prashant had offered to sleep in the room with me. Premkumar frowned. He had only about an hour before teaching began at the university. We mounted his moped and drove to Triveni, the holy spot where the three rivers met. Premkumar murmured a prayer and we watched as the ashes sank slowly into the water.

When Premkumar and his family arrived in Amta, the rains had not yet started but most of the other relatives had abandoned their journey when the floods began. Not even Ramji Upadhyaya had come, the pakhwaj player with whom Vidur Mallik had played his whole life. He had been ill himself when he heard of his comrade's death, word had it.

'It will be to your eternal credit that you made it here when even the Indians had turned round and given up,' Premkumar told me. 'It is a merit that can never be wiped from your account.'

I stretched out on one of the wooden pallets on the veranda in front of the house and tried to sleep. It was impossible. I had hardly slept a wink since disembarking from the aeroplane in Delhi, five days and nights ago. It was too hot to sleep. Flies settled on my body and eager villagers kept coming to take a look at me.

As soon as I opened my eyes, they began to talk to me. They pointed at the photograph of Vidur Mallik, its frame wreathed in flowers, that hung above me on the wall. 'When we see that photo, it's as though he were still here,' they said, 'as though he has just gone away for a while and will be back soon.'

An old uncle who lived in the next house hobbled over on his stick and grilled me about everything that had happened in Germany in the last twenty years. Sweat dripped from my body. I was drowsy and losing focus. Even the evening brought no relief. As soon as the sun set, squadrons of mosquitoes dive-bombed me. They came from the pool that spread out in the dusk in front of the house.

I could see them in the light from the petroleum lamp. They were tiny and impossible to fend off. If I wrapped myself in a cloth, my skin was slick with sweat within minutes. Their bites hurt like hell. After a little while, I was so thoroughly bitten that I made no further effort to defend myself but simply endured the pain. I had no choice.

All night I tried to find some way to lie on the hard wooden boards without my hip bones aching. Whenever I opened my eyes, I saw the stars. A child lay next to me on the wooden boards and a dog had curled up to sleep underneath.

FLIGHT THROUGH DARKNESS

Heathrow Airport, 4 August 1999

Suddenly there was a dull thud and a man sitting at the next table who hadn't been there before. He stared ahead, glassy-eyed, and began to moan softly.

He had just fallen from the balcony above this cafe at Heathrow Airport. A few seconds ago I had seen him from the corner of my eye, leaning over the railing, but I had thought nothing of it. Now he was suddenly sitting at the next table. He had fallen ten feet and ended up on a chair at the next table just as though he had walked up and sat down on it. His arms were hanging down over the back of the chair. It must have been extremely painful to have fallen from such a height but there was no sign of this on his face. He stared ahead dully, as though under anaesthetic.

It took a while for those sitting round to realize what had just happened. At first glance, you really couldn't tell that the man had fallen from the balcony. He just sat there, moaning softly. He didn't say a word, gazing dead ahead. Then people formed a cordon, called out to one another. Someone fetched a doctor and the ambulance man, who carried the chap off on a stretcher.

I was in the cafe to wait for Vidur Mallik and his sons. Premkumar's wife Rashmi was also supposed to come along, and his son Prashant, just turned eighteen, was visiting Europe for the first time. I was nervous. Since they had only got their visa at the last moment, there had been no time to arrange the work permit that they would need to give concerts in Great Britain, and I wasn't sure whether they might not be stopped at immigration and sent back. The man who had fallen seemed an ill omen for the journey ahead of us. We had been invited to a festival that would be taking place in Cornwall in a few days.

The festival was Crispian Mills' idea. I had no idea who Crispian Mills was but Michael, who had called me up from England in January and introduced himself as Crispian's manager, told me what was what. Crispian Mills was the lead singer of a pop group called Kula Shaker. I had never heard of Kula Shaker either but Michael told me that the group was causing something of a stir among British teens. Their first CD had sold over a million in the UK, last summer they had been number two on the hit parade, just after the Spice Girls, and next up they would open for Robbie Williams—so Michael told me. He reckoned they were a band with a big future.

Mills had a thing about India and sprinkled his songs with Sanskrit words. The band took their name from Kulashekhara, a ninth-century king of the south Indian Chola dynasty who had been a famous devotee of Krishna. An American hippy who had supposedly once lived with John Lennon had predicted to Mills that his band would enjoy staggering success if they took Kulashekhara's name. Three weeks later, RCA offered to sign them up but they decided for Columbia instead. Their second CD had just come out.

Michael told me that Mills was planning a festival for August's solar eclipse. It was to take place on the southern tip of Cornwall, on the Lizard Peninsula, which was apparently the central point from which to watch this cosmic event. Michael went on to say that Indian music was very important for Mills and that Talvin Singh from London's Asian Dub scene had already been booked and so had the legendary Indian flautist Hariprasad Chaurasia. A little while ago, Mills had been in Vrindavan to make a video for MTV and he'd heard of Vidur Mallik. He was a great fan of the sanctuary there, he even had a guru, who had taken him into his temple. Mills wanted to give Krishna and the culture of Braj a special place at his festival, which is why he wanted to invite Vidur Mallik.

I knew Braj, I knew the temple and I knew the priest who had shown such favour to Crispian Mills. He had been my neighbour for years.

Vrindavan, 1980

It's so far off the beaten track that there isn't even a railway station to connect it to the outside world. Anyone wanting to reach Vrindavan has to get off at Mathura Junction and make his way onward for the next seven or eight miles by share taxi, by rickshaw, auto rickshaws or horse-drawn tonga.

When I went to Vrindavan for the first time in 1980, I chose to ride by tonga. The journey took an hour, jolting and juddering along—time to sit and think. As soon as we had left the houses of Mathura behind us, I could look round from my place on the box seat next to the driver and see the tangled mass of low trees and shrubs stretching out right and left of the road. Dust whirled up beneath our carriage wheels, birds twittered, a peacock swept through the bushes. A troop of monkeys crossed the street ahead of us, one baring his teeth when he saw me watching as I passed.

Every Indian has heard of it but no one seems quite sure how the name of this little temple town should be spelt. When I passed the turn on the Delhi–Agra expressway, the name on the signpost read Vrindaban, but if you turned round and looked at the other side of the sign that you see when coming from Agra, the first letter is *B*. In English transcription, the consonants are chopped and changed according to some inscrutable system, although in Sanskrit the word is always written with two *V*s. Vrindavana is the vana, the forest, where the vrinda grows.

Ocimum sanctum, also called holy basil, is a dark-leaved shrub, distantly related to European basil but with a much sharper, almost bitter taste. The plant's vernacular name is tulsi; its leaves are used to make a herbal tea to cure coughs in the cold season. The coach-man was wearing a mala carved from tulsi wood round his neck, which identified him as a Vaishnav. Krishna is the avatar of the sustaining aspect of the godhead. Tulsi is Krishna, for the god lives in the plant. We were driving through a holy forest.

The coachman told me that there was not merely one holy forest but twelve. He knew them all and had driven his tonga all over. The ancient Bhagvata Purana had described the forested land where the god played his flute when he descended to earth but no one quite knew where until seers such as the Bengali Chaitanya and the blind singer Surdas saw it in their visions and recognized it in the groves of Braj. They founded a cult which persists today in Vrindavan and the villages round. Every year, half a million pilgrims from all across India flood to this land. Peak season for pilgrims is at the full moon in spring and in autumn. The pilgrims gather in Vrindavan at the September full moon to see Krishna in his manifold forms at the maharas, the great dance of the god with his countless devotees; first though, they undertake the yatra on foot through the twelve holy forests of Braj to see the mystery plays, as children act out Krishna's and Radha's adventures at the original locations.

The coachman told me about the pilgrimage, Braj Chaurasi Kos, on which pilgrims cross this whole visionary landscape in forty days. A kos is an old unit of distance, and the route that leads through the holy land is eighty-four-kos long, about a hundred and ninety miles. Most pilgrims go on foot, while luggage and the infirm are taken by bus or tonga.

The horse's hooves clattered on the asphalt. At the halfway point, next to the red temple named for the Birla industrial dynasty, the coachmen drew up by a horse trough and let his beast drink.

'Yeh Vrindavan Dham ko marama na jane koi— dal dal pata pata par radhe radhe hoi,' he recited, plucking a leaf from the branch at his side. 'No one knows the secret of Vrindavan Dham—on every twig, on every leaf is Radha's name!' He showed me the leaf. The light veins in the dark green leaf indeed looked like Devanagari script.

There was a barrier across the road at the entrance to town, a tree trunk weighed down with a stone at one end. Next to it sat a few men, most with shaven heads, some with locks flowing over their shoulders. Their shirts, buttoned at the side, glowed in every hue from orange to dark red; they wore quilted caps or scarves wound about their brows and looked as though they had stepped from a mediaeval miniature.

In front of them was a huge set of iron scales, which might have been used for weighing sacks of grain. One of the men pointed at my luggage and wanted to know what was in there.

'A cassette recorder,' I answered.

'A-ha,' the man said. 'Electronics.' He put my cassette recorder on the scales and jotted down the weight, then scribbled a few words on a pad, tore off the sheet and handed it to me.

'Two kilograms, electronics—that's twenty-four rupees.'

When the mahant of the Sankat Mochan Temple in Benares had founded the dhrupad mela there and it had become an annual event, other temples became encouraged to do the same. Vrindavan was the obvious next place to join in since, after all, Swami Haridas had lived as a hermit on the banks of the Yamuna, here in the forest of Vrindavan, while his pupil the great Tansen was one of the nine jewels of Emperor Akbar's court. Vrindavan is the home town of dhrupad.

The coachman drove his tonga through the little town's narrow alleyways and set me down at a gateway. The festival would take place in a hall built by Maharaja Jai Singh, founder of Jaipur, for his retreats here in the holy land. The complex is called Jai Singh Ghera and stands on the bank of the Yamuna, by the Chir Ghat where Krishna is said to have stolen the gopis' clothes as they bathed in the river; it was here that they came to him, one by one, to fetch their saris. A tree on the bank is festooned with bright cloths that the pilgrims have tied to the branches.

The festival lasted seven days and seven nights. Hundreds of dhrupadiyas had accepted the invitation, never before had so many been gathered in one place. It was the greatest dhrupad mela in living memory. They played and sang until well past midnight and in the early hours of the morning, the voices and sounds of the pakhwaj could be heard again from their rooms. One of the guest houses was directly over the stage and others were scattered across the precinct. The concerts took place in a hall, open to the garden on two sides. I had never heard of most of the musicians. The tradition was much stronger than I had imagined—it would take years to document the music and the cassettes that I had brought with me were nowhere near enough to record all the concerts.

'You see, that's the difference between Western music and Indian music,' an Indian friend told me when

238

he saw my quandary. 'In India, the tapes run out but the music keeps on, while in the West it's just the other way round—the music stops but the tapes keep running!'

Shri Chaitanya Prema Samsthana, which hosted the mela, is a cultural and religious foundation attached to the Radha Raman Temple. Shrivatsa Goswami, who had organized the festival, invited me to stay on. I told him that some of my friends in Delhi had founded the International Society for Traditional Arts Research, dedicated to the research and documentation of traditional music. They had secured funding for an archive of dhrupad compositions but I doubted that an archive on its own would do much to keep the tradition alive.

I knew some of these archives. Many of them held rare recordings, and from time to time enthusiasts tried to copy these, to put them out on records or at least save them from oblivion. These attempts almost always got bogged down. Endless bureaucratic delays got in the way.

'What would my archive be worth if I simply shared it with others?' the director of such an academy in Delhi had asked me. The collection had been built up with state funds but he regarded it as his private property. The guardians of these archives knew just how much effort it had taken to get their recordings. Sometimes it could take years to persuade an ustad or a guru to sit down in front of a microphone, and it took not simply financial payment but real skills of persuasion. A cassette recorder and microphone were expensive items and there was a shortage of cassette tape. Power cuts were a constant threat and, often enough, the musicians just didn't want to play. Confronted with a microphone, a musician would remember how much he had sacrificed for the composition and in the end, the recordings would vanish into the archives, never to be seen again. It would be better to use the funds of the society to establish and fund a school. If the tradition was really to live on, one had to bring gurus and students together.

Shrivatsa Goswami agreed, telling me that one of the aims of Shri Chaitanya Prema Samsthana was to bring the old arts back to Braj, their birthplace, and dhrupad was certainly one of those. It had reached the princely courts when a singer from these sacred groves had taken it there. We decided to run the school together. Vidur Mallik became our first guru and we called the school a gurukul, a family of learning, for the old Indian custom was that gurus and students lived together.

Shrivatsa Goswami allowed us to use an empty building in the Radha Raman Temple precinct, where his family had lived before they moved across to the Jai Singh Ghera which had more space. The Goswamis, descended from the temple founder, owned houses all round the temple district.

The Radha Raman Temple is at the centre of a spacious precinct, secluded behind high walls. Visitors must first climb some high steps to reach the great gate that leads to the temple grounds. In a little sentry post next to the gate, one member of the extensive priestly clan of the Goswamis had set up a small photography studio. He was a real artist, retouching his portrait photographs by hand and adding colour if the client so wished. His masterpiece was a panorama of the holy town, a collage made up of many smaller photographs that he had taken, years ago, on the other side of the river. He also sold original photographs of Radha Raman, the avatar of Krishna who dwelt in the temple.

Once you have climbed the steep steps to the gateway, your path leads on to the heart of the temple precinct. The houses to your left and right are old, the sandstone mellowing from red to yellow to brown to grey. There are inscriptions on the stone and above a doorway you may see the numbers of a magic square. The windows are all barred—here, people live in cages to protect themselves from the monkeys, who come swarming over the high wall across from the temple, the wall which shelters Nidhivan, the treasure grove. In this wood, it is said, four hundred years ago, Swami Haridas found the black statue of Krishna that he called Banke Bihari, the flautist from the forest. Later it came to reside in the temple of that name, on the other side of town.

Nidhivan is a sacred grove. At night its gates are closed, for it is said that Radha and Krishna retire to sleep in the depths of the wood. In a little temple deep among the trees is their bed, where pilgrims give gifts of all those things that Indian women need for their toilette—pots of sindur, the vermilion that married women wear on their foreheads, colourful glass and plastic bangles, tikas, the dots women wear between their eyebrows. Inquisitive pilgrims who enter the walled grove at night to watch the divine lovers at play are found the next morning, stark mad, so the locals say.

At the end of the alleyway, a second gate leads to the temple square. Usually, you can find a cow standing there, chewing peacefully the fodder the priests leave, though she doesn't turn her nose up either at chewing the plastic bags which fly about on the breeze. Visitors must stoop to enter through the low temple door. Then they find themselves in the broad open courtyard in front of the throne of Radha Raman. The marble floor is tiled black and white and a spray of tulsi stands nearby on a pedestal. The priests distribute a few leaves to each pilgrim at the services as prasad.

Indian temples from the Mughal era are modelled after mediaeval princely courts, where the whole building is oriented about the ruler's throne. Pilgrims, and musicians, take their place within balustrades of colourful painted sandstone. The ruler sits on a couch on a marble platform, at eye level to his court; Radha Raman, the lover who delights in his beloved Radha— a black statue, about one foot tall. They say that it was not made by human hand but that the divine image simply materialized in 1542, when Gopal Bhatt, a brahman from South India came here following his visions. He found the statue in this place and the temple has been built round it over the centuries. This happened in May, at full moon, and ever since, the statue has been bathed in gallons of milk on this night.

In Vrindavan's other temples, Radha and Krishna are always united, their murtis shown together as a pair. The Radha Raman statue however manifested without the beloved, and the temple's theology asks that worshippers create the unseen beloved with their devotion.

The statue's throne is on a low pedestal and silver cows and other objects are placed about it according to the seasons and the festivals. There are ceremonies eight times a day, which mark Krishna's daily customs, beginning as the god awakes, takes his ritual bath, dons his clothes and is served breakfast. Then Krishna joins his playmates and roams the groves of Braj until he returns for lunch, takes rest, plays for the rest of the day and is sung back to sleep in the evening. The day is thus divided into eight praharas of three hours each, as are the ragas sung at each service.

At each ceremony, the statue is dressed in new clothes. The priests draw a curtain across the altar as they dress him, for his worshippers are not meant to see the god's nakedness. Usually, only a few people sit in the temple but there is always a much greater crowd at the most important morning and evening pujas, waiting in front of the curtain to see the god in his new attire. The service ends with the priests spraying water on the crowd and handing out clay dishes full of sweetmeats.

From the temple square, in a corner on the right, a short flight of stairs leads up to the house where I lived in the eighties, with Vidur Mallik and our Indian and Western students.

Berlin, Spring 1999

Vidur Mallik visted the Radha Raman Temple every day. I could well imagine that the neighbours had told Crispian Mills about the singer who was there so often.

Michael told me that Mills hadn't had time to meet Vidur Mallik personally but wanted to invite him and his family to the festival in Cornwall for August's total solar eclipse. Could I help him to organize the journey? Before hanging up, Michael said 'Radheshyam,' the courtesy used by the Brajvasis, which identified him as a Krishna devotee. The same day, he sent me a fax. 'As promised, I will keep you informed of developments with this project in a timely way.'

That was the last I heard from Michael. Maybe Mills had fired him. When I called Vidur Mallik, he confirmed that he had been invited to the festival by an Englishman called Mathura Das.

In May, Kula Shaker played in Berlin and I tried to meet Mills. The lady who organized the concert told me that the band was rather retiring and not much interested in meeting the public. I went anyway. A gaggle of teenagers was standing in front of the doors at the Columbia concert hall. As I went in, the warm-up band was still playing. Then Kula Shaker took the stage. Mills bestraddled the stage in the midst of a psychedelic light show, flailing away at his guitar. I could understand next to nothing of the lyrics and went back home.

In June, Mills rang me in Berlin and told me that he was taking charge of Vidur Mallik's appearance at the Cornwall festival, the family should book their flights right away. It was all going to plan, he said.

The newspapers had been full of the impending solar eclipse for months now. On the morning of 11 August 1999, the moon's shadow would pass over the Earth, entering Europe at the southernmost tip of Great Britain and leaving again at the Black Sea. Then it would cross Iran and Pakistan and finally vanish into the sea on the east coast of India. This cosmic connection between Cornwall and India had given Mills the idea for the festival.

In Britain, the total solar eclipse would only be visible from the southernmost tip of the island, a narrow strip running through Devon and Cornwall. The last total solar eclipse visible from anywhere in England had happened in 1927 and the next one would be on 23 September 2090. The chance to watch the solar eclipse of 11 August was a unique opportunity that would not come again in the lives of most of those involved.

'If you are planning to go to Cornwall or Devon for the 1999 eclipse, I must sound an immediate note of caution,' I read in *Patrick Moore's Guide to the 1999 Total Eclipse*, which I had bought in Heathrow. 'So far as I know, virtually every hotel, guest house and bed and breakfast in the zone of totality is already booked up. I may be wrong, of course, and there are always last-minute cancellations, but the West Country shows signs of being overcrowded around the time of the eclipse. Drive down, then, and select a suitable site? There will be problems here too. Even in an ordinary year the roads are jam-packed, and in the days just before the eclipse the situation is bound to be frustrating. Public transport ought to be the answer, but I fear that trains and coaches may be hopelessly overcrowded, even though the railway companies and tour operators are laying on many extra services, and special trains and coaches are being chartered to ferry people down to the south-west of England for the eclipse. It may be that some roads will be officially closed during "eclipse week", and the only advice I can give is to make your plans carefully. If you have to drive, start out several days early if you can.'

England, August 1999

Crispian Mills had heeded this advice. The Malliks were to arrive a week before the eclipse, and he had included a recording session at Peter Gabriel's Real World Studios near Bath, on the way down to Cornwall.

They were the last ones off the plane, after all the other passengers had already gone through. They looked exhausted, their faces drawn. There had been a seven-hour stopover in Dubai and part of their luggage had been lost en route.

Mills had kept his word though. A liveried chauffeur took us to the elegant, silver-grey Chevrolet minibus waiting in the car park. We were joined by Mathura Das, Mills' friend who had visited the Malliks in Vrindavan. He was a long-haired Englishman, bedecked with necklaces and Eastern trinkets. He was to accompany us to the festival.

Two and a half hours later, the bus dropped us in front of a house in the studio grounds. Mills shook locks of hair off his face as he greeted us and told us that there was a Mongolian yurt ready and waiting at the festival, where we would certainly be much more comfortable than in a hotel. Then he disappeared somewhere, since organizing the festival took a great deal of attention. The next morning, I went over to the studios, which stand in an idyllic park. Hariprasad Chaurasia, the flautist, was just having breakfast. He glowered at me when I told him that the Malliks had a session that same day. As far as he was concerned, we were in the wrong studio—we had the Big Room, surrounded by water, pride of place in a studio much talked about for its elegant design and technical perfection. He wanted to be in there himself but Mills had booked it for us and we couldn't help it that the flautist had to make do with a smaller studio. Maybe, we had got the bigger studio because there were more musicians in our group. Be that as it may, throughout the day I heard the flautist grumbling about the allocation to the Indian girls who were to sing overdubs for his solo pieces.

On our journey to Cornwall, the roads were utterly empty. The congestion which Moore had predicted just wasn't there. We turned off the motorway onto a country road that led across a broad plain until at last a big top appeared on the horizon, made fast to a whole forest of massive tent poles decked with bunting. The blue tent was huge and could easily have held fifteen thousand people, but behind its wire-mesh fence the festival site seemed deserted. A few security guards stood at the gate, and each of us got a heat-sealed pink plastic band round our wrist.

One of the sentries led us backstage, to an area protected by a tall wire-mesh fence, where we found the yurt which Mills had arranged for us. It was spacious but didn't have a kitchen. We had stopped at a supermarket on the way to buy rice, vegetables and everything that we would need to make Indian vegetarian food but there was no stove.

The other problem was the shower and toilets. They were right next to us; we could look through the wire mesh that fenced off the backstage area and see the queue but to get there we had to hike the long way round and show our pink wristbands at several checkpoints.

We tried to make the best of these drawbacks. Das—who obviously knew something that we didn't—had brought along a camping stove, enough to boil water for tea but not to make a meal for seven people. There were hardly any festival-goers to be found. Rumour had it that the BBC had been saying that the roads down to Cornwall were all jammed up, which was why any potential audience was staying at home. Mills was nowhere to be seen. We asked Das for a telephone number where we could reach him but there was no such thing. 'Crispian's really hard to reach,' he said. 'Maybe he'll get in touch soon.'

With Prashant, I took a turn round the festival site. A knot of fairground booths and little tents had gathered about the central big top. Just as promised, it was a global village, with a 'leading-edge cybertent', an authentic Irish pub, jazz cafes, a big wheel, a bungee jump, wigwams and espresso bars and tents for reiki healing, storytelling and basket-weaving. Pass between the Arabic bazaar and the Celtic craft shop and you reached the sci-fi FutureZone. The festival had promised groovy bars and funky cafes and a banner at the entrance proclaimed 'Lizard '99 excites the senses and soothes the soul.' There were fifteen smaller stages grouped round the huge tent for 'mega dance acts', indie pop, reggae and blues, and a long list of musicians was signed to appear. Mills' friend showed me the stage where we were due to play but other than a few scattered hippies, the whole site was empty. This global village looked like a ghost town.

Over time, a little campsite grew up next door where English hippies smoked their hashish. A girl in the next tent got out her cello. Das had brought along his guitar, and the two of them twanged and plunked away.

We stayed in the Mongolian yurt for three days and nights, waiting for someone to explain to us what was happening here. The Malliks dealt with the situation with good humour and passed the time by singing. We saw more and more signs that the festival was a washout. We heard that Hariprasad Chaurasia had been booked into a hotel nearby but since the organizers hadn't paid for his room, he had left. We couldn't leave though. All that we had with us were the return tickets. We waited for word from Mills but he didn't get in touch.

On the last night, something started to happen. Grumbling bass notes could be heard from the big top and from time to time we caught snatches of a violin solo. As they came back, the hippies told us that Nigel Kennedy had played, for no fee, as a consolation for all those who had made it to the festival.

The next morning, the elegant Chevrolet minibus that had brought us down to Cornwall drew up again. The chauffeur told us that he was to bring us to Mills.

The minibus drew up in front of a romantic English cottage. Mills stood by the door, while his wife, whom he had married in Vrindavan, waited inside. When she saw us, she burst into tears. It was from her that we found out that the festival had been a flop. Mills, she told us, had set his heart on bringing his love for Braj to a wider audience but he had been led up the garden path by the festival organizers. Mills apologized and said that he much regretted that there would be no concert. He had no money left but if we liked we could stay the night in his cottage. He had already changed the booking for the Malliks' flights and he would do his very best, he said, to pay our train tickets back up to London himself.

Heathrow Airport, 11 August 1999

The Malliks flew back on the day of the eclipse. I watched them go through the gates, a week after they had arrived, and then I went to the cafe where the man had fallen from the balcony at the beginning of the journey.

I looked at the clock. It was just before 11 in the morning and the eclipse was due to begin at 11.03 a.m. London was not in the zone of totality but the sky was already growing dark. A yellow glow enveloped the cafe. Through the window, I could see an aeroplane taking off.

I knew how frightened Indians can be of a solar eclipse; Indian belief has it that the two demons of the lunar nodes, Rahu and Ketu, swallow the sun. Once, I had watched a solar eclipse from the terrace of my house. I was the only human figure far and wide; the city was entirely silent and no cars were driving. People had drawn their curtains but I knew that my landlady would be sitting behind closed curtains and watching the eclipse on television. Now the Malliks were sitting in a metal tube that flew through the darkness. Perhaps they had drawn the blinds down over the cabin windows but most likely, the passengers had not even noticed the eclipse, in all the bustle of take-off.

VI

Amta, Saturday, 3 August 2002

As dawn broke, I tossed and turned on my wooden pallet, half asleep. 'You know atom?' a voice asked. It was the uncle who lived next door. Last time I had been in Amta, the great-uncle had been alive. He too had been a musician and had once played the esraj, which is played like the sarangi—but he was ancient, too old to hold the instrument in his trembling fingers. When I practised on the veranda in the morning, he would come to listen, drawn by the sound of my instrument, and tell me about his teacher, singing for me the pieces that his guru had taught him long ago and making me play them on my sarangi.

'Uranium 235, you know?' the voice asked. 'Supercharged energy. No existence! It is only radiation, no substance at all.' He repeated the same sentences several times in English until he was quite sure that I was awake. Then he explained in Hindi, telling me that there had once been an Indian sage who had discovered the secret of the atom long before the Europeans. No European had visited Amta for decades and now he was taking the opportunity to tell me that Indians had discovered the secret of the atom long ago. More than two thousand years ago, the Indian sage Kanad had asked what would happen if we could split matter ever and again and had concluded that matter consists of tiny particles that cannot be seen with the naked eye, which he called paramanu.

The topic fascinated the uncle. He had been a teacher once, earlier, although he had lost the job after only a few months. Since then he had lived here in the village. His son Ramesh, a broad-shouldered fellow with a long, pockmarked face and a brigand's moustache, played pakhwaj and had found a post at the ladies' college in Darbhanga.

'Half my working life is gone,' he told me, 'in confusion', when he found occasion to draw me aside. 'I must see that I spend the other half well.' He would have liked to add that I could make that second half of his life so much more pleasant by bringing him to Europe and fixing a job for him there but he knew that it would come to nothing. 'You won't forget me when you're back in Germany?' he asked instead.

'How could I forget you, Ramesh?' I asked in turn, ignoring the unspoken question. The Malliks were a ramified clan and he knew as well as I just how impossible it would be to fly them all to Europe. I tried to explain to Ramesh that his lifestyle was much more secure than mine. Where I lived hand to mouth, he had some land, a house and a job.

'What would you do in Europe?' I asked. The question was not entirely fair—a journey to the West would have added to his prestige—but then I remembered that he had once said that nowhere else in the world could you make such music as in his village. 'Didn't you once tell me,' I asked him, 'that in Amta even the goats bleat in the melodies of ragas? You'd miss that in Europe.'

In fact, he wasn't so badly off. There were plenty in Amta who had no work at all. Three-quarters of the inhabitants were illiterate. There was a preponderance of old people since most of the young had left the village to find work elsewhere. Some had gone all the way to Delhi and got themselves a little shop, or a taxi, and by such means the Yadav herdsmen caste had overtaken the Malliks and from cattle and water buffaloes had worked their way up to become wealthier than the original land-lords. They were politically active; the Bihari chief min-ister who now sat in prison while his wife ran the show was a Yadav and he helped out his own people. They couldn't hold a candle to the Malliks when it came to prestige, though, and there was still a noticeable social gulf in the village, less to do with the Malliks being brah-min and much more because they were still seen as palace musicians. Even today, villagers descended from the other castes whom the Malliks had settled here addressed them not by name but as the reverential 'malik'. It was a sign of respect, how a vassal speaks to his lord, even if the tables had actually been turned.

A few years ago, the Indira Gandhi National Centre for the Arts in New Delhi had started a research project on the cultural significance of Indian villages. The study had chosen thirteen villages for preserving artistic traditions intact, among them Amta, seen as a model of the musicians' village. An anthropologist,

Professor Balanand Sinha, took a particular interest in the Malliks' village, since he was himself Bihari by birth, the son of a wealthy zamindar; the Malliks had played for his ancestors. In economic terms, Amta was an underdeveloped village. Once upon a time, it had had electric power but the transformer had burnt out and never been replaced. There was no school and no doctor; the only thing that distinguished Amta from other villages was the continued presence of the musical dynasty who had founded the village. This was quite exceptional, the professor wrote, one of very few instances—perhaps the only one—where musicians continued to derive an income from lands granted to them in Mughal times.

I had his study in my luggage. It was a work of impressive depth and gave precise figures. The village had three thousand inhabitants, of which forty-one men and eleven women had finished school. Six villagers in all—five men and one woman—had attended university. The great majority of the villagers were landless labourers. One hundred and twenty families owned enough land to live off. Some villagers made a living as weavers, barbers or cobblers but only five of the village's three hundred families still made a living from their music.

The study gave an inventory of the village property. The professor had counted two hundred water buffaloes, fifty-five cows, seventy goats, forty-three pigeons, nine geese and a single chicken. After the livestock came material capital; one jeep, one diesel generator, one battery-powered television set, two sewing machines, two irons, two oxcarts, fifty manual water pumps, one hundred and eighty-four spades. The list contained no more than four musical instruments.

Professor Sinha wrote that it was not the number of musicians that made the village so significant but their quality. He described the relationship between the Malliks, the former landlords, and the descendants of the other settler castes, in anthropological terms as a relationship between centre and periphery. The Malliks had been able to preserve dhrupad as the centre of tradition and the other residents of the village continued to form a periphery that simply supported this centre. When music was played in Amta, they gathered round to listen, and as they walked the fields behind their plough they imitated the thundering gamaks that the singers could make deep in their bellies, down below the navel. They were proud of the particular significance that the Malliks gave to their village, even though the tables had been turned economically.

'Amta is a wonderful place for music,' Ramashish Pathak had told Professor Sinha. He was the pakhwaj player whose house I could see across the pond. 'But the musicians are leaving the village since it can't offer them a living. We're forced to go to the cities. Most of us would move back to Amta at the drop of a hat. We still live in the village anyway, mentally; it's only our bodies that live in the city.'

I went to see Pathak, who had come back to the village for the puja, although he now spent most of his time in Laheriasarai, a suburb of Darbhanga. 'I only moved there so that my children could go to school,' he told me. 'But when I play drums all night in the city, the way I am used to here in the village, the neighbours complain about the noise. When I play in the village, folk come from the fields and listen. The city music schools certainly hand out their diplomas, which help you get a job, but when you listen to the school graduates sing and play, you notice straight away that something is missing from their music. It's a dimension that you only find out here in the country, where you can concentrate totally on music. If UNESCO or some other institute were to fund a music school here in Amta, we'd all come back.'

He pointed to a thatched building that stood near his house. After Ram Chatur Mallik's death, the regional government had approved funding to build a hall to keep his legacy alive. The villagers had built it, but the hall stood empty, just like the school building and the hut that was to have been a health centre. There were no teachers or doctors—they had all gone to the cities.

Professor Sinha concluded his study by remarking how the process of urbanization was disrupting the centre–periphery relationship, while the musicians' pleas that their tradition be preserved went unheard. When a new government was elected, the directors of the Indira Gandhi National Centre for the Arts were fired, the project was wound up and the study was locked away in the bookshelves.

The day was more tolerable than the night, when the mosquitoes began to swarm from dusk. There was no point trying to sleep. Although the air was humid, not a drop of rain fell. Sweat streamed from my body. The village men wore dhotis wound about their legs and only put on an undershirt when they were expecting visitors. It was much too hot to do anything. I spent the day on the veranda, under the garlanded picture of Vidur Mallik.

'I only began to sing dhrupad because of him,' Prashant said, sitting down next to me on the wooden boards. 'I never really wanted to be a singer. Certainly not a dhrupad singer. Khayal, if anything.'

He had been born in Allahabad, where his father taught at the university music department. 'I wanted to study microeconomics,' he continued. 'But when I visited my grandfather in Vrindavan, I heard how he taught his students. It really impressed me, the way he treated them, as people, not just musicians.'

I too had seen how Vidur Mallik gave lessons. He even took on rickshaw drivers as students. 'Would you like to learn to sing?' he would ask the men who hummed hymns to Radha and Krishna as they pedalled him across town from his house to give lessons. 'Are you interested in classical dhrupad? I teach every day from five to eight, in the afternoon—come along if you like!' he would offer.

And come they did. Not mainly because they were interested in dhrupad but because this man had made such an impression on them with his offer. What kind of guru teaches a rickshaw driver these days? What could they possibly pay him for lessons? But this meant nothing to Vidur Mallik. Quite the opposite; he even bought one of the men a rickshaw to help him earn a living and the only condition was that he should take him to classes every evening.

'It wasn't just the rickshaw drivers who loved him, even the fruit sellers and greengrocers in the bazaar!' Prashant added. 'Everyone in Vrindavan knew him! They all called him Guruji—the sadhus, the rickshaw drivers, the street traders. Not because he was a musician but from respect. In the evening he would often go off to the ashrams where the sadhus lived and invite them home to eat. Whole gangs of them would turn up at his house, twenty sadhus, twenty-five, with matted hair and torn clothes. My grandmother would clap her hands to her head. "Where did you drag them in from?" she would ask him. She was upset that she'd have to cook for them all. If she didn't cook, then grandfather would do it himself. For him, it was a way to come closer to God; he always wanted to give something, never take. Not even from us, his family. He never paid any attention to how he dressed. Once I asked him why he didn't wear a silk kurta on stage, like other musicians, and he laughed at me. "Have they come to hear me sing or to look at me?" he asked. "Would a silk kurta make me young, like you?" He wanted everything to be as simple as possible. What drew me to him was his way of life. You know what it's like when you visit other great Indian musicians! You find a big house, full of tasteful decoration and comfortable sofas, so that visitors can see how rich and important the owner is. That was just what my grandfather didn't want. When you went to his house in Vrindavan, it was as though you were back in the village. Two rooms, tiny windows that hardly let in any air, and he slept on a wooden pallet with a thin sheet. He'd put an old cushion on to make it his bed and that was that. He wanted to be seen as what he was.'

'And do you know what would happen when he went to Radha Raman Temple in the evening?' Prashant asked me. 'A whole pack of children would be waiting for him at the gate. "Baba! Baba!" they'd shout when he came and they'd beg money from him. Whenever he left the house, he put a few coins in his pocket to have something to give the children. They didn't even wait for him to hand them out, they'd stick their hands straight into his pockets and rummage about till they found the coins. "Wait, wait. Everyone will get something," he'd say. "How can you put up with it?" we'd ask him, but he wouldn't be put off. "Here in Vrindavan, all the children are avatars of Radha and Krishna or the gopis," he told us. He loved to give them something, and once he'd got an idea in his head, nothing in the world could dissuade him.'

The first time Prashant had come to Vrindavan, his grandfather had made him go barefoot. 'Why are you wearing shoes? Vrindavan's dust is holy, it will do you good to feel it on your feet,' he had said. Then he wanted Prashant to take his shirt off too. His grandson asked why. 'What?' he replied, 'You learn English in school but you don't know the ways of your forefathers? When you come to Vrindavan for the first time, you must put aside all worldly possessions.'

'So there I was, walking beside him through the streets wearing nothing but a pair of short trousers.'

Prashant shook his head. 'It was unbelievably embarrassing. "Who's that?" people would ask. He'd tell everyone that I was his grandson and could speak English but that I'd forgotten the ways of my forefathers. At the same time though, he was very proud that I could speak English and he'd egg people on to speak English to me to test me out. It was incredible but that's why I loved him. My grandfather was my first guru. When I decided to study with him, it was the best decision I ever made in my life.' I looked at Prashant as he sat next to me on the veranda. His eyes were shining.

Gradually, I began to think about my return journey. My flight was in a week. It had taken me five days to get from Delhi to Amta and I would most likely have to reckon with the same, or worse, for the return journey.

'No problem,' Ramkumar told me. 'There's a jeep in the village. It might not actually work at the moment but there are motorbikes as well, and they can get you to Darbhanga.' Premkumar chipped in that he would come with me since he had to get back to work at university in Allahabad. There might even be trains running again from Darbhanga, we would wait and see. Granted, word had it in the village that the transport strike was still on but no one worried much about that. Today was the first free day after the thirteen days of puja for Vidur Mallik. Tomorrow there was to be another ritual to cleanse the house, so that life could resume.

In the evening, Ramesh Mallik came by, with a turban wound about his head, to invite us for a chillum. It was a friendly invitation that could not be refused, part of his daily round.

While we smoked, we remembered all those old people who had smoked before us. Premkumar's grandfather had been in the habit of smoking a chillum every evening, only three puffs, no more, saying that it helped him to clear his weeping eyes. The hashish helped the old man with his tears, with the balance of his humours. As soon as dusk crept in, squadrons of mosquitoes zoomed in on me again. Even the chillum didn't help me sleep. I lay awake for a long time, looking up at the black night sky where stars glimmered and shone like the glow-worms over the pond.

DO THESE CLOWNS HAVE ANYTHING
TO DO WITH YOU?

Schönefeld Airport, Berlin, October 2000

'Do these clowns have anything to do with you?' asked the officer in the green cap. 'They think that they can enter Germany without a penny in their pocket!'

'Yes, they're mine,' I reassured him. 'Didn't they show you the letter of invitation?'

'How many forged letters do you think we get to see every day here!' he barked back at me. 'They imagine they can enter the country just like that. Who are you, anyway? Are you sure you want to cover their costs? Then take these jokers along with you right away or we'll put them on the next plane back to Moscow!'

It had been more than an hour since the Aeroflot flight had touched down at Berlin Schönefeld but my Indian guests still hadn't come through the gate. When the frosted-glass doors opened, the usual assortment of arrivals from all points East trotted out into the Berlin morning air, a crowd of grey, tired faces. The last to leave were a pair of Russian blondes with their entourage, draped with gold chains and looking as though they had got up that morning in a Moscow bordello. After that, the doors stayed closed.

I couldn't believe that the Malliks hadn't arrived. Passengers from Delhi to Berlin had a long stopover in Moscow. The food wasn't up to much and Premkumar had told me that last time they took this flight, a couple of drunken Russians had thrown up in the cabin. He found it quite revolting, but it was the cheapest flight. Perhaps they had been delayed somehow in Moscow?

There was no one at the Aeroflot counter to give me any information about my missing arrivals. I sat down on a bench and thought what I could do. That evening the Mallik family were to be showcased at the World Music Expo, WOMEX, the world music fair at Berlin's Haus der Kulturen der Welt.

The frosted-glass doors which usually glide apart to let arriving passengers through stayed firmly closed but halfway up there was a narrow strip of clear glass. By bending down, I could peer through this gap and see a slice of the hall where the luggage carousels turn. A little way off, I spotted a group of Indians sitting on their suitcases, surrounded by police. It was the Malliks. Next time the doors swung back, I hallooed.

They waved back and told the immigration officials that someone had come to pick them up. One of the uniformed officers let me through. Next to the Malliks squatted another, older Indian. He looked like a professor on his way to a congress but immigration wouldn't let him through. He was due to be sent back as well because, like the Malliks, he didn't have any

German money. I asked whether I could help but he declined, dispirited.

The group of Indians were the only travellers who had been detained; all the other Aeroflot passengers had long left the departure hall. 'Is this some sort of special treatment for arrivals with dark skin?' I asked the officer.

'D'you want to get lippy with me?' he snorted. 'Take 'em along with you and clear orf out!'

I was relieved that they'd arrived. We were booked for a tour that would take us through several German and Swiss cities, then onward to London and New York. If they had been turned back now, the whole tour would have fallen through. I couldn't have raised the money to fly them in a second time.

I had been organizing tours for the Malliks for several years. They had come to the West more than a dozen times now, playing hundreds of concerts everywhere from the Royal Albert Hall to circus tents and Berlin's backstreet clubs. We hadn't grown rich; mostly the tours just about paid for themselves, sometimes there was a little left over for the musicians. From time to time, a festival or a cultural foundation would cover the travel costs but that was the exception. Mostly, I borrowed money to pay for the flights ahead of the tour, never certain that I would get it back, but in the end, it always worked out. The Malliks told me that I had the goddess' blessing, that I was part of her divine plan.

I had put my head on the block this time as well. WOMEX had sent an invitation but that wasn't enough on its own. To be able to apply for a visa, the Malliks had to have their return flights already booked, so I had sent them a wire transfer to Delhi for the flights. Now it only remained for the visas to be issued but it was never quite sure whether they would be. We always had some problem or other with the German Embassy in Delhi. There was never any telling what refinements the diplomatic staff would resort to in order to refuse a visa or, if they couldn't, delay it as long as possible.

This time I really thought I'd done everything right. As well as sending letters of invitation straight to the musicians, the WOMEX organizers had also faxed copies of all the documentation to the German Embassy in New Delhi, giving names and addresses and dates of birth, performance dates, sponsors' letters, a friendly covering letter emphasizing how well regarded the musicians were and what the festival was all about, flight dates including return flights—everything imaginable.

The next day, Anita, our Delhi travel agent, sent one of her staff over to the embassy with the passports, flight tickets and all necessary forms to apply for the visas. She knew that this kind of thing would take hours, so she had specially hired a factotum for such purposes. He wasn't allowed inside. An Indian employee standing on the pavement outside the embassy was marshalling applicants into several queues and sending them onward as the fancy took him to the officials within. Germans, and other Western tourists, were of course exempt from the procedure, they could just go in. Indians had to pay to be allowed to join the queues. The travel agency's man waited to see whether he couldn't get in somehow. Several hours later, he had got as far as the visa department but the clerk at the counter there refused to accept the applications. He told Anita's man quite firmly that there had been no invitation from Germany. The agent went back to her office empty-handed.

I was woken at six o'clock next morning by a call from Delhi. Anita told me what her chap had told her about his fruitless efforts and that she had called the embassy next thing. The visa-department man had told her that this was quite so, they couldn't begin to process the Malliks' applications since there was no invitation from Germany. Apparently, the documents hadn't been faxed through yet, Anita told me, and could I get onto this so that her man wouldn't have another day's waiting in vain. She asked me not to mention that applicants had to pay to get into the embassy—if this got out, it would only make trouble for her agency.

Since I was quite sure that WOMEX had faxed the documents over to Delhi the day before, I called the embassy myself. A sleepy Indian voice answered the telephone. He said that he would try to connect me to the visa department and then hung up.

I waited five minutes, then called the number again.

'No one picks up phone,' the voice said.

'I know,' I replied, 'Why is that?'

'No one picks up phone,' he repeated. When I asked him to put me through to the cultural attaché, he hung up, after which the line remained dead.

I called the WOMEX organizers and asked them to fax the documents through to the embassy again. Anita sent her messenger boy off once more, with the same result—he waited for hours and in the end, the application was not even accepted. At last, the WOMEX people managed to get the visa official on the phone, who confirmed that he had heard of these applicants but couldn't take up their case since he had no idea who WOMEX were. Their letterhead showed that they were affiliated with the Haus der Kulturen der Welt, and the house website proclaimed that this is where the Federal Republic of Germany receives the world's artists and cultural luminaries as guests. One mouse click would have told the man that WOMEX was an official event of the Haus der Kulturen der Welt but he hadn't looked. He told me that he would need a notarized copy of an entry from the companies register, after which he could proceed.

It took two days to get the copy made and faxed to Delhi. Anita called the embassy man again. He told her that it simply would not do to send her factotum, he had to interview the applicants in person. A friend who worked at the German Foreign Office told me that this was routine these days. They kept an especially close eye on musicians. A group of Indians claiming to be a musical ensemble had entered Germany and then vanished without trace. Since then, all Indian musicians were treated as suspect.

One look at the Malliks' passports would reveal that they had visited Germany a dozen times since 1983. The WOMEX cover letter confirmed that a jury had chosen them to represent Indian music at the fair. The previous year, Premkumar Mallik had been in Berlin as a guest artist of the German Academic Exchange Service. All this was in the cover letter, but the visa man insisted on verifying this for himself.

The Malliks lived scattered all across North India. The father lived in Vrindavan, his brother-in-law, the pakhwaj player Ramji Upadhyaya, lived in a village near Gaya, Ramkumar was in Amta, Premkumar was a university professor in Allahabad and had taken a short sabbatical for the tour, booking his train tickets to Delhi well in advance. They were all due in Delhi on the weekend before the flight but now they had to arrange to be there a week earlier since the process would take several days. The embassy official declared that he would need some time to issue the visas.

They managed to reach Delhi within three days. The next day, they were waiting at the embassy door but once again they found that their applications were not to be accepted. A counter clerk told them that there were no documents from Germany to confirm their invitation.

The next day, I called the secretary general of the Haus der Kulturen der Welt, who said that he was surprised that the Malliks couldn't get their visas. He knew them from previous performances in Berlin. I cajoled him into sending a fax to the German ambassador in Delhi, asking for the visas to be issued speedily.

Since time was running out, the Malliks set off for the Swiss Embassy the next day, needing a separate visa for Switzerland. They joined the queue of applicants while Anita sent her man with the passports to the German Embassy, imagining that now the secretary general had put a word in, the visas would be issued right away. He was then to take the Malliks' passports across to the Swiss Embassy, not far away. With a little luck they would be able to apply for their Swiss visas and pick them up the next day, just before they flew.

Just to be on the safe side, the WOMEX organizers called the German Embassy. This time another man took the call and told them that he too couldn't see why the visas had not already been issued, since all the necessary paperwork was to hand. When the travel agency's messenger got to the counter, he was told exactly the opposite. The visas could not be issued because there were no papers from Germany. Again.

When I heard about this on Friday, I went back to the Haus der Kulturen der Welt. The head of the music section got in touch with the foreign office. He found someone ready and willing to take on the case. One hour later, he called back with the assurance that the visas would be issued. That could only be done on Monday though, for the embassy was closed by now. They used to issue some emergency visas on Saturdays, he explained, but they couldn't do that these days because the computer was always switched off at weekends. He wished us the very best of luck.

We had that luck. The applications were accepted on Monday morning and the Malliks picked them up that afternoon. They went to the airport at ten at night and at two in the morning they were sitting on the plane.

The next day I was standing in front of the automatic doors at Berlin Schönefeld arrivals hall. 'Yes,' I told the officer in the green cap. 'These clowns are mine.'

VII

Amta, Sunday, 4 August 2002

In the morning, I steered the conversation back to
the return journey. I had found neither jeep nor motor-
bike anywhere in Amta. It was a good twenty miles to
Darbhanga and I couldn't imagine walking that distance in the heat. On top of which, the transport strike
was still on. No one in the village really knew whether
the train from Darbhanga to Delhi would be running
again by now.

No one, other than myself, seemed to mind. Premkumar retired for his morning puja, while Ramkumar
muttered something about a vehicle that might perhaps
be got from the next village over. Besides which, there
was a rickshaw in Amta and that could take me to
Darbhanga. I wanted to see it but he waved my concerns
away. Why trouble today about tomorrow's business?

I rather doubted that we would set off tomorrow.
There are very strict precepts in India about when you
can travel in which direction, on what day of the week.
The Malliks had rather old-fashioned ideas on the matter and I knew that it was against their rules to set off
westward on a Monday.

Today, everyone was busy with preparations for the afternoon puja. This was not a funerary rite but a ritual to return life to its normal course. Ever since their father had died, the house had counted as ritually unclean and while the funeral observances were underway, they could not even cook food in the house. Now the women bustled into the inner courtyard and began to prepare a meal there again. They smiled at me as I came into the courtyard. I was something of a hero in their eyes for having made it to Amta.

When I had heard of Vidur Mallik's death, I knew that I would miss out on something if I did not go to Amta but I didn't know what. Now I was in Amta and I still didn't know what I was doing here. I had reckoned that the journey would give me a chance to reflect on how my story was bound up with that of Vidur Mallik and his family, perhaps to reach some kind of resolution. But it had been an exhausting journey. It had taken all my efforts to get here and now that I was in Amta, there were no easy answers.

Vidur Mallik was not a man to reveal his depths quickly. When he began to teach at the gurukul we had established in Vrindavan, I began to tape his songs. At first he had great reservations—the tapes from the time document his reluctance—but after a while his tongue began to loosen and out came a flood of notes, syllables, rhythms, a river into which he could dive any time he wished. When he sang the old dhrupads, there were moments when his music was ravishingly beautiful, when the syllables flowed from his lips and built up into majestic palaces, but I loved just as much, perhaps even more, to listen to him singing a Bihari folk song while he drummed away on an upturned lota.

'It was as though my grandfather's lips had a magic power,' said Prashant, pointing at the picture on the wall above us. 'Whatever he said came true.' He told me how earlier that year he had taken part in All India Radio's annual competition for young musicians. 'They get hundreds of cassettes sent in, it's not easy to win the first prize. Even when you work hard, you don't know whether you are in with a chance.' His grandfather had listened to him sing the pieces. 'Don't worry, you'll win the prize,' he told him. 'Not only first prize, they'll also give you a special commendation.' His prediction was fulfilled; Prashant was crowned the best dhrupad singer of his generation.

His sixteen-year-old sister, Priyanka, had also been invited to a competition in May organized by Zee TV in Bombay, along with five hundred other young musicians. The judging took place in a hall. Prashant had gone along with his sister and, as he told me, they almost didn't let him in. In the end he got into the hall by pretending that he too was taking part in the competition.

The jury sat at a table on stage. Every entrant had a minute to sing. Because it would take hours for everyone to have thier turn, clapping and applause was forbidden. 'When Priyanka took the stage,' Prashant told me, 'she started by singing "Ek Radha Ek Mira" from the film *Ram Teri Ganga Maili*. The jury listened without interrupting her as they had the other competitors.

When the song was over, they began to clap, even though they'd banned it.' He laughed.

'Then they asked Priyanka who she was and where she came from. She answered that she had studied classical music with her grandfather, Pandit Vidur Mallik. "How's that?" asked the president of the jury. "Isn't he a dhrupad singer?" She told him that Grandfather and Father had taught her not only dhrupad but all four styles of classical music, as we do in our family. We call it choumukhi, the four faces of music—dhrupad, khayal, ghazal and bhajan. Only someone who has mastered all four styles is really a singer. The jury president asked her to sing one of her grandfather's songs, and she sang the bhajan "Sada Shyama Shyama", one of his compositions. They all clapped again, the audience as well this time. Then she had to sing a song by Shubha Mudgal, and the president asked her to give Grandfather his best regards.'

The uncle from next door came over and sat down on the veranda chair. 'Uranium 235, you know?' he said, taking up his theme from the day before. 'Supercharged energy, no existence!' He wagged a finger at me and repeated, emphatically, 'No existence!'

Kali-babu hobbled across, leaning on a stick. When Ram Chatur Mallik died, his family had given the singer's servant the use of a hut here in Amta. While the old man was alive, singer and servant had been inseparable. Even back then, Kali-babu hadn't been able to see much and now, he seemed almost blind. His eyes were hidden by thick, dusty lenses. He felt my arms and my face with his hands to find out whether it was really me sitting in front of him. Then he hobbled back to his hut.

Images flashed through my mind and vanished again. I thought of the dream that I had had in Delhi. Singers must die twice, the angel had told me. It was an oracular sentence and could be taken many ways. One interpretation was about the singer whose family had said farewell to him in these thirteen days. He had died once, as Chandrabhushan, and been reborn as Vidur, but Vidur Mallik was not dead yet. He would only die his second death when his family had forgotten him and that would take a very long while yet. The spring had not run dry.

The last time I had seen my guru had been in Allahabad. It was at the Kumbh Mela, celebrated in Allahabad since time immemorial. Kumbh means a vessel, and this mela is named for the brimming vessel of amrit that appeared from the ocean of milk. The gods had called the demons to help them find this treasure, the nectar of immortality. They churned the Kshira Sagar in a way that Indian milk sellers still use when there is no electricity, making lassi by winding a string round a wooden querl. Pull the string from both sides alternately and the querl turns, making a light foamy drink.

To whisk the ocean of milk, the world serpent Sheshanag wound itself round the mythical Mount Meru. The serpent was the string, the mountain was the querl and the demons tugged at the serpent king's head while the gods pulled at his tail. As soon as the pot of nectar appeared, the demons let go of the serpent's head, grabbed the vessel and tried to run away. The gods followed them. In the course of the struggle that ensued, four drops of the holy liquid spilt from the kumbh and fell to earth in four places in India—in Haridwar, Nasik, Ujjain and in Prayag, as Allahabad had been called until Emperor Akbar renamed the city in 1584.

The date of the Kumbh Mela is determined by Jupiter's orbit, rather under twelve years, and more exactly, by the alignment of the sun and moon. The Kumbh Mela in Allahabad always begins when Jupiter enters the sign of Vrishabh, which Westerners know as Taurus, and ends when the sun enters Makara, or Capricorn. If the moon is also in Makara, then this marks a Maha Kumbh Mela, though this convergence only happens every hundred and forty-four years.

The Maha Kumbh Mela of January 2001 was one such. Millions of people thronged in the greatest gathering of human beings in our planet's history. Estimates of the number who made their way to the mela over the course of its six weeks vary from thirty to seventy million but there was little sign of this in the Mallik household in the backstreets on the other side of town.

Vidur Mallik had come to Allahabad with Mataji, and as usual, he had made himself at home in the reception room where Premkumar received guests and pupils. Mostly he lay stretched out on the bed below the display cabinet with its imitation-silver trophies, framed certificates, miniature Taj Mahal, knick-knacks and soft toys. A television set stood on a little table in the corner and during the day the children watched World Wrestling Federation, Zee TV music or Amitabh Bachchan's quiz show. Every evening, the family gathered in the room to sing. The routine was always the same—first the grandchildren would sing, then the sons, then the grandfather and last of all, they would all sing together. I knew many of the songs by heart but there were always new pieces that I had never heard. Some of these were sung only rarely, ragas that only this family knew, some sung for particular occasions and some of them new compositions that father and sons seemed to be able to create almost off-handedly. There was no end to this, no fathoming the stream of their tradition, never a sign of the other shore, always something new to discover. I taped some of these evenings on video, but as I sat on the veranda of the Amta house I saw a picture that is not on any tape.

The high point of the mela fallss on the day of the new moon. We set off early in the afternoon, three generations of the family—grandparents, children, grandchildren and other relatives. We joined the great crowds of people on foot, making their way determinedly but unhurriedly over many miles to the sangam, where the Ganga and the Yamuna meet the mythological underground River Saraswati. This day is called Mauni Amavasya, the new moon of silence, since the ritual bath at the sangam used to be taken in silence, though this observance has long been abandoned. As we crossed the great bridge that spans the riverbanks, loudspeakers blared into our ears from their high poles, an endless litany of names, people lost in the crowds whose friends and family were looking for them. We had a view of the tent cities that had sprung up to cover the sandy river banks. Thousands upon thousands of tents, as far as the eye could see, but we had only an inkling of the real size. The newspaper reported that the tents covered an area of more than twenty square miles.

The closer we came to the sangam, the thicker the crowd of bodies all around. People spilt down the banks and into the river so that it was impossible to tell where the water began. Hundreds of boats drifted on waves that glittered in the setting sun. In among the people, we took off our clothes, caught hold of one another's hands so as not to lose our group and found our way to the water. We dipped and went under, five times in all. I was surprised at how cool the water was. Flowers and plastic bags lapped against the shore but further out, the water was clear.

Time seemed to stand still for a short while, only the blinking of an eye, the moment between breathing in and breathing out. I felt that I was part of an eternal cycle, a rhythm that endured through all generations. Our ancestors had been here before us, we had come back to this same place and our children's children too. It was the same spot where—a year and a half later, though now we could not know it—Vidur Mallik's ashes would be scattered to the waves.

We dried our clothes at the shore and made our way home. I walked behind the grandfather. Every man has his own gait; I would have known Vidur Mallik's feet, his walk, among thousands, and this is the image that stays in my mind like none other—his feet treading the dusty ground. They were broad feet, the toes turned a little outwards. He put them down carefully and confidently, one pace, another, like a farmer walking his fields. There was a scent that came with the image—the dust which his feet disturbed bore that faint smell which you only smell in India.

It was hard to leave Allahabad. My girlfriend had come with me on this trip and we were even married at the Kumbh Mela—without our knowledge, according to Indian custom. Premkumar and his wife Rashmi, when they took us by the hands, had placed us between themselves, man with man and woman with woman, and dipped beneath the waves at the same moment. When we surfaced, they told us that we were now married; the conjugal spark had jumped from them to us, and the water was our witness. The family rubbed sindur onto Lisa's forehead and on the way back home, Prashant bought a colourful cardboard trumpet, a children's toy, which he gave us as a wedding present. It unrolled two paper arms when you blew into it. We laughed. It was a fleeting moment, there was no further ceremony, but the time and the place where it happened gave the event its own truth.

The next evening, we had trouble getting the Delhi train. Our flight to Germany was imminent but we had not managed to get a reservation, although we were on the waiting list, on number 108. The most important day of the mela had passed and hundreds of thousands of people thronged towards the railway station. We joined the seemingly endless column of people marching onward in the dim neon light. It looked like a migration, like an exodus, a whole nation on the move but with no hint of panic. It was very calm. The only sounds were the murmur of voices, soft calls, then a steam train hooting in the distance.

The square in front of the railway station was so full of people that it seemed impossible even to set one foot in front of the other. Somehow we managed to push our way through to the station building itself, balancing our suitcases on our heads. The scheduled departure time was long past but the train still stood at the platform. No one seemed to know what was going on, so people simply squatted down and waited. We climbed over their backs, putting our feet down where there was a tiny patch of ground free. We could see faces, arms, legs through the barred windows of the compartments. The train was hopelessly overcrowded and the compartment doors had been barred from the inside. We hammered on doors, showing bystanders the paper which ensured us our place on the waiting list, but they shook their heads helplessly, shrugging and pointing at the barred doors.

At that moment, a compartment door opened. A short, bald Indian man peered out through the crack. He wore a dhoti and round glasses and looked remarkably like Mahatma Gandhi. The crush of people behind him almost thrust him out of the train, which was just getting underway, but he held tight to the grab bar by the door. 'Come quick!' he called to us. 'I have a spare ticket—if you can make do with one seat for the two of you, you can have it!' Then he pulled us into the train as it gathered speed, the door was barred once more and we were on our way to Delhi.

This time too, I thought as I sat on the veranda in Amta, I'd find some way. There had always been a way. Meanwhile, the sun was directly overhead and it grew hotter every minute. I reminded Ramkumar of my flight and he smiled reassuringly. It was far too hot to take any decision.

The Malliks could not themselves perform the Satya Narayan puja that was due today. They had kept all their traditional knowledge of the Hindu formulas and rituals and used these on occasion but for their own family ceremonies they had to call in others.

The family priest was fetched, a little old man who spread out his paraphernalia on the veranda, by the front door, with great ceremony. It took hours to get everything ready—dried cow dung, copper pots of ghee and sindur, sandalwood, grass, a bundle of betel leaves, grains of rice, coconuts. Late in the afternoon, the family gathered round the fire that the priest had lit in a little open hearth of brick and stone.

Seen from outside, it didn't look like an especially solemn occasion. I saw a group of exhausted people gathered about the fire, while the old priest threw grass into it, dripped melted butter and milk and other fluids from his little brass spoon and murmured mantras. Most of those squatting on the ground round the priest were women. Ramkumar was sitting across from the priest, watching the little man in the yellow shirt go through the ritual, and was the only one wearing a fresh dhoti. It was a long ritual, taking hours to perform. The murmur of voices and the repetitive actions made me sleepy.

Then Ramesh put his head round the corner and waved to Prem-kumar and me. We followed him to his house. Ramkumar had given up alcohol, along with meat, and so was not invited, since this time Ramesh served us not with a chillum but with whisky. He led us into his hut so that the private ritual would not be too obvious. The three of us sat down on the clay floor, then Ramesh fetched out a bottle and poured the dark brown liquid into three metal cups.

We looked at one another. Premkumar made the toast. 'We have become the gurus now. From now on, we must find the way ourselves, there is no one to show it to us.'

What he said was true, and it was not an uplifting thought. We were entirely on our own now.

THE MALLIK FAMILY TREE

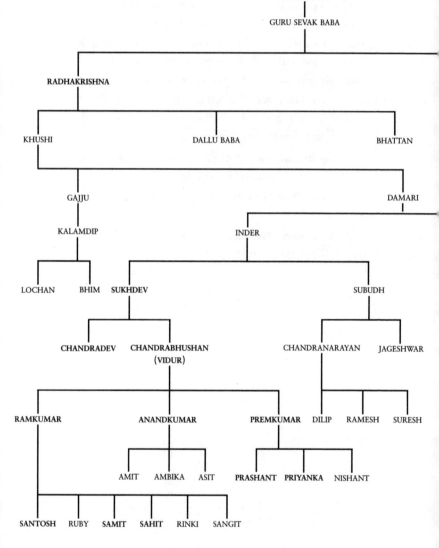

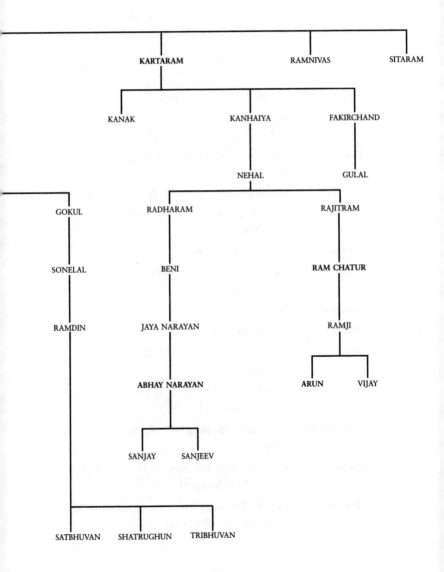

GLOSSARY

achkan	A man's knee-length formal jacket
akash	Sky; the fifth element in Indian cosmology, known as aether in Classical Europe
alap	The introductory section of the performance of a raga
arti	A form of worship usually by a Hindu priest in which the sacred flame is waved in front of an idol
bara peg	A large peg of whisky
baul	A group of wandering mystic singers from Bengal
bhagwan	God
bhajan	A religious song
bhang	An intoxicating drink made with ground cannabis
bidi	An Indian cigarette made of tobacco rolled in the leaf of the tendu tree
cante jondo	'Deep song', the song style of Andalusian gypsies
chaiti	A semi-classical song sung in the month of Chaitra (March–April)
chapati	A small, flat and round piece of bread usually rolled out and baked over a gridle

chillum	A clay pipe for smoking cannabis
churidar	Tight trousers worn with a kurta
dal	Lentils
damaru	An hour-glass-shaped clapper-drum
darbar	The court of an Indian ruler; a court ceremony
darshan	The sight of a god; the blessing attained by seeing the god
Devanagari	The alphabet and written form of some Indian languages including Hindi and Sanskrit
dham	A holy place
dharma	Religion; duty and correct behaviour, morality and social order in Hinduism and Jainism
dhobi	A laundryman or laundrywoman
dhoti	A long piece of cloth worn by men, tied round the waist with the lower part passed between the legs and tucked in at the back, so that the knees are covered
dilruba	A bowed stringed instrument
Diwali	The festival of lights, celebrated in the month of Ashwin (September–October)
Domra	The chief of the workers, especially of lower castes, who tend to funeral pyres
Durga Puja	The festival of the goddess Durga, which is celebrated in the months of Ashwin or Kartik (September–October)
esraj	A bowed stringed instrument
gamak	An ornamented note in North Indian classical music
gandharva	The class of demi-gods proficient in music and war

ganja	A form of hashish usually smoked
gharana	Musical dynasty; the musical tradition passed on across generations of one's family or pupils
ghat	A quay-side on the river; bathing stairs
ghazal	A love song in Urdu
ghee	Clarified butter
goli	Globule
goshala	A shelter for cows
gur	A coarse dark brown sugar made by evaporation of the sap of palm trees.
guru	A teacher
gurudhan	A gift given by the guru
gurukul	A school where the guru and shishya live together
Guruma	Honorific form of address to a guru's wife
harmonium	A portable keyboard instrument with a bellow
Holi	The spring festival of colour, celebrated in the month of Phalgun (February–March) in eastern, northern and western India
jaghir	A piece of land given permanently by a Mughal emperor or by the British government to a person or body that would administer it
jiva	In Hinduism, the immortal essence of a living organism
kajri	A semi-classical song sung in the rainy season
Kali-yuga	In Hinduism, the last and worst of the four ages of human history when people will be immoral and corrupt and lack faith
khayal	A North Indian classical style of song, more recent than dhrupad

kothi	A house; brothel
Krishna	The Black One, an incarnation of the god Vishnu born into the Yadav clan in the Mahabharata
kurta	A loose-fitting shirt worn over a salwar or churidar by women, or over a pyjama by men
laddu	A round sweet made from ghee, sugar and other ingredients
lakh	One hundred thousand
Lakshmana	Brother of Rama
lassi	A cooling drink made with yoghurt and water
lila	In Hinduism, the playful activity of the divine spirit; a form of popular theatre showing incidents from the lives of Rama and Krishna
lingam	Black stone sacred to Shiva; a phallic symbol
lota	A water pot used for cleansing after defecation
lungi	A garment consisting of a piece of cloth, worn wrapped round the hips and reaching the ankles
mahant	Chief priest
Maha Shivaratri	The great night of Shiva, new moon in the month of Phalgun (February–March)
mala	A garland or necklace
mantra	A sacred prayer or incantation
Mataji	Honorific form of address to a mother
mehfil	A gathering for some form of entertainment
mela	A Hindu festival or fair
mohalla	A quarter of town; neighbourhood
moksha	Liberation from the cycle of rebirth in Hindu and Buddhist philosophy

mullah	A Muslim scholar
murti	A statue or image of a god
naubat	An ensemble of drums and wind instruments, especially the shehnai
nautch girl	A professional dancing girl
Om	The mystic sound denoting the Hindu trinity; the origin or root of all sounds; the symbol representing the Supreme Being
paan	Betel leaf, usually folded into the shape of a tri angle and filled with spices for eating
pakhwaj	A long clay drum played by beating the two ends with the hands
pandit	A person with great knowledge about the Shastras; title for a wise man or master, a Hindu singer or musician
papadam	A fritter made with chickpea flour
paramanu	Atom
Parvati	Daughter of the mountains; Shiva's consort
peshwa	The chief minister of the Maratha confederacy
prahara	A measurement of time by which the day is divided into eight parts of three hours each
pralaya	In Hindu mythology, the destruction of the universe
prasad	Offering of food made to a god and then distributed among the worshippers
puja	A Hindu ceremony of worship
Puranas	The 18 books containing Hindu myths, legends and the genealogy of gods, heroes and saints
Radha	The beloved of Krishna

raga	In Indian classical music, a pattern of notes used as a basis for improvisation; there are specific rules for the playing of ragas, and for the time and season at which they should be performed
Raja Bahadur	A princely title
Rama	An incarnation of Vishnu; the hero of Ramayana
sadhu	A holy man
sangam	Meeting; a confluence of rivers, especially of Ganga, Yamuna and the mythical Saraswati at Allahabad
sangeet	A song; music
Sangeet Shastra	A textbook on music
sannyasi	A monk
sarangi	A bowed stringed instrument
Saraswati	The goddess of music and learning; also the mythical underground river
sarkar	Government; an honorific form of address for an overlord or a person in authority
sati	A widow who burns herself on her husband's pyre; the practice of burning a woman alive on her dead husband's pyre
satisthan	Place where a sati is honoured
sattra	Feeding of brahmins
Shakti	Strength; The female principle of divine energy
Shankar	A name of Shiva
shastriya sangeet	Classical music based on the textbooks
shehnai	A wind instrument
sherbat	A sweet drink
shishya	A disciple

Shiva	The third god in the Hindu trinity, the destroyer
shruti	The smallest perceptible interval; a mictrotone in Indian classical music; in Hindusim, a group of texts that are believed to have been made known to the humans by the gods
siddhi	A miraculous power given to someone who has become concerned only with spiritual matters
sindur	Vermilion powder that married Hindu women put on the parting of their hair
Sita	The consort of Rama
sitar	A large, long-necked stringed instrument with movable frets, played with a wire pick
surbahar	A larger version of the sitar which produces a deeper sound
sutra	A thread; in Sanskrit grammar, law or philosophy, a brief statement that requires comments and notes
tabla	A paired set of small drums played with the hands, usually to accompany other music
tadi	Toddy, palm-wine
tanpura	A stringed instrument that provides accompaniment to songs or other instrumnts
thali	A metal plate for serving food
thandai	A cooling drink made from hashish
thumri	A romantic song in North Indian classical music
tihai	A closing phrase in music, repeated thrice
tika	A decorative mark worn on the forehead

tilak	A mark worn on the forehead by a Hindu to indicate caste or sect; the engagement ceremony
tonga	A light covered carriage with two wheels, pulled by a single horse
tulsi	Holy basil, a plant sacred to Krishna
Upanishads	Part of the Vedic literature that interprets the nature of God and existence
Vac	The sacred word
vahan	A steed of the gods; a vehicle
Vaidyanath	The lord of healers; a Shiva shrine near Deogarh
Vasant Panchami	A spring festival, the fifth day of the month of Magh (January–February)
veena	A stringed instrument sacred to Goddess Saraswati
Vishwanath	The lord of the world, the reigning deity at Benares
Yadav	A cattle-herding caste
yatra	A journey or procession; pilgrimage
yoni	Symbol of the vagina
zamindar	A landlord responsible for collecting money and paying it to the government

In Praise of the Goddess: Devotional Songs from North India

Recorded at Rundfunk Berlin-Brandenburg (RBB), 17–18 July 2005, Celestial Harmonies 13267-2, 2006, CD, produced by Peter Pannke.

Premkumar Mallik: voice, harmonium and tabla; Prashant and Nishant Mallik: voices; Priyanka Mallik: voice and tanpura; Ravishankar Upadhyaya: tabla and pakhwaj; Rashmi Mallik: tanpura

1   Raga Durga, chhota khayal, drut Ektaal: 'Devi Durge Bhavani', 11:50

2   Raga Gurjari Todi, bada khayal, vilambit Ektaal: 'Paar Karoge'; chhota khayal, drut Tintaal: 'Tuma Sanga Lagi', 26:39

3   Raga Bilaskhani Todi, chhota khayal in madhyalaya Tintaal: 'Jagata Janani', 13:28

4   Raga Adana, Sultaal: 'Triveni Kalindi', 10:16

5   Raga Bhairavi, bhajan, Jhaptaal: 'Dayani Bhavani', 10:51

The Prince of Love: Vocal Art of North India

Recorded at former Sender Freies Berlin (now RBB), 24 June 1997, Celestial Harmonies 13238-2, 2004, CD, produced by Peter Pannke.

Premkumar Mallik: voice and harmonium; Ravishankar Upadhyaya: tabla and pakhwaj; Peter Pannke: tanpura

1 Raga Todi, alap, 11:39

2 Raga Todi, dhrupad: 'Adi Brahma Nirakara', 6:37

3 Raga Abhogi Kanada, alap, 12:53

4 Raga Abhogi Kanada, dhamar: 'Braja Mein Dekho Dhuma Machi Hai', 5:49

5 Raga Vasant, Sultaal: 'Ranga Jhama Banaye', 6:59

6 Raga Jog, chhota khayal: 'Sajana More Ghara Aye', 11:26

7 Raga Jog, tarana, 6:38

8 Raga Mishra Pahadi, thumri: 'Vaida Nipata Anari', 8:30

9 Kabir bhajan: 'Bita Gaye Dina Bhajana Bina', 7:40

The Fast Side of Dhrupad

Recorded at Sender Freies Berlin, 16 May 1993, Wergo SM 1517-2, 2004, CD, produced by Peter Pannke.

Vidur Mallik: voice; Ramkumar and Premkumar Mallik: voices and tanpuras; Ramji Upadhyaya: pakhwaj

1 Raga Bhairav, alap, Sultaal: 'Narayana Hari Tu', 11:50

2 Raga Ramkali, alap, Jhaptaal: 'Aja Sakhi Bhora', 11:37

3 Raga Asavari, alap, Tevra taal: 'E Nanda Lala', 9:58

4 Raga Puriya Dhanashri, alap, Jhaptaal: 'Jao Ji Jao', 10:14

5 Raga Bhimpalasi, alap, Sultaal: 'Shambhu Hara Re', 11:33

6 Raga Multani, alap, Sultaal: 'E Mana Re', 9:26

7 Raga Adana, alap, Sultaal: 'Triveni Kalindi', 12:01

The Nightingale of Mithila: Love Songs from Vidyapati and Other Joys

Recorded at Sender Freies Berlin, 1 October 1994, Navaras NRCD 0144, CD, produced by Peter Pannke.

Vidur Mallik: voice and harmonium; Premkumar Mallik: voice and tanpura; Anandkumar Mallik: tabla; Amelia Cuni: tanpura

1   Vidyapati thumri: 'Kunja Bhavana Se', 10:15
2   Raga Khamaj, thumri: 'Chhavi Dikhlaja', 13:08
3   Raga Khamaj, Dadra taal: 'Nazariya', 9:35
4   Mirabai bhajan: 'Giridhara Nagara', 7:55
5   Raga Bhairavi, thumri: 'Basiya Ne Tere', 14:37
6   Raga Bhairavi, Dadra taal: 'Sakhiyana Sanga', 10:12
7   Bindu bhajan: 'Sada Shyama', 8:03

Dhrupad from Darbhanga

Recorded at Vrindavan by Gottfried Düren and Peter Pannke, 1982, produced by Peter Pannke, Museum Collection CD17, Department of Ethnomusicology, Museum for Folklore, State Museum of Prussian Cultural Heritage.

Ramkumar and Premkumar Mallik: voices and tanpuras; Ramji Upadhyaya: pakhwaj; Vinod Mishra: sarangi; Nattilal Sharma: harmonium

   1/1   Raga Bhup Kalyan, alap, 15:50
   1/2   Raga Bhup Kalyan, dhrupad: 'Jhuthi Bata Samjhhi Kari', 8:10
   1/3   Raga Bhup Kalyan, dhamar: 'E Sakhi Rama Lala', 8:19
   1/4   Raga Bhup Kalyan, Sultaal: 'Tala Drdha Mudra', 2:22

Abhay Narayan Mallik: voice; Ramkumar and Premkumar Mallik: voices and tanpuras; Ramji Upadhyaya: pakhwaj; Vinod Mishra: sarangi

   1/5   Raga Darbari Kanada, alap, 29:00
   1/6   Raga Darbari Kanada, dhrupad: 'Aho Raja Birama Shaha', 6:52
   2/1   Raga Shadav Vasant, alap, dhamar: 'Bhamara Chai Rakhiyo', 11:54

Vidur Mallik: voice; Ramkumar and Premkumar Mallik: voices and tanpuras; Ramji Upadhyaya: pakhwaj; Vinod Mishra: sarangi; Sundarlal: harmonium

2/2 Raga Jay Jayanti Malhar, alap, 34:25
2/3 Raga Jay Jayanti Malhar, dhrupad: 'Nayo Megha, Nayo Neha', 15:10
2/4 Raga Jay Jayanti, dhamar: 'Khelata Hori Braja ki Gori', 11:33

Dhrupad of Darbhanga

Recorded at Vrindavan, by Gottfried Düren and Peter Pannke, 28 March 1982, produced by Peter Pannke. VDE CD 1006/ AIMP LXIII International Archive of Popular Music, Museum of Ethonography, Geneva.

Vidur, Ramkumar and Premkumar Mallik: voices; Ramji Upadhyaya: pakhwaj; Vinod Mishra: sarangi

1 Raga Deshi, alap, 10:26
2 Raga Deshi, dhrupad: 'Abadha Pura Nagari Ke Raja Shri Ramachandra', 10:46
3 Raga Vrindavani Sarang, alap, 2:09
4 Raga Vrindavani Sarang, dhamar: 'Eri Daiya Aba Na Ja Braja Mein', 9:20
5 Raga Vrindavani Sarang, Sultaal: 'Tala Sura Ke Bheda Na Janata', 8:46

Ramkumar and Premkumar Mallik: voices; Ramji Upadhyaya: pakhwaj; Vinod Mishra: sarangi

6 Raga Lalit, alap, 6:31
7 Raga Lalit, dhrupad: 'Dekho Sakhi Vrindavana Mein Mohana Rasa Rachayo', 5:48
8 Raga Lalit, dhamar: 'Shri Gopala Nanda Lala Ho Tum Darasa Ko Behala', 8:52

Secret Colours

Recorded at Sender Freies Berlin, 1 October 1994, Shalimar
SHLMR 7775, CD, produced by Peter Pannke.

Vidur Mallik: voice; Premkumar Mallik: voice and tanpura;
Anandkumar Mallik: tabla; Amelia Cuni: tanpura

1　Raga Vasant, alap, vilambit Jhaptaal: 'Navala Raghu-
　　natha', 12:44
2　Raga Vasant, chhota khayal, madhya Ektaal: 'Phulawa
　　Binata', 8:54
3　Raga Vasant, tarana, Tintaal, 11:01
4　Raga Shahana, alap, vilambit Jhaptaal: 'Guthi Lavari',
　　16:19
5　Raga Shahana, drut Ektaal: 'Nagara Sagara', 9:20
6　Raga Shahana, tarana, 13:05

Vidur Malik: The Lyrical Tradition of Dhrupad

VOL 1, Makar MAKCD 002, 1994, CD.

Vidur Mallik: voice; Ananadkumar Mallik: pakhwaj

1　Raga Bairagi Bhairav, alap, 14:32
2　Raga Bairagi Bhairav, dhrupad, 7:59
3　Raga Bairagi Bhairav, dhamar, 7:29
4　Raga Bairagi Bhairav, Sulfaktaal, 10:47
5　Raga Nand, dhamar, 10:11
6　Raga Shahana Kanada, dhamar, 12:01
7　Raga Bhairavi, Jhaptaal, 6:01

The King of Dhrupad: Ram Chatur Mallik in Concert

Recorded at Jai Singh Ghera, Vrindavan, by Gottfried Düren
and Peter Pannke, 27 March 1982, Wergo SM 1076-50, CD,
produced by Peter Pannke.

Ram Chatur and Abhay Narayan Mallik: voices; Purushottam Das: pakhwaj; Vinod Mishra: sarangi; Nattilal Sharma: harmonium; Ramkumar Mallik and Rameshchandra Chaturvedi: tanpuras

1 Raga Vinod, alap, 34:36
2 Raga Vinod, dhrupad: 'Piya Ghara Nahin Ali Ri', 6:24
3 Raga Sindhura, dhamar: 'Ladili Tu Mana Na Kijau', 12:01
4 Raga Paraj, dhamar: 'Eri Dapha Bina Mridanga Bajata Dhamara'; Sulfaktaal: 'Darasana Kaum Naina mere', 7:22

North India: Pandit Ram Chatur Mallik

Pias, Air Mail Music SA 141001, 1997, CD.

Ram Chatur and Abhay Narayan Mallik: voices; Ramashish Pathak: pakhwaj

1 Raga Darbari Kanada, 26:15
2 Raga Multani, 27:30

Ram Narayan in Concert: Sarangi Solo

Recorded at School of Music, Munich, by Ulrich Kraus, 14 February 1976, Wergo SM 1601-2, CD, produced by Peter Pannke.

Ram Narayan: sarangi; Suresh Talwalkar: tabla; Jürgen Saupe: tanpura

1 Raga Marwa, alap, 25:25
2 Raga Marwa, gats, Tintaal and Ektaal, 23:49
3 Raga Mishra Pilu, alap and gats, Chachar and Tintaal, 26:26

Raja Chatrapati Singh: Pakhwaj Solo

Recorded at Jai Singh Ghera, Vrindavan, 23 March 1982, and at LOFT, Munich, 27–28 May 1987, by Gottfried Düren, Wergo SM 1075-50, CD, produced by Peter Pannke.

Raja Chatrapati Singh: pakhwaj; Ratanlal and Surya Pratap Singh: ghanti; Sundarlal and Gauri Shankar: harmonium; Allyn Miner: surbahar

1   Ganesh Paran and Lakshmitaal, 22:15
2   Krishnataal, 7:18
3   Shiva Paran and Brahmataal, 21:52
4   Tha Chautaal, 6:54

R. Fahimuddin Dagar: Dhrupad

Recorded at the Swiss Embassy, New Delhi, 19 April 1988, by Gottfried Düren, Wergo SM 1081-2, produced by Peter Pannke.

R. Fahimuddin Dagar: voice; Gopal Das: pakhwaj; Jyoti Pandey and Amelia Cuni: tanpuras

1   Raga Marwa, alap, 31:51
2   Raga Marwa, dhrupad: 'Sangata Dvara Sura Soda Leta', 13:57
3   Raga Marwa, dhamar, 'Eho Ali Dhuma Machi Hai', 26:26

Kamalesh Maitra: Ragas on Drums

Recorded at Sender Freies Berlin, 6 November 1991, Wergo SM 1602-2, CD, produced by Peter Pannke

Kamalesh Maitra: tabla tarang; Kumar Bose: tabla; Laura Patchen: tanpura

1 Raga Shri, alap, 11:15
2 Raga Shri, gat, Chartaal ki Sawari, 16:30
3 Raga Mishra Bachaspati, alap and gats, vilambit and drut Tintaal, 41:32
4 Dehati, 5:14

Honeywind: Sounds from a Santal Village

Recorded in India, by Andres Bosshard and Peter Pannke, and mixed at Sender Freies Berlin, November 1994, Wergo SM 1612-2, produced by Peter Pannke.

Peter Pannke: Music for Unborn Children; A Harmonic Experience

Recorded at Radio Bremen, electronic realization by Walter Bachauer, 1982, Wergo SM 1074-50.

Mechthild Kampik, Tina Rusvay, Werner Durand, Peter Pannke: tanpuras

1 Teil, 23:10
2 Teil, 24:00

Morungen: Songs from a Visionary Musical

Recorded at Sender Freies Berlin, 19 March 1992, 9–11 February, 25 March, 16 April 1994, Wergo SM 1087-2, produced by Peter Pannke.

Peter Pannke: voice, sarangi, kemence, djoza, esraj; Barbaros Erköse: clarinet; Farhan Sabbagh: oud; tanbur, riqq, bendir; Fernando Grillo: double bass; Kamalesh Maitra: tabla, pakhwaj and sarod; Güngör Hosses: darbukka; Annalisa Adami and Laura Patchen: tanpuras

1 Riqq solo, 3:13
2 Owe war umbe, 5:32

3 Instrumental duo, 1:43

4 Ich horte uf der heiden, 4:32

5 Taksim on the clarinet, 3:53

6 Si ist ze allen eren, 7:11

7 Taksim on the oud, 2:19

8 Vrowe mine smerze siech, 4:18

9 Samai Muhayyar, 6:22

10 We wie lange soll ich ringen and sargam; 6:59

11 West ich ob es verswiget möchte sim 2:52

12 Soror Mystica 8:15

13 Uns ist zergangen, 10:14

Troubadours United: Road of the Troubadours

Recorded at Sargam Studio, Lahore, November 1997, University of Bombay, and at Propast Studio, Prague, July 2001, Enja ENJ-9436-2, recorded and produced by Peter Pannke.

Barbaros Erköse: clarinet; Louis Soret: voice, flute, nay, bag-pipes, doira, lyra, soprano sax, violin and oud; Iyad Haimour: bendir, oud, kanoun and riqq; Premkumar Mallik: voice, harmonium, tabla; Peter Pannke: voice, Persian setar, cümbüs and tanpura; Anandkumar Mallik: tabla and pakhwaj; Martin Gordon: electric bass on bonus tracks

1 Klingsor's Return, 2:28

2 Farai un vers de dreyt nien, 4:54

3 Chevalerie, 3:16

4 Hinduba, 6:51

5 Sanson Ke Svaron Se, 4:43

6 Mayasam, 3:23

7 Peshrev farahfaza, 4:29

8 Une porte sans clé, 2:35

9 Von den elben, 4:29

10 Istorik 3:29
11 Also auf nach Vrindavan, 1:35
12 Padagaresa, 4:39
13 Wünschet daß ich wohl gefahr, 4:33
14 Bab khemis, 2:50
15 Viel Süsse, 6:27
16 Obsession (bonus track /video clip), 3:57

10 Istorik 3:29

11 Also auf nach Vrindavan, 1:35

12 Padagaresa, 4:39

13 Wünschet daß ich wohl gefahr, 4:33

14 Bab khemis, 2:50

15 Viel Süsse, 6:27

16 Obsession (bonus track /video clip), 3:57